Roses For Canadians For Dummies®

Cheat Sheet

Rose Jargon

Bareroot roses: Sold in early spring or late fall while dormant and without soil on their roots.

Bicolour: A two-coloured rose, usually with two or more colours on opposite sides of the petals.

Blend: A multicoloured rose with two or more colours blending together on both sides of the petals.

Bud: An unopened flower. A *bud eye* is dormant vegetative growth that forms in the upper angle where a leaf joins a cane.

Bud union: A swollen or knobbly area on the lower trunk of a rose plant, where the flowering variety joins the rootstock.

Cane: A structural branch of a rose plant, usually arising from the base of the plant.

Deadhead: To remove spent blossoms from a bush.

Double flower: A rose with more than one row of petals.

Hardiness: The capability of a rose to withstand cold temperatures without being killed or injured.

Hip: The seed pod that forms after a rose's petals fall off. Some may turn bright orange or red and are quite colourful in fall and winter.

Leaflet: A part of a leaf. Rose leaves are usually divided into 5 to 7 leaflets, but some have as many as 19 or as few as 3.

Own-root roses: Roses that grow on their own roots and are not budded onto a separate rootstock.

Reverse: The underside of a rose petal.

Rootstock: The roots onto which a rose variety is budded. A rootstock increases the adaptability of the rose, giving it increased hardiness, vigour, soil tolerance, and other advantages.

Semi-double flower: A rose having two or three rows of petals.

Single flower: A rose having a single row of petals.

Sucker: A vigorous cane that arises from the rootstock of a rose. Its leaves look different from the rest of the plant, and you should remove it.

Variety: A specific type of rose. For example, 'Mister Lincoln' is a variety of hybrid tea with fragrant red flowers.

The Ten Most Popular Roses

According to one of the largest growers of roses for home gardeners, these roses have been the top sellers for the last several years:

- 🌸 **'Blaze':** Red climber
- 🌸 **'Bonica':** Pink shrub
- 🌸 **'Chrysler Imperial':** Red hybrid tea
- 🌸 **'Double Delight':** Red and white hybrid tea
- 🌸 **'Iceberg':** White floribunda
- 🌸 **'Mister Lin...**
- 🌸 **'Peace':** Ye...
- 🌸 **'Queen Eliz...**
- 🌸 **'Simplicity':**
- 🌸 **'Tropicana':** ...ange hybrid tea

...For Dummies®: Bestselling Book Series for Beginners

Roses For Canadians For Dummies®

Cheat Sheet

Rose Types

Climbers: Vigorous, sprawling rose plants that need the support of an arbour, fence, or trellis to stay upright.

Floribundas: Free-blooming shrubs that produce tons of flowers, usually borne in large clusters.

Grandifloras: Vigorous bushes producing large, beautifully formed flowers that are more likely to be borne in clusters than one to a stem. 'Queen Elizabeth' is a classic grandiflora.

Hybrid teas: The most popular type of rose bush, with beautiful long-stemmed flowers that are ideal for cutting.

Miniatures: Small in leaf and stature but big in amount of bloom. Grow only 10 to 90 centimetres (4 to 36 inches) high but make great landscape plants, especially as edgings and in containers.

Old garden and species roses: A huge group of roses varying in plant habit and flower type. Most bloom only once a year. Many have extremely fragrant and/or uniquely formed flowers.

Polyanthas: Small, compact shrubs producing large clusters of flowers.

Shrubs: A diverse group of quite varied plants. Includes many new excellent landscape varieties known for their easy care and abundant bloom. Also includes some of the hardiest roses.

Tree roses: Any of the preceding types of roses that are trained to look like small, round-headed trees.

Positive Thinking for Beginning Rose Gardeners

- Roses are tough; you don't need to baby them.
- Many roses are disease resistant; they don't need frequent spraying.
- If a rose isn't growing as well as you'd like, yank it out and replace it with a variety that does.
- Foolproof rose plan: If it doesn't rain, water once a week. Fertilize every four weeks. Whack 'em back in early spring. Smell them often.
- Ask questions. Find a rose society meeting near you and join up; they can help. And don't forget your local nursery.

Your Growing Zone

These plant hardiness zones are based on average annual minimum temperatures for Canadian growing zones.

Temperature in ° C	Zone	Temperature in ° F
−45 to −40	2	−40
−40 to −3	3	−40 to −30
−35 to −29	4	−30 to −20
−29 to −23	5	−20 to −10
−23 to −18	6	10 to 0
−18 to −12	7	0 to 10
−12 to −7	8	10 to 20
−7 to −1	9	20 to 30

The ...For Dummies logo is a trademark, and ...For Dummies is a registered trademark of IDG Books Worldwide, Inc. The CDG Books Canada logo is a trademark of CDG Books Canada, Inc. All other trademarks are the property of their respective owners.

...For Dummies®: Bestselling Book Series for Beginners

 TM

References for the Rest of Us!™

8/99

Roses
For Canadians
FOR
DUMMIES®

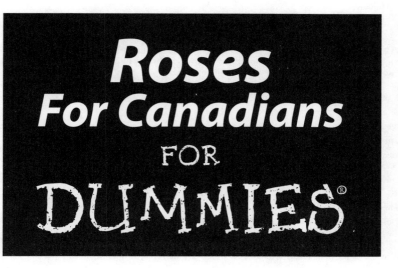

Roses
For Canadians
FOR
DUMMIES®

by **Douglas Green**
The Editors of *Canadian Gardening*
Lance Walheim
The Editors of The National
Gardening Association

CDG
BOOKS
CANADA

CDG Books Canada, Inc.

◆ Toronto, ON ◆

Roses For Canadians For Dummies®

Published by
CDG Books Canada, Inc.
99 Yorkville Avenue
Suite 400
Toronto, ON M5R 3K5
www.cdgbooks.com (CDG Books Canada Web Site)
www.idgbooks.com (IDG Books Worldwide Web Site)
www.dummies.com (Dummies Press Web Site)

Canadian Cataloguing in Publication Data

Green, Douglas

Roses for Canadians for dummies

Includes index.
ISBN: 1-894413-15-6

1. Rose culture – Canada 2. Roses – Varieties. I. Walheim, Lance. II. National Gardening Association (U.S.). III. Title

SB411.5.C3G73 2000   635.9'33734'0971   C00-930700-1

Distributed in Canada by CDG Books Canada, Inc.

For general information on CDG Books, including all IDG Books Worldwide publications, please call our distribution center: HarperCollins Canada at 1-800-387-0117. For reseller information, including discounts and premium sales, please call our Sales department at 1-877-963-8830.

This book is available at special discounts for bulk purchases by your group or organization for resale, premiums, fundraising and seminars. For details, contact CDG Books Canada, Special Sales Department, 99 Yorkville Avenue, Suite 400, Toronto, ON, M5K 3K5; Tel: 416-963-8830; Email: spmarkets@cdgbooks.com.

For press review copies, author interviews, or other publicity information, please contact our Marketing department at 416-963-8830, fax 416-923-4821, or e-mail publicity@cdgbooks.com.

For authorization to photocopy items for corporate, personal, or educational use, please contact Cancopy, The Canadian Copyright Licensing Agency, 1 Yonge Street, Suite 1900, Toronto, ON, M5E 1E5; Tel: 416-868-1620; Fax: 416-868-1621; www.cancopy.com.

Trademarks: For Dummies, Dummies Man, A Reference for the Rest of Us!, The Dummies Way, Dummies Daily, and related trade dress are registered trademarks or trademarks of IDG Books Worldwide, Inc. in the United States, Canada and other countries, and may not be used without written permission. All other trademarks are the property of their respective owners. CDG Books Canada is not associated with any product or vendor mentioned in this book.

is a trademark under exclusive license to CDG Books Canada, Inc., from International Data Group, Inc.

About the Authors

Douglas Green is an Ontario writer and photographer, in addition to being a very active gardener. As the proprietor of Simple Gifts Greenhouses, a specialty greenhouse and nursery growing unusual annuals and perennials, he learned the secrets of cultivating a huge array of domestic and exotic plants. The author of *Tender Roses for Tough Climates*, as well as a contributor to such publications as *Harrowsmith* and *The Garden* (magazine of the British Royal Horticultural Society), Doug provides readers with his personal tried and true garden wisdom. He writes a weekly Internet newsletter — *Garden Magic* — circulated worldwide to over 4,000 subscribers at www.simplegiftsfarm.com.

Canadian Gardening is one of Canada's most popular gardening magazines. Published since 1990, *Canadian Gardening* is the industry leader and has become the definitive source for novice and expert gardening enthusiasts. For more information, check out the Web site at www.canadiangardening.com.

Lance Walheim graduated from University of California, Berkeley with a degree in botany and shortly thereafter began writing and researching books on gardening. He's contributed to more than 40 books on topics ranging from citrus growing to rhododendrons. He has authored three previous books on roses.

The National Gardening Association is the largest member-based, non-profit organization of home gardeners in the United States. Founded in 1972 (as "Gardens for All") to spearhead the community garden movement, today's National Gardening Association is best known for its bimonthly magazine *National Gardening*. Reporting on all aspects of home gardening, each issue is read by some half-million gardeners worldwide.

ABOUT CDG BOOKS CANADA, INC. AND IDG BOOKS WORLDWIDE, INC.

Welcome to the world of IDG Books Worldwide and CDG Books Canada.

IDG Books Worldwide, Inc., is a subsidiary of International Data Group, Inc., the world's largest publisher of computer-related information and the leading global provider of information services on information technology. IDG was founded more than 30 years ago and now employs more than 9,000 people worldwide. IDG publishes more than 295 computer publications in over 75 countries (see listing below). More than 90 million people read one or more IDG publications each month.

Launched in 1990, IDG Books Worldwide is today the #1 publisher of best-selling computer books in North America. IDG Books Worldwide is proud to be the recipient of eight awards from the Computer Press Association in recognition of editorial excellence and three from *Computer Currents'* First Annual Readers' Choice Awards. Our best-selling *...For Dummies®* series has more than 55 million copies in print with translations in 31 languages. In record time, IDG Books Worldwide has become the first choice for millions of readers around the world who want to learn how to better manage their businesses.

In 1998, IDG Books Worldwide formally partnered with Macmillan Canada, a subsidiary of Canada Publishing Corporation, to create CDG Books Canada, a dynamic new Canadian publishing company. CDG Books Canada is now Canada's fastest growing publisher, bringing valuable information to Canadians from coast to coast through the introduction of Canadian *...For Dummies®* and *CliffsNotes™* titles.

Every one of our books is designed to bring extra value and skill-building instructions to the reader. Our books are written by experts who understand and care about our readers. The knowledge base of our editorial staff comes from years of experience in publishing, education, and journalism — experience we use to produce books to carry us into the new millennium. In short, we care about books, so we attract the best people. We devote special attention to details such as audience, interior design, use of icons, and illustrations. And because we use an efficient process of authoring, editing, and desktop publishing our books electronically, we can spend more time ensuring superior content and spend less time on the technicalities of making books.

You can count on our commitment to deliver high-quality books at competitive prices on topics you want to read about. At IDG Books Worldwide and CDG Books Canada, we continue in the IDG tradition of delivering quality for more than 30 years. You can learn more about IDG Books Worldwide and CDG Books Canada by visiting www.idgbooks.com, www.dummies.com, and www.cdgbooks.com.

Eighth Annual Computer Press Awards ≥ 1992

Ninth Annual Computer Press Awards ≥ 1993

Tenth Annual Computer Press Awards ≥ 1994

Eleventh Annual Computer Press Awards ≥ 1995

IDG is the world's leading IT media, research and exposition company. Founded in 1964, IDG had 1997 revenues of $2.05 billion and has more than 9,000 employees worldwide. IDG offers the widest range of media options that reach IT buyers in 75 countries representing 95% of worldwide IT spending. IDG's diverse product and services portfolio spans six key areas including print publishing, online publishing, expositions and conferences, market research, education and training, and global marketing services. More than 90 million people read one or more of IDG's 290 magazines and newspapers, including IDG's leading global brands — Computerworld, PC World, Network World, Macworld and the Channel World family of publications. IDG Books Worldwide is one of the fastest-growing computer book publishers in the world, with more than 700 titles in 36 languages. The "...For Dummies®" series alone has more than 50 million copies in print. IDG offers online users the largest network of technology-specific Web sites around the world through IDG.net (http://www.idg.net), which comprises more than 225 targeted Web sites in 55 countries worldwide. International Data Corporation (IDC) is the world's largest provider of information technology data, analysis and consulting, with research centers in over 41 countries and more than 400 research analysts worldwide. IDG World Expo is a leading producer of more than 168 globally branded conferences and expositions in 35 countries including E3 (Electronic Entertainment Expo), Macworld Expo, ComNet, Windows World Expo, ICE (Internet Commerce Expo), Agenda, DEMO, and Spotlight. IDG's training subsidiary, ExecuTrain, is the world's largest computer training company, with more than 230 locations worldwide and 785 training courses. IDG Marketing Services helps industry-leading IT companies build international brand recognition by developing global integrated marketing programs via IDG's print, online and exposition products worldwide. Further information about the company can be found at www.idg.com. 8/24/99

Dedication

Doug dedicates this book to his children, Christina, Jennifer, Robert, and Elizabeth, who did the weeding while he did the writing.

Lance Walheim and the editors of the National Gardening Association dedicate this book to anyone who can't walk by a rose without sticking his or her nose into it.

Authors' Acknowledgments

Doug thanks the editors at CDG Books Canada, Inc. — Kim Herter and Joan Whitman — for doing such a great job and smoothing the way to make the book happen.

He appreciates all those who reviewed the book for accuracy and relevance to Canadians.

Although rose lovers seldom agree on the best varieties, the best blooming roses, or the most fragrant roses, we all agree that the rose is a wonderful flower.

Doug sends a special thanks to Harry McGee for going over the manuscript with a fine red pen.

Lance Walheim and the National Gardening Association say many thanks to the American Rose Society for the information obtained from many of their chapters, members, and publications. In addition, they thank Weeks Roses, Upland, California; Jackson & Perkins, Medford, Oregon; Sequoia Nursery, Visalia, California; Garden Valley Ranch Nursery, Petaluma, California; and the Pasadena Tournament of Roses, Pasadena, California.

They thank Ann Hooper, a special consultant; Tom Carruth of Weeks Roses; F. Harmon Saville of Nor'East Miniature Roses; David P. Kidger of Primary Products; and American Rose Society Consulting Rosarians Martha Chapin, Dr. Thomas Cairns, Robert Ardini, Malcolm Lowe, and Louise Coleman. At NGA, editors Emily Stetson and Regan Eberhart, as well as Charlie Nardozzi helped keep the book on track, and thanks are extended to the NGA and the staff of the magazine *National Gardening:* David Els, Michael MacCaskey, Linda Provost, and Larry Somers.

Effusive thanks to the team at IDG Books Worldwide, Inc., which includes in Chicago: Kathy Welton and Stacy Collins. In Indianapolis, Pam Mourouzis and Tammy Castleman contributed enormously to this book — many thank-yous to you both.

Publisher's Acknowledgments

We're proud of this book; please register your comments through our IDG Books Worldwide Online Registration Form located at http://my2cents.dummies.com.

Some of the people who helped bring this book to market include the following:

Acquisitions and Editorial

Acquisitions Editor: Joan Whitman

Assistant Editor: Kim Herter

Copy Editor: Lisa Berland

Technical Reviewer: Harry McGee

Photography

Cecil Lamrock — miniature roses; Joyce Fleming — 'Roberta Bondar' rose; Doug Green — 'John Cabot' rose; Anthony Tesselaar and Sally Ferguson of Ferguson Caras — Dream and Flower Carpet series roses; Janet Davis — cover photograph and all remaining interior photographs

Production

Production Manager: Donna Brown

Production Editor: Rebecca Conolly

Layout and Graphics: Kim Monteforte, Heidy Lawrance Associates

Proofreader: Pamela Erlichman

Indexer: Liba Berry

Illustrations: Ron Hildebrand

Special Help

Michael Kelly, Tammy Castleman, Tom Hopkins, Beth Parlon, Dr. Felicitas Svejda, Amy Black

General and Administrative

IDG Books Worldwide, Inc.: John Kilcullen, CEO; William Barry, President

CDG Books Canada, Inc.: Ron Besse, Chairman; Tom Best, President; Robert Harris, Vice President and Publisher

IDG Books Technology Publishing Group: Richard Swadley, Senior Vice President and Publisher; Walter Bruce III, Vice President and Associate Publisher; Steven Sayre, Associate Publisher; Joseph Wikert, Associate Publisher; Mary Bednarek, Branded Product Development Director; Mary Corder, Editorial Director

IDG Books Consumer Publishing Group: Roland Elgey, Senior Vice President and Publisher; Kathleen A. Welton, Vice President and Publisher; Kevin Thornton, Acquisitions Manager; Kristin A. Cocks, Editorial Director

IDG Books Internet Publishing Group: Brenda McLaughlin, Senior Vice President and Publisher; Diane Graves Steele, Vice President and Associate Publisher; Sofia Marchant, Online Marketing Manager

IDG Books Production for Dummies Press: Michael R. Britton, Vice President of Production; Debbie Stailey, Associate Director of Production; Cindy L. Phipps, Manager of Project Coordination, Production Proofreading, and Indexing; Tony Augsburger, Manager of Prepress, Reprints, and Systems; Laura Carpenter, Production Control Manager; Shelley Lea, Supervisor of Graphics and Design; Debbie J. Gates, Production Systems Specialist; Robert Springer, Supervisor of Proofreading; Kathie Schutte, Production Supervisor

Dummies Packaging and Book Design: Patty Page, Manager, Promotions Marketing

◆

The publisher would like to give special thanks to Patrick J. McGovern,
without whom this book would not have been possible.

◆

Contents at a Glance

Cartoons at a Glance

By Rich Tennant

page 63

page 285

page 95

page 9

page 305

page 193

Fax: 978-546-7747

E-mail: richtennant@the5thwave.com

World Wide Web: www.the5thwave.com

Table of Contents

Introduction

*I*f you asked ten people to name their favourite flower, probably nine would name the rose. Think about it for a second. What other flower offers so much? There's the wonderful, almost sensuous way a rose opens — the petals slowly unfurling, so softly, so gently. And the colours are so intense, so vivid, and sometimes just so wild. And what about the fragrance? Even though rose fragrance seems to surround us in perfumes, air fresheners, and what have you, there's still nothing more refreshing or revitalizing than sticking your nose in a rose and taking a deep breath. Oh, the fragrance!

But our meagre attempt at describing the beauty of roses as perfect flowers can never stand up to those of poets, painters, artists, and writers, who for centuries have tried to capture that beauty in words and pictures. Even though roses have been loved for so long and are so popular today, their use and appreciation as flowering shrubs — hardworking plants that can form the backbone of a landscape as hedges, ground covers, and sources of season-long colour — may be only in its infancy.

It is easy to be bewildered by how huge and versatile this group of plants is. Roses are wonderful landscape plants that are unmatched for the length of the season in which they bloom and the amount of colour they produce. But who really thinks of them as utilitarian plants? Not enough people, that's for sure.

And no matter what you've heard, roses are easy to grow. In fact, many roses are tough plants that fit perfectly into the low-maintenance gardens of the modern world. Sure, they need a little care, but what plant doesn't? The pleasure they give in return is well worth it.

About This Book

This book aims to change the way you think about roses. They are *not* finicky plants that need constant attention and a social security pension to keep them healthy. Roses are plants for the 21st century — blooming unselfishly, pleasing the eye and nose, and asking only for your appreciation in return. Even though the rose family is huge, the goal of this book is to make roses easy to understand. We tell you not only how to distinguish one type of rose from another, but also how to best use each type and colour, whether you want one plant for a bouquet or 100 plants for a hedge. This book can help you make roses work for *you*.

And you don't have to read this book cover to cover to understand the wide world of roses. You'll find a great deal of interesting and useful information, but we've put it together in a way that is easy to access. If you have a question, you can answer it quickly and then put the book down until you need it again.

The first thing we want you to realize is that a rose is not just a rose. Even if you already grow roses, maybe have for years, you can still find plenty of new information to excite you.

Before you get your hands dirty, and get to know roses — how the plants grow, how the flowers form, and what makes them smell so good — you'll likely have a lot of questions. They are all answered in this book, and in easy-to-understand language. All the things you need to know to grow roses in Canada are right here.

Conventions Used in This Book

Rose gardeners, or any gardeners for that matter, have their own jargon. Although most words are straightforward and down to earth (most of you won't have any trouble figuring out *watering, fertilizing,* or *pruning,* for example), one area is a bit trickier: the names of specific plants. To ensure that we all know which plant we're talking about, gardeners have a system of plant naming based on Latin.

So following conventional garden nomenclature, we list the common names of plants in normal type, usually lowercased (dog rose, for example). Every plant is a member of a larger horticultural family, sharing general horticultural characteristics with other members. For roses, that family is Rosaceae. All roses share the same family, but, interestingly enough, other common garden plants are also members of the rose family, including apples, hawthorns, and potentilla.

Plant families are divided into groups of closer relatives, indicated by a group or genus name. This genus name is always written in italics with the first letter capitalized. Thus, the genus name for rose is *Rosa* and the genus name for apples is *Malus*.

The next name is the species name. Like the genus, this name is written in italics, but the first letter is lowercase. Only some of the oldest roses, such as *Rosa multiflora*, are described by species. Most modern roses are grouped by class instead of species: hybrid teas, floribundas, grandifloras, climbers, and so on. You'll find out more about those in Chapter 1. Within each group are the varieties. We won't bore you with all the reasons why, but these are usually enclosed in single quotation marks. These names, like 'Queen Elizabeth' and 'Double Delight', are types of names that you will become most familiar with. On a rare occasion, a *botanical rose variety,* meaning that the rose was found flourishing in the wild rather than having been created by a rose breeder, is listed as the third part of the botanical name, in italics with the first letter lowercased. But you need not lose sleep over that.

Foolish Assumptions

In writing this book, we're assuming a few things about you and your experience with roses:

- ✔ You've been one of the lucky ones to receive a bouquet of roses from a florist, or you've envied those friends, relatives, or co-workers who were.
- ✔ You enjoy gardening or want to give it a try.
- ✔ You've tried growing roses before, but may not have been very successful with them, or you heard roses are so difficult to grow that you've been afraid to try them out.
- ✔ You're interested in growing your own roses, or you already grow them and want to expand your collection of these wonderful flowers.
- ✔ You've stuck your nose in a rose and enjoyed its exquisite fragrance.
- ✔ You think that roses are very colourful and want to bring some of that colour into your own garden or home.

How This Book Is Organized

This book is organized into parts, each of which contains several chapters. If you already know a bit about roses, you may want to skip the chapters in Part I since you're probably familiar with basic rose anatomy and the various rose classifications that exist. Use the Table of Contents as a guide to find the topics that interest you most. Each chapter is designed to be read on its own or in sequence with the other parts of the book — you don't have to read or re-read anything if you don't want to — decide for yourself what information you want to look at first. The sections below give you a quick outline of what's in store.

Part I: Roses 101

Roses are a diverse group of plants. Having a basic understanding of the different classes of roses, from the beautifully formed hybrid teas to the floriferous shrub roses to the sprawling climbers, and how they grow and bloom, helps you appreciate their versatility. Part I tells all about rose plants, rose flowers, and rose fragrance. It also explains why where you live influences which roses you can grow and how you grow them.

Chapter 1 gives you a basic introduction to rose types and the lingo used to describe them, and tells how you can use roses in the landscape.

Chapter 2 introduces you to rose flowers: how they form, which colours they come in, and what distinguishes their character.

Chapter 3 is about rose fragrance and how to enjoy it fully. It tells you which varieties smell best and why.

Chapter 4 gives you everything you need to know about rose climates. It includes lists of varieties that are proven performers in your geographic area and gives you tips on how to recognize the best place to plant them in your yard.

Part II: Using Roses in Your Garden

Here's where we put roses to work in the garden.

Chapter 5 tells you how to use roses in the landscape as hedges, screens, edgings, ground covers, and everywhere else you'd never think to plant them.

Chapter 6 is about combining roses with other plants, such as flowering perennials and herbs.

Chapter 7 tells you the basics on growing roses in containers, from which type of pot and soil to use to choosing the best varieties and caring for them.

Part III: All the Roses You Need to Know

You can choose from literally thousands of rose varieties. In this part, we help you make the best choices. Each chapter contains lists of popular rose varieties with full descriptions, all organized by flower colour.

Chapter 8 covers hybrid tea type roses, probably the most widely known variety. You've definitely seen this kind of rose in your local florist's window in all its long-stemmed perfection.

Chapter 9 introduces you to grandifloras, a sort of cousin to the hybrid tea.

Chapter 10 discusses polyantha and floribunda roses — everything from their origins to our favourite varieties.

Chapter 11 brings miniature roses to light — their versatility and hardiness may surprise you.

Chapter 12 explores the characteristics of climbing roses and recommends the most hardy varieties for Canadian climates.

Chapter 13 describes the diverse range of shrub roses and the best growing techniques to keep them blooming.

Chapter 14 presents the great-grandparents of the rose family — species and old garden roses.

Chapter 15 identifies the extra-hardy Canadian-bred roses in the Explorer and Parkland series.

Colour Pictures

In the centre of this book, you'll find colour pictures of roses. Whereas all the roses described in the text are arranged by type, here the roses are arranged by colour. We've also included Agriculture Canada's Plant Hardiness Zone Map so you can determine which hardiness zone you live in and can choose the right roses for your climate.

Part IV: Growing Healthy Roses

This part gives you the nuts and bolts on everything you need to know about growing roses, from picking them out at the nursery to keeping them free from pests and diseases.

Chapter 16 describes the different ways roses are sold and which may be the best for you.

Chapter 17 takes you through the proper techniques for planting roses.

Chapter 18 covers the basics on watering and mulching. Don't worry; we tell you how much water to apply and how often to apply it.

Chapter 19 is about the nutrients you can apply to keep your roses healthy and blooming on and on.

Chapter 20 makes pruning roses simple. It's all here — the tools you need, when to prune, and no-nonsense talk on the exact technique.

Chapter 21 helps you get your roses through chilly winters.

Chapter 22 is about insects and diseases and what to do to prevent them while still keeping your garden a healthy and happy place.

Chapter 23 shows you how to increase your rose collection and, if you're so inclined, even create your own unique varieties.

Chapter 24 is about drying rose flowers and using them to make wonderfully fragrant potpourris.

Part V: The Part of Tens

This part contains all the rest of the fun stuff that doesn't fit neatly anywhere else.

Chapter 25 answers the most commonly asked questions about roses — no-nonsense, quick, and to the point.

Chapter 26 is the anti-primer on roses — things you should *not* do if you want to grow healthy roses. With these tips in mind, you'll be sure to avoid the most common gardening blunders.

Chapter 27 focuses on one of the best ways to use roses: as cut flowers.

Chapter 28 is a light-hearted look at roses and rose gardens that have made history.

Part VI: Appendixes

One thing about growing roses — they grow on you, and fast. You always want more information about where to find them, tricks for growing them right in your neighbourhood, even how you can show them off when everything goes right and you grow the perfect flower.

Rose societies are everywhere — the flowers are that popular. Join one and you have a wealth of information and expertise at your fingertips. You can also enter your flowers in rose shows. In Appendix A, we tell you what rose societies offer and how to sign up.

Mail-order catalogues often sell everything you need, from the most obscure rose varieties to the latest irrigation technology. And you don't have to leave home to shop. In Appendix B, we list Canadian rose growers, many of which offer mail-order services through catalogues and Web sites. In addition, we list online sources of rose information and suppliers who specialize in gardening equipment we think you may want to have. Appendix B also contains useful provincial contact information for soil testing, insect control, and growing conditions in your area.

Icons Used in This Book

We use the following icons throughout the book to point out particularly important information:

Helps you avoid common pitfalls or dangerous situations.

Demystifies gardening lingo. (Although we've made this book as jargon-free as possible, you need to know some terms.)

Gives addresses and/or phone numbers for ordering special gardening equipment, supplies, or specific plants. (You can also find sources in Appendix B.) Information next to this icon may help you find useful tidbits for your rose growing.

Flags helpful information that even some experienced gardeners may not know.

Marks varieties that are pictured in the colour section of this book.

Where to Go from Here

If you're just beginning and want to find out why the rose is one of the most beloved flowers, go to Part I. If you want to know how to use roses in the landscape or grow them in containers, go to Part II. Head to Part III if you're trying to decide which rose to buy. Go to Part IV if you want to learn all there is about growing roses, from buying them in nurseries to planting, watering, and fertilizing to controlling common pests. If you're just looking for some fun facts about roses, go to Part V.

Part I
Roses 101

In this part . . .

The rose has been called the Queen of Flowers, and people have treasured it for as long as people have been in existence. Cro-Magnon man probably brought a bouquet of roses back to the cave for his mate. And she was undoubtedly as thrilled to receive them as people are today.

Rose hobbyists, otherwise known as rosarians, would have the world believe that roses require more fertilizer, more water, more love, more attention, more time, and more money than any other flowering plant — probably because rosarians usually enter their blossoms in rose shows and are in a never-ending search for the perfect rose. Although we admit that rosarians grow some pretty spectacular roses, we also want to assure you that everyday gardeners can get great results with very little effort.

This part familiarizes you with the unique language and culture that have developed around rose culture and tells you how roses are classified, how the plants grow, how the flowers form, what colours they come in, and which varieties are fragrant and why.

We also have to do some geo-positioning. Most roses grow and bloom anywhere they get proper care. But one of the tricks of growing great roses with a minimum of hassles is to choose varieties that are well adapted to your climate. And that means knowing a little about your climate — whether the summers are hot and dry, hot and humid, or cool and humid, and whether the winters are frigid and icy or merely almost icy and uncomfortable.

Once you become weather-wise, you can choose the right varieties — for example, ones that are hardy enough to survive your cold winters, that resist disease where it's hot and humid, or that bloom beautifully despite cool summers. To give you suggestions, this part also provides lists of recommended roses for different types of climates.

Chapter 1

Everything You Need to Know about Roses

● ●

In This Chapter

▶ Why roses are easy to grow

▶ Where roses come from

▶ Why you need to know the definition of budding

▶ Which roses you should grow

▶ How roses are grouped

▶ Where new rose varieties come from

● ●

*W*hether you just want to mix a couple of roses in with your other perennials or you get so hooked that you want to make roses your hobby, you won't find any plant that is more beautiful or as satisfying. Roses are fun and easy to grow, particularly if you know a little about them before you start.

Of course, no book can include everything about roses, but we think that this one comes close to having all you need to know in order to buy, plant, grow, and care for just about any rose. But then again, we would.

If you want to go out and dig a hole this very minute, stop. Read this chapter first. But if you've already dug yourself into a hole by jumping in without knowing what you were doing, remember the old adage:

If at first you don't succeed, read the directions and try again.

Are Roses as Hard to Grow as Everyone Says?

If you gain one thing from this book, you should be able to answer anyone who tells you that roses are hard to grow. Plain and simple, roses get a bum rap in this department, but like many stereotypes, this one does contain a grain of truth. As you peruse this chapter — and throughout this book — you'll quickly gain a sense of how many different kinds of roses you can buy, and you'll find out how different from each other they are.

We may be stretching the point, but we'll make an analogy with cars (any automobile enthusiast can relate). Some cars are expensive, and some aren't. Some look great, and some don't. Some are easy to maintain, and some aren't. Yet they're all cars. If you were wary of working on cars, you wouldn't buy an antique Jaguar or Triumph. You probably wouldn't buy a new Lamborghini, either.

If you don't want to fuss over your roses after you plant them, don't choose the fanciest, most beautiful, most fragrant long-stemmed rose. Look for something a bit more . . . well, practical. And please don't assume that an "easy" rose doesn't look so good. 'Champlain' is one of the easiest (and hardiest) repeat-blooming roses to grow, and it's also one of the most beautiful red roses. We're only saying that out of the thousands of roses available, some are the easiest, most trouble-free plants you'll ever meet, and yet some will need the indulgent fussing that some gardeners love to provide.

Which Rose Should I Grow?

Good question — and exactly the subject of a good portion of this book. Unfortunately, no one can answer this question for you. You have to become familiar with what's available, develop some preferences (for a colour or fragrance, for example), and give some thought to the type of rose that's likely to thrive in your garden (or how much care you're willing to provide).

We think that colour is a great place to start, and that's why we organize the pictures in this book according to the colour of the roses. You can look there among the roses of a colour you like and then refer to the chapters that describe the specific roses. Also, you can find lists of roses throughout this book: ones that look good, smell good, grow well, are cold hardy, and what have you. Chapter 4 includes several lists of roses for different uses.

Finally, again and again in this book, we recommend that you consult with a local rose expert (a *rosarian*) if possible and visit public gardens that offer substantial displays of roses. Either way, you'll know for a fact that a particular rose grows well — or really struggles — in your area.

Where Do Roses Come From?

Botanists believe that roses in some form flourished long before humans inhabited the earth, and it's thought that people have cultivated roses for more than 5,000 years. Many of these early roses, called *species roses* (you can read about them in Chapter 14), are still around. But humans have been applying their genius to rose culture (growing) and rose hybridizing (breeding) for a long time. Now gardeners can have the best of both worlds — species and old garden roses as well as modern hybrids.

Most rose plants that you can buy today are grown by *commercial rose growers* in huge rose fields in fairly temperate climates. In North America, nearly all the rose plants are grown commercially in California, Arizona, and Texas, as well as by smaller nurseries in British Columbia and Ontario. Many Canadian roses are imported either from the United States or Holland. These plants are field grown for two years before they're harvested while leafless and dormant (their normal winter rest period). They are stored *bareroot* (a descriptive term meaning that they have no soil on their roots) in huge, moist, refrigerated facilities to keep them from growing before being shipped to gardeners, nurseries, and garden centres nationwide in winter or early spring. You can find out more about all this rose-buying stuff in Chapter 16.

What Are Roses Made Of?

For all their perceived mystery, roses are pretty simple plants, as Figure 1-1 shows. They consist of *roots* that feed the plant, taking up water and nutrients from the soil, and *canes* (or stems). These canes grow from above the bud union to produce the desired flowers. Note that if the canes come from below the bud union, they are called suckers and are pruned off. The leaves and branching canes grow from *bud eyes,* small buds that sprout at intervals along the cane. The leaves are usually produced in five-leaf *leaflets,* although, to make your life interesting, rose leaflet numbers vary from variety to variety. As a plant thrives, new canes sprout both from the crown of the plant and from the junction of the cane and the leaflets.

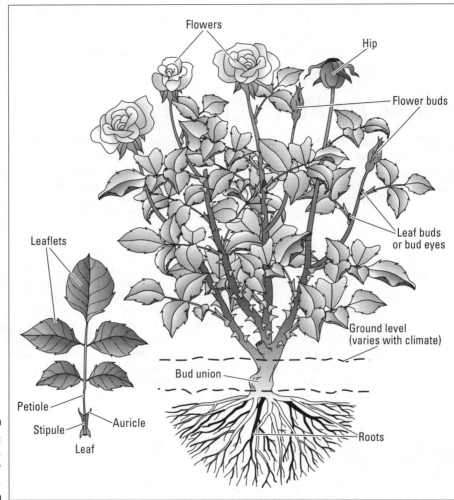

Figure 1-1:
The anatomy of a rose.

Rose flowers are called *roses, flowers, blooms,* or *blossoms.* A rose flower stays on the plant and looks like a rose for a certain length of time, depending on the variety. When the flower fades, falls apart, or otherwise dies, it is called a *spent bloom* and should be cut off the plant to encourage repeat flowering. Cutting off dead flowers is called *deadheading.* The rate at which a rose plant can form a new flower is called *repeat.*

Most *modern roses* — those that have been bred since the late 19th century — are *ever-blooming* or *recurrent,* which means that they are repeat bloomers and flower continuously throughout the growing season. Many older rose varieties bloom only once a season. To find out more about rose flowers, see Chapter 2.

What's This Budding Thing All About?

Many types of roses are grafted, or, more correctly, budded, onto a rootstock, as opposed to growing on their own roots as most perennials do. A *rootstock* is simply a rose that produces a good, hardy root but not a heavy-flowering top. We cut off the poor top (replacing it with a bud from a good rose) but use the excellent root to encourage good growth on the heavy-flowering plants we want to grow. Not only do some roses (usually the more tender varieties) perform better on hardy rootstocks, new plants don't have to take a long time to establish extensive root systems in your garden. Growers get a larger percentage of roses to thrive on rootstocks than they do when growing roses on their own roots.

Commercial growers take canes from the varieties they want to propagate. They cut the *bud eye*, or the junction of the cane and a leaf, from the cane and insert it under the bark on the cane of a rootstock plant. When the canes and foliage are cut off the rootstock plant, all the plant's energy goes toward making the newly budded eye grow. The bud eye from the desired variety has all the genetic material needed to create a new plant that's identical to the original.

The point at which the bud is inserted into the bark of the rootstock plant is called the *bud union*. On mature plants, the bud union looks like a knob. As the plant grows in your garden, new, large canes grow from the bud union.

In cold climates, the bud union is the part of the plant that's most important to protect in winter. Plant the bud union up to 15 centimetres (6 inches) below the ground in cold-winter climates or protect it by covering it with a mound of soil during the winter months. (For more about growing roses in cold regions, see Chapter 21, "Protecting Roses Where Winters Are Cold.")

How Are Roses Grouped?

The plant family Rosaceae is the third largest plant family. This family includes many ornamental landscape plants, as well as fruits such as apples, cherries, and raspberries, that are characterized by the shape of the *hip* (the part of the flower where the seeds develop) and by having petals in groups of five. Within the Rosaceae family, roses are members of the plant genus *Rosa*. Within that genus, roses can be grouped into seven different classifications based on their characteristics:

- Hybrid tea
- Grandiflora
- Polyantha and floribunda
- Miniature
- Climber and rambler
- Shrub
- Species and old garden

Each rose classification has its own special qualities. Deciding which rose to grow depends on how you plan to use it and on your personal preferences. Some rose gardeners grow only one or two types of roses, and others grow many types. Our advice is to try growing one or two in each class and see which rose types you prefer. Here are the basic differences between the various types of roses, listed in alphabetical order:

- **Climbers** (see Figure 1-2) don't really climb like clematis or other true vines that wrap around or attach themselves to supports. They do, however, produce really long canes that need to be anchored to a fence, trellis, or other support. Otherwise, the plants sprawl on the ground. Flowers bloom along the whole length of the cane, especially if the cane is tied laterally, such as along a fence. Some climbers bloom only once in the spring, but many modern climbers produce flowers throughout the growing season. Climbing roses are described in Chapter 12.

The old-world class system

The World Federation of Rose Societies does not recognize the seven-category system of rose classifications — preferring instead to use two classes: 1) large-flowering roses and 2) cluster-flowering roses. Seems simple enough doesn't it? You won't see this classification being used in North American nurseries or catalogues (or this book), but we tell you about it in case you're reading European books or magazines and they bring it up.

Figure 1-2:
A climbing rose trained as a pillar.

The keepers of rose knowledge

The history of roses is obviously a rich one, and keeping track of new varieties and of new developments is an important job of rose societies. In Canada, the Canadian Rose Society maintains a membership of interested rose growers, publishes the thrice-yearly *Rosarian* magazine and the yearly *Rose Annual*, holds rose shows, and provides local rose growers and societies with information. To keep track of new roses, the International Registration Authority — Roses (IRAR) is run by the American Rose Society. It registers new varieties of roses to ensure that accurate records are kept regarding rose names, descriptions, and ownership, as well as trademark and patent information.

For more information about the Canadian Rose Society, and similar groups in other parts of Canada, see Appendix A.

✔ **Floribundas** (see Figure 1-3) have smaller flowers that usually grow in clusters on short stems. The bush is usually quite compact and blooms continually throughout the growing season. Most floribundas are budded, but commercial growers are beginning to grow them on their own roots. Choose floribundas if you need fairly low-growing plants that produce great numbers of colourful flowers. Floribundas are featured in Chapter 10.

Figure 1-3:
A floribunda
rose plant.

✔ **Grandifloras** (see Figure 1-4) are usually tall-growing plants with hybrid tea-type flowers that are smaller than hybrid teas. The flowers often grow in clusters, but the stems on each flower within a cluster are long enough for cutting. Grandifloras are almost always budded and are a good choice if you like lots of bloom for colour in the garden and stems for cutting, all on the same plant. We talk about grandifloras in Chapter 9.

Figure 1-4:
A grandiflora rose plant.

✔ **Hybrid teas** (see Figure 1-5) have large flowers that usually grow one to a long stem. The bush can grow quite tall, with an upright *habit* (a term we use to describe the shape or look of a plant). Hybrid tea roses are usually budded onto a hardy rootstock. The plant flowers continually throughout the growing season. Hybrid teas are a great choice if you like large flowers with a real rose form (the centre is higher than outside petals) and if you like to make rose arrangements or have cut flowers in the house. Chapter 8 features hybrid teas.

Figure 1-5:
A hybrid tea
rose plant.

✔ **Miniatures** (see Figure 1-6) are small plants, usually between 15 and 90
centimetres (6 and 36 inches) in height. Their leaves and flowers are in
perfect proportion. Extremely popular, they are not usually budded but
grow on their own roots, making them hardier in cold climates. Most mini
varieties bloom profusely and are a great choice if you need lots of colour
in a small space. You also can grow miniatures indoors in pots on a sunny
windowsill or under fluorescent lights. Miniature roses are covered in
Chapter 11.

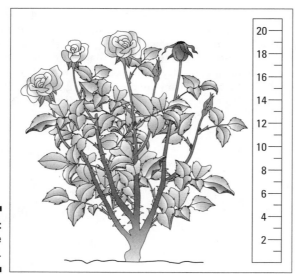

Figure 1-6:
A miniature
rose plant.

✔ **Old garden roses** (also called heritage, antique, or classic roses) are divided into two categories — those discovered or hybridized before 1867 and those discovered or hybridized after 1867. The classification *old garden roses* comprises many subclasses of roses, including alba, bourbon, China, hybrid perpetual, damask, and the species roses. By far the largest percentage of old garden roses bloom only once during the growing season. Old garden rose aficionados enjoy the history and study of these lovely and often fragrant plants. We cover them in Chapter 14.

✔ **Polyanthas** are the forerunner of modern floribundas. They are usually moderately sized in Canada, and covered with small, miniature-type flowers. The usual habit is compact, hardy, and generous-blooming. The variety we see most often is 'The Fairy', which is a wonderful variety, covered with small pink flowers on a plant that can spread to a few metres in height and width. Because they are so similar, we group the polyanthas with the floribundas in Chapter 10.

✔ **Ramblers** are the forerunners of today's large-flowered climbers. The large, hardy, free-growing plants generally bloom only once in early summer, although there are several repeat bloomers such as 'Super Excelsa'. In warmer parts of the United States they often grow wild, but unfortunately ramblers are not reliably winter hardy without protection in most parts of Canada. Although not many garden centres carry them, you can still find ramblers in specialist rose catalogues. You can find more about them in Chapter 12.

✔ **Shrubs** (see Figure 1-7) have become very popular in recent years because most are quite hardy and easy to grow. They are generally large plants, and most, particularly the modern shrubs, bloom profusely throughout the season. They are great for landscaping. If you have a large space that you want filled with colour, the shrub category offers a great deal of choices. For more information, see Chapter 13.

Figure 1-7:
A shrub rose.

✔ **Tree roses,** or standards, aren't included among the basic categories because nearly any rose that is grafted (more specifically, budded) onto a tall trunk is a tree rose. Most often, hybrid teas, floribundas, and miniatures are used as tree roses. These plants really aren't even trees. Most just have that lollipop tree look, as shown in Figure 1-8, but are only 60 to 180 centimetres (2 to 6 feet) high. They are wonderful either in the ground or in containers but are very susceptible to winter damage, and in cold climates you must either bury the entire plant (tops and all) in the ground or overwinter it indoors in a cool storage area.

Figure 1-8:
A tree rose.

When you go to a garden centre to choose your rosebushes, knowing which classification of rose you want is important. The classification dictates its use in your garden. You don't want to plant a once-blooming old garden rose in a spot where having season-long colour is important. The *variety* you choose (see the following section) depends on your personal preference as to colour, hardiness, and so on.

Where Do Rose Cultivars Fit In?

Within each classification of roses there are many different *cultivars*. These differ from each other in colour, fragrance, growth vigour, and hardiness, but not in the basic flower construction or growth habit. Sometimes you'll see a cultivar referred to as a variety. While botanically incorrect, in common usage they are the same thing. Most of us use the incorrect term *variety* and only those who prefer horticultural correctness to plain speaking use *cultivar*. Technically, a cultivar is a ***culti*vated *var*iety**, while a variety is the category of plant name that comes between the subspecies and the forma. Having said that mouthful, unless you have a botanist hanging over your shoulder, don't worry about which term you use. While it is technically incorrect, we'll use *variety* throughout this book just to make life easier for us all.

For example, the variety 'Olympiad' is classified as a hybrid tea rose. So if you're looking for a lovely red rose that has a classic rose form and grows on long stems for cutting, you may want to consider the hybrid tea 'Olympiad'. Cultivars or varieties of all types or classifications of roses are described in Part III of this book.

Where Do New Roses Come From?

Many new varieties of roses are introduced to the gardening public each year. Some of them are so fabulous that you can't resist seeing them grow in your own garden. But who invents new rose varieties? Rose breeders, more correctly called *rose hybridizers,* are unique people. First, there aren't many of them — perhaps fewer than 100 in the whole world. Some are amateurs — usually *rosarians* (people who are very serious about growing roses) who take their hobby a step further and try their hand at hybridizing. Some are independent hybridizers, who develop new varieties and sell them to commercial rose growers. But the most successful (and financially secure) rose hybridizers are employed by commercial rose growers who can better afford to support large-scale hybridizing programs and the years of development needed to bring a new rose to the market.

Roses are crossbred by pollen exchange. The hybridizer must be an expert in rose genetics in order to choose existing varieties whose desirable characteristics will be passed on to a new variety and whose undesirable characteristics will not.

After pollen is exchanged, the rose hip must be left to ripen. When it is harvested, the hip is cut off the plant and broken open, and the seeds are stored for a few weeks before they're planted in flats in a carefully controlled greenhouse.

Rose denominations

To further complicate the issue of rose names, here's a tidbit of information that won't affect you in any way unless you want to grow roses commercially or want to be a contestant on *Jeopardy!*: Each variety of rose has a *denomination*, or code name. The denomination identifies the rose plant no matter what commercial name the plant is given. Sometimes, roses that are bred in Europe are introduced into Canada under another variety name (and vice versa). For example, the floribunda 'Livin' Easy' is also called 'Fellowship'. But the denomination is the same in Europe and in Canada.

The denomination consists of three capital letters that indicate the company that owns the rights to the rose, plus a bunch of usually meaningless lowercase letters that indicate the particular cultivar. The floribunda 'Livin' Easy' (or 'Fellowship' in Europe) is ultimately identifiable by its denomination, HARwelcome. *HAR* indicates that the rights to the plant are owned by Harkness & Company in England, and *welcome* tells you that the plant is the orange floribunda you know and love. (Note that *welcome* is not part of the rose name but part of the denomination — just to keep things clear between us.)

Rose breeders and commercial rose growers go through all this rigmarole because they patent their new varieties of roses. In Canada, plant breeder's rights last for 18 years, so the owner of the rights can collect a royalty on each plant that's sold here for 18 years. These rights, which vary from country to country, protect the breeders and encourage new plant development. So, no matter the name or where it is sold, patents and international treaties protect the breeder.

Next time you buy a rosebush, notice the metal tag that's attached. The denomination is printed under the variety name, either in parentheses or after the abbreviation cv (for *cultivar*). For example:

- Timeless™ (JACecond)

- Scentimental™ cv. WEKplapep

JAC is the abbreviation for Jackson & Perkins, and *WEK* is the abbreviation for Weeks Roses.

In one hybridizing season, hundreds of thousands, perhaps half a million, seeds are planted. From the seedlings, eventually only three or four are deemed worthy of selling to gardeners.

New seedlings are tested for several years to ensure that the new variety grows well in all climates, is not a haven for every pest and disease that comes along, and has pleasing flowers and a desirable growth habit. It's not unusual for a new rose variety to be tested for ten years or more before it comes to market.

How does a rose get its name?

Who really thinks up those wild names you see in catalogues? Most of the time, the breeder names the rose, but sometimes other considerations come into play.

We asked Joyce Fleming, a rose breeder in Southern Ontario, how she names her roses. Most of her rose introductions are named after her family, but her best rose to date was named after Canadian astronaut Dr. Roberta Bondar. This yellow climbing rose was named because Joyce thinks, "Canadians need to honour their heroes — especially their women heroes." Dr. Bondar agreed to have this rose named after her, in fact given the choice of two roses, she chose the yellow climber. After you see the picture of this yellow rose, you'll agree that 'Roberta Bondar', a tall-growing, heavily blooming rose, is well and aptly named. A hero indeed!

Of course large rose nurseries name their roses so that they will sell well. Which would you be more inclined to purchase? A rose called 'Dream' or one called 'Seagull'; a rose called 'Fragrant Delight' or one called 'Tower Bridge'? In business terms, a mediocre name can ruin a great rose just as a good name can sell a mediocre rose. One of the best-selling roses of all time was introduced immediately after World War II. Its name? 'Peace'.

Once a new rose's name is chosen, it is registered with the American Rose Society to ensure the name and description is original and correct. After the name has been accepted as not having been used before, the breeder can register the rose under Canadian Plant Breeder's Rights legislation. This registration expense is not undertaken lightly by small breeders such as Joyce Fleming. In fact, Joyce has not patented any of her roses due to the cost. Rose growing and naming can be big business.

Chapter 2

It's All about Flowers

*F*lowers are the reason people grow roses. Rose flowers come in almost all colours and many shapes. Depending on the kind of rose you buy, the plant may flower once or all season long. No matter what kind of roses you like, the flowers are endlessly fascinating. But to make sure that the rose you buy has the colour, shape, size, and blooming schedule that suits your yard, your climate, and your expectations, you should know what to look for.

Rose flowers have enthralled human beings through the ages. In fact, the Empress Josephine — you know, Napoleon's main squeeze — made rose gardening the "in thing" for generations of gardeners, right up until today. She started in 1798 and attempted to collect every known variety of rose for her garden at Malmaison, near Paris. When she died in 1814, she had collected 250 different varieties.

Today, you can find thousands of rose varieties, all, in one way or another, descended from the early roses.

What endear roses to people are the colour, the shape, the substance, the fragrance, the size, and the overall appeal of the flowers. In this chapter we thought we'd give you a little background to help you understand and appreciate the huge variety of roses that are available.

Anatomy of a Rose

Like most plants, the flowers of a rose plant are its sexual anatomy. The petals of each blossom surround the sexual parts of the plant, which include both male and female organs. Yep, roses have both male and female parts, all in one lovely flower, making them able to self-pollinate.

Figure 2-1 shows a cross-section of a rose flower. The *stamens,* which are so lovely in many varieties of roses, are the male parts of the rose. The *anthers,* at the top of the stamens, produce the pollen that fertilizes the *ovules,* or eggs, which are at the bottom of the pistils, inside the hip of the flower. Rose flowers can self-pollinate, but the resulting new plant is rarely as good as the original. You can find out more about the sex life of roses in Chapter 23.

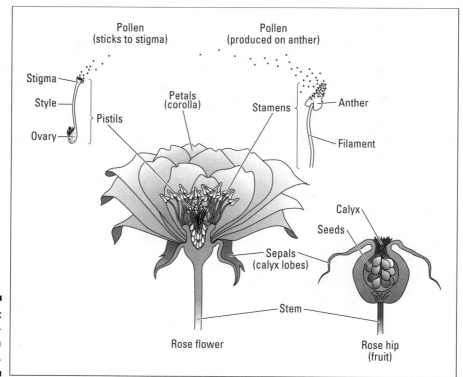

Figure 2-1:
A cross-section of a rose flower.

The *sepals* are leaf-like structures that protect the rose buds, covering them before they open. They slowly separate to reveal the colour of the developing flower and finally pull away entirely, allowing the petals of the bud to unfurl. The sepals are often a very attractive part of the flower, particularly if their feathery ends extend above the top of the bud. When they drop, allowing the petals to open, they can be a very decorative underpinning to a beautiful flower.

Petalling Around Town

You can find much beauty in all the parts of a rose flower, but what most people consider perfection in a rose bloom is the petals — the colour, the substance, the arrangement of the petals, and the fragrance.

A rose can have no petals at all, like the famous green rose, *Rosa chinensis viridiflora*. Really, what seem to be the petals of the flower are actually lots of sepals. Many people consider the green rose uglier than several miles of bad road, but others find a strange beauty in its greenness. The green rose is of the China family of roses, and, as with all Chinas, has a well-deserved reputation of being quite frost-tender. This plant will not survive typical Canadian winters. Bury the entire rose quite deeply or take it indoors to a cool room. Unlike most other old garden roses, however, the Chinas, including the green rose, bloom all season long. (See Chapter 21 for details of overwintering.)

Or a rose can have so many petals that it won't open in anything but the hottest weather. Sometimes these many-petalled roses are so fabulous that they're worth growing, even if you see only a few blooms a year during a heat wave. The most notorious rose for having so many petals that many of the flowers end up as squishy rotten balls at the top of a strong cane is the hybrid tea 'Uncle Joe'. The plant is a large one, often reaching 180 to 210 centimetres (6 or 7 feet) tall, with wonderful, clean foliage. In hot weather, when the flowers do open, they are among the most beautiful of the red hybrid teas.

Because roses are all about flowers, we couldn't resist adding pictures of some of our favourites to this book. They're easy to find — look for the colour section of different-textured paper. The photographs are arranged, sensibly we think, by colour so that you can easily compare features of roses with the same colour flowers.

The most common petal formations fall into three categories:

✔ **Single:** Many beautiful roses have only a single row of petals. Like the wonderful 'Dainty Bess', a single hybrid tea with five large, pale pink petals surrounding bright red stamens, roses that are single can be very lovely. 'Eyepaint' is another beautiful single rose. See Figure 2-2 for an example of a single rose.

Figure 2-2:
A single
rose has a
single row
of petals.

✔ **Semi-double:** Roses that are considered semi-double may have only two or three rows of petals, as shown in Figure 2-3. The pink floribunda 'Simplicity', which performs well as a hedge rose, has semi-double flowers.

Figure 2-3:
A semi-
double rose
has two or
three rows
of petals.

✔ **Double or fully double:** These roses have lots of petals, as Figure 2-4 shows. A rose is considered double if it has more than 35 petals. Double roses are generally larger and showier than singles or semi-doubles. The red hybrid tea 'Mister Lincoln' has wonderfully double flowers, as do the Austin roses.

Figure 2-4:
A double rose has many petals.

Whether you choose roses with single, semi-double, or double flowers makes no difference. If you like them, they're perfect.

Top Form

The way a flower's petals unfurl is called *form*. Whether or not a rose is considered to have good form depends on the kind of rose you're looking at, as well as your own idea of what's attractive. Many people think that the quartered form that's often found in old garden roses is very attractive. Other people prefer the complete lack of form that's found in other old garden roses, with floppy petals that jut out in every direction. Many old garden roses with little or no form are very charming.

But really, when we talk about rose form, we're talking about modern roses. Modern roses, including hybrid teas, floribundas, grandifloras, and miniatures, can have two types of form:

- **Exhibition or formal:** Many-petalled rose flowers with great exhibition (formal) form are often called *exhibition roses*. They are gracefully shaped, with the petals symmetrically arranged in an attractive circular outline, tending toward a high centre. The arrangement of the unfurling petals should be symmetrical and evenly spaced, with no evident gaps. The centre of the bloom should be perfect — well defined, high, and pointed. From the side view, you should notice a symmetry of structure as the petals unfurl uniformly from the high, pointed centre. The outer row of petals should be as close as possible to a horizontal plane.

  Each variety has its own inherent characteristics. Exhibition roses are at their perfect phase of bloom when they are one-third to one-half open.

- **Decorative or informal:** Decorative (informal) form is evident when a rose does not have a well-defined, high, pointed centre. A decorative rose may be ruffled or cupped and can have a low centre. Decorative roses usually have fewer petals. These roses are often referred to as *garden roses,* as opposed to exhibition roses.

Climate conditions, culture, and weather can affect rose form. But if you want to grow roses with consistently good form, you must choose varieties that are genetically graced with good form. Unless you're planning to exhibit your roses at a rose show, however, form really doesn't matter much, as long as it's pleasing to you.

Once you get involved in the rose hobby, though, you may find that form becomes more important to you. If so, you want to buy varieties that are known as exhibition varieties. Doing so isn't as difficult as it sounds. If a rose has exhibition form, the catalogue description generally says so. Not quite as many roses with exhibition form are available as roses with decorative form, but you still have plenty to choose from.

Following is a list of hybrid teas that we think are top-notch in the form department:

- **'Royal Highness':** Light pink hybrid tea
- **'Marijke Koopman':** Medium pink hybrid tea
- **'Tower Bridge':** Medium red hybrid tea
- **'Savoy Hotel':** Light pink hybrid tea
- **'Touch of Class':** Orange-pink hybrid tea
- **'Victor Borge':** Orange blend hybrid tea
- **'Warm Wishes':** Orange-pink blend hybrid tea

Miniature rose form is judged like hybrid tea form. Here's our list of top exhibition minis:

- ✔ **'Antique Rose':** Medium pink miniature
- ✔ **'Just for You':** Deep pink miniature
- ✔ **'Millie Walters':** Orange-pink miniature
- ✔ **'Rise 'n' Shine':** Medium yellow miniature
- ✔ **'Rainbow's End':** Yellow and red miniature
- ✔ **'Work of Art':** Orange blend miniature

But Does It Have Substance?

Substance is a quality in a rose that is extremely important to the stability and durability of its form and to its *keeping quality,* or vase life. Substance is the amount of moisture in the petals, and it is manifested in the texture, firmness, crispness, thickness, and toughness of the petals. You can determine the presence of substance in rose petals by feeling thickness in the petals, by an opalescent sparkle and sheen in pastel-coloured roses, and by a velvety appearance in red roses.

When you feel substance by touching a rose's petals, you can't help but be impressed with the thick velvetiness of some varieties. They truly are a work of art. The people we know should have as much substance as some roses do!

A Horse of a Different Colour

Colours of roses! So many exist that we hardly know where to begin. Three factors affect the colour of roses:

- ✔ **Hue:** The component that gives visual impact to the eye and distinguishes one colour from another.
- ✔ **Brightness:** The clarity and vividness of the colour, and the absence of cloudiness or muddiness.
- ✔ **Chroma:** The purity and intensity of the hue. Ideal chroma has the least amount of grey or white in the hue.

So ideal hue is a combination of ideal brightness and ideal chroma. This really doesn't help you pick the rose you like; it just gives you some more ammunition for your next cocktail party.

The International Registration Authority for Roses divides rose colours into 18 colour classes. Every rose fits into one of these categories, and when introducers register their roses with the International Registration Authority — Roses, they must specify one of these 18 colour classes. Mail-order rose companies may describe colours of roses in terms that are more accurate or whimsical, such as "candy apple red" or "salmon orange," but the *official* colour class is one of the 18 listed here:

- ✔ White (includes near white and white blend)
- ✔ Light yellow
- ✔ Medium yellow
- ✔ Deep yellow
- ✔ Yellow blend
- ✔ Apricot (includes apricot blend)
- ✔ Orange (includes orange blend)
- ✔ Orange-pink
- ✔ Orange-red
- ✔ Light pink
- ✔ Medium pink
- ✔ Deep pink
- ✔ Pink blend
- ✔ Medium red
- ✔ Dark red
- ✔ Red blend
- ✔ Mauve (includes mauve blend)
- ✔ Russet

Although these 18 colour categories are the official colours of roses, we've simplified them. In the colour section of this book, we group roses into six colour groups: red, pink, orange, yellow, white, and multicoloured or blends. In describing the varieties in Part III of this book, we stick to the same simplified groups and use adjectives that we hope will help you imagine the rose better. And as Chapter 4 points out, rose colour can change slightly when a rose is grown in different climates. That's why "official" colour descriptions sometimes vary from the colour in a photograph or the colour of the rose in your own garden.

Black and blue...

When someone develops a blue rose or a black rose, the International Registration Authority for Roses will have to add new categories. But we probably won't see those colours during our lifetime. Most every hybridizer has about given up on black because the dark tissue of the petals absorbs so much heat that the flower dies before it opens.

As for blue, well, a couple of research groups send out media releases every year or so saying that they almost have a blue rose. Then their funding gets a shot in the arm. It's pretty unlikely, though, that a true blue rose will appear in the foreseeable future. The problem is that roses have no natural blue pigment. The pigment that makes mauve roses mauve is really a red pigment that is altered by the pH in the rose's cells. An interesting note: The red pigment in mauve roses doesn't photograph well, showing up as pink on film. That's why the colour of many mauve roses is not quite accurate in some catalogue photos.

Making a blue rose will require some big-time gene splicing, and because biologists haven't even identified most of a rose's genes, splicing 'em will be pretty hard. Also, the chemical response to the pH in the cell, once altered, would have to react favourably with the process of photosynthesis and with the plant's metabolism. A plant scientist could make this project his or her life's work. But if the scientist were successful, he or she would be rich beyond anyone's dreams!

Oh, and for the record, a *blend* is a rose that has different shades of one colour, or two or more different colours, on the same flower. They are usually grouped by the most dominant colour. If a rose is several shades of one colour, we describe it in Part III under that colour. If a rose has several colours, we call it a multicoloured rose in this book.

Where Do Rose Flowers Come From?

So now you know what makes a good rose a good rose, but how do those naked-looking sticks you plant in the spring get to the flower stage? The process is nothing short of a miracle.

With the three major fertilizer nutrients, nitrogen, phosphorus, and potassium, working in concert with the micro-elements in the soil that plants need to promote photosynthesis (you remember from high school science: light and carbon dioxide go in the leaf, and water and oxygen come out), your rose plant develops new canes from two places:

- From the crown of the plant (the bud union on budded roses)
- From the bud eyes located at intervals along the canes

Rose flowers form at the top of a new cane. You can watch the tiny bud as it forms and grows.

Hybrid tea roses

Hybrid teas usually form flowers one-to-a-stem in early spring, but subsequent bloom during the summer often produces two or more buds to the sides of the large main bud. The energy the plant must expend to make the side buds grow takes vitality away from the larger central bud, so all the flowers are small.

If you want your hybrid tea flower to reach its full size and potential, you must *disbud* it when the tiny side buds are forming. You can disbud easily by snapping off the side buds when they are very small. Doing so allows the main bud to reach its maximum size. If you like a larger quantity of flowers and don't care about their size, don't bother to disbud.

Floribunda roses

Floribundas usually form flowers in clusters, often called *sprays*. A cluster forms at the top of a cane, just like a single flower. But instead of only one bud, there are several. As the buds grow, the centre or *terminal* bud grows faster than the others in the cluster and opens several days sooner than the others in the cluster. If you want all the flowers to open at the same time, you must nip out the centre bud. From that point on, all the buds in the cluster mature at the same time. (See Figure 2-5 for an example of a floribunda cluster.)

Explorer roses

When Agriculture Canada rose researcher Dr. Felicitas Svejda wanted to name the new class of roses she was developing, she thought first of the nature of our country. She said, "Canada was developed by rugged people exploring new and rugged areas; nobody had gone there before our Canadian explorers." Her roses, bred for ruggedness, disease resistance, and summer blooming, seemed a good fit to match these early adventurers. So the roses bear names like 'Captain Samuel Holland', 'William Baffin', and 'George Vancouver'. "I thought about naming them after painters," she said, "but for ruggedness, the explorers had to take precedence." As an amateur painter, she added, "Besides, anybody can paint."

Figure 2-5:
A cluster of
floribunda
roses.

Having all the flowers in a cluster open at the same time is important only if you're going to exhibit the spray in a rose show or if you're going to use the entire spray in a flower arrangement.

So When Do They Bloom, Anyway?

Few flowering plants are *ever-blooming*, meaning that the flowers keep developing and blooming from spring to late fall. But roses do bloom all season, making them among the most desirable of garden plants. At least, most modern hybrid teas, floribundas, grandifloras, miniatures, and modern shrubs are ever-blooming, while the majority of old garden roses are either once-flowering (per year) or *recurrent*, which means that they bloom once in the spring and again in the fall.

You can expect your roses to bloom for the first time about six weeks after growth starts in the spring. The flower needs that long to form and mature. The first bloom in the spring, when all your roses are in full bloom, is always the most spectacular, making that time of year — whenever it may be in your area — a favourite time for everyone who loves roses. Modern roses continue to produce flowers throughout the season, and the process for repeat flower development takes the same six weeks or so. Luckily the plants always have flowers at different stages of growth, making for a continuous display.

Roses That Bloom Once a Season

Roses that bloom once a season are called *non-recurrent*. They are usually old garden roses — those discovered or hybridized before and a little after 1867. Some old garden roses, namely the hybrid musks, damask perpetuals, noisettes, Chinas, teas, and about 60 percent of the rugosas, are repeat blooming. But all the others, like the albas, centifolias, damasks, and gallicas, bloom only once.

"So why grow 'em?" you may ask. You grow them for the amazing display they put on when they do bloom. It is as if they're saving up all their energy for a whole year and then throwing it all away in an explosion of bloom. Old garden roses that bloom only once produce 50 times more flowers than ever-blooming roses, and you have to love them for their exuberance.

They do it right the first time!

Although these roses bloom only once a year in spring, when they do flower, they'll knock your socks off! (See their photos in the colour section, and go to Chapter 14 for more details.)

✔ **'Harison's Yellow Rose'**, *Rosa harisonii*: Cupped, soft yellow blooms with golden stamens.

✔ **'Königin von Dänemark'**: Alba rose. Flesh pink flowers with a darker centre. Very full, medium-sized, fragrant blooms. Vigorous grower.

✔ **'Madame Hardy'**: Damask rose. Flowers are pure white, occasionally tinged flesh pink, with a green pip. Cupped, large blooms in clusters. Very fragrant. Vigorous growth.

Chapter 3

Rose Fragrance

● ●

In This Chapter

▶ Understanding what makes a rose fragrant

▶ Enjoying different scents

▶ Knowing how and when to enjoy fragrance

▶ Recognizing the James Alexander Gamble Fragrance Award winners

▶ Choosing fragrance favourites

● ●

*F*ragrance isn't the main reason people grow roses, but it sure is a nice benefit. Many of the world's most beautiful roses have little or no fragrance, and they're wonderful to grow and look at. But many people think that fragrance is an important characteristic and seek out only fragrant varieties.

An estimated 25 percent of all roses have no fragrance or only a small amount, 20 percent are intensely fragrant, and the remainder lie somewhere in the middle. So if you shop only for fragrant roses, you may be missing out on some of the world's best varieties.

This chapter can help you to pick out particularly fragrant varieties and make the most of their tantalizing fragrance. Just follow your nose!

A quest for scent

In recent years, rosarians have asked rose hybridizers to try to breed fragrance into new varieties, especially hybrid teas, which as a group are notoriously scentless. And probably not one rose hybridizer in the world doesn't try. But breeding for fragrance isn't as easy as it sounds. It isn't a single gene that is responsible for fragrance, but a series. And that series is elusive. You might think that if you crossed one fragrant rose with another, you'd get a fragrant rose. Not so. In fact, when you cross two fragrant varieties, you're just about guaranteed to get no fragrance at all! So when a hybridizer does come up with a new fragrant rose, it's cause for excitement throughout the rose world.

Locating Rose Scent

Nearly all the parts of a rose can emit fragrance — even the thorns, although we rarely put our noses close to them. On moss roses (see Chapter 14 for more information about them), the fragrance is concentrated in the moss, or the hairs on the hip and sepals (Chapter 2 explains the anatomy of a rose flower). But most often, fragrance, or at least the highest concentration of it, is in the petals of a rose.

Fragrance in roses is, like everything else in the living world, a series of chemicals. It is determined by the chemicals present in the plant and by their complex reaction with one another and with the atmosphere. Several chemical groups are responsible for floral fragrance, including

- Aromatic alcohols
- Aldehydes
- Fatty acids
- Phenols
- Carbonic acid
- Essential oils and resins

Certain hydrocarbons, such as citronellol and phenylethyl, have been identified as being responsible for certain scents, but this chemical stuff is complicated (and you probably don't care, anyway). Better to know how your nose interprets those chemicals in everyday terms.

Knowing Them with Your Nose

There are just about as many rose fragrances as there are noses. Certainly, everyone gets something different when they bury their nose in a rose. But several individual scents have been more or less definitively identified. It is thought that a connection exists between fragrance and other rose characteristics, with darker roses being generally more fragrant than lighter-coloured ones, heavily petalled roses having a stronger or more intense scent, and red and pink varieties being more closely associated with classic rose scent. Yellow and white roses more often emit orris, nasturtium, and violet aromas, along with other flowery and lemony scents, and orange roses are often associated with a fruity scent. You can, however, count on exceptions to all these "rules."

The following list includes the most commonly identified scents and at least one rose that is considered representative of that fragrance:

- **Apple:** 'New Dawn', 'Honourable Lady Lindsay'
- **Apple and clove:** 'Souvenir de la Malmaison'
- **Apple, clove, parsley, and lemon:** 'Eden Rose'
- **Apple, rose, and clove:** 'Zéphirine Drouhin'
- **Bay:** 'Radiance'
- **Classic rose scent:** 'Parfum de Lowe', 'Scentsational', 'Seattle Scentsation'
- **Clove:** 'Dainty Bess'
- **Fern and moss:** 'Queen Elizabeth'
- **Fruit:** 'Fragrant Plum'
- **Lemon:** 'Confidence', 'Lemon Spice'
- **Lily of the valley:** 'Madame Louis Lévêque'
- **Linseed oil:** 'Persian Yellow'
- **Nasturtium:** 'Buccaneer'
- **Orris:** 'Golden Masterpiece'
- **Orris and raspberry:** 'Kordes' Perfecta'
- **Orris and violet:** 'Golden Dawn'
- **Quince:** 'Sutter's Gold'
- **Raspberry:** 'Angel's Mateu'
- **Rose and clove:** 'Chrysler Imperial', 'Dolly Parton', 'Fragrant Cloud'
- **Rose and lemon:** 'La France', 'Mirandy', 'Tiffany'
- **Rose and nasturtium:** 'Sarah Van Fleet'
- **Rose and parsley:** 'American Beauty'
- **Spice:** 'Soleil d'Or', 'Scentimental', 'Ain't She Sweet', 'Secret'
- **Violet:** 'Margaret McGredy'
- **Wine:** 'Vandael'

Unfortunately, not all these roses are widely available, or even described in this book. But the next time you go to a public rose garden, you may want to compare the fragrances of different roses. Doing so is kind of fun, especially for kids.

Enhancing Your Sniffing Pleasure

Although fragrance is a genetic characteristic that's present in some roses and not in others, other factors affect the strength of the fragrance within a fragrant variety. Excellent growing conditions, including planting in good soil and correct soil pH, are vital to ensure that fragrance can reach its full potential. Even more important is the amount of moisture in the soil. Rose fragrance is sweetest when plants have adequate water. So that's just another good reason why you should read Part IV, "Growing Healthy Roses."

Temperature, humidity, wind conditions, and time of day also affect fragrance strength. Scent is more pronounced on warm, sunny days, is significantly reduced on cloudy days, and is hard to detect when the weather is overcast, cold, or raining. And roses emit more fragrance later in the day than they do in the morning.

Chapter 27 tells you how to get the most out of cut roses for bouquets. Once a rose is cut, its fragrance stays with the petals, but the scent is strongest when the room is warm and the air is more humid than dry.

Choosing Fragrant Varieties

Because fragrance is a great selling point, mail-order rose catalogue descriptions never keep fragrant varieties a secret. To further narrow your choices, you can always look for those that have been awarded the James Alexander Gamble Rose Fragrance Award.

The following list includes all the roses ever to have won the prestigious Gamble Fragrance Award:

- **1961:** 'Crimson Glory', red hybrid tea
- **1962:** 'Tiffany', pink and yellow blend hybrid tea
- **1965:** 'Chrysler Imperial', red hybrid tea
- **1966:** 'Sutter's Gold', orange-yellow hybrid tea
- **1968:** 'Granada', red multicoloured hybrid tea
- **1970:** 'Fragrant Cloud', orange-red hybrid tea
- **1974:** 'Papa Meilland', red hybrid tea

- **1979:** 'Sunsprite', yellow floribunda
- **1986:** 'Double Delight', red and white bicoloured hybrid tea
- **1997:** 'Fragrant Hour', orange-pink hybrid tea

Winning fragrances

Roses that have been awarded the James Alexander Gamble Award will be identified in catalogues — with the notation Gamble Award or Gamble Fragrance Award.

No roses won the award between 1986 and 1997 because of the rigid qualification requirements. Not only must a nominee be fragrant, but it also must possess a number of other attributes, including vigour, pest and disease resistance, form, substance, colour, and extreme popularity for more than five years. These qualities are why almost all the Gamble Award winners are still available at your local garden centre or favourite mail-order nursery.

You may have noticed that most of these roses are hybrid teas. As we said earlier, many hybrid teas don't have strong fragrance, which is true. But isn't it also interesting that some of the most fragrant roses are hybrid teas? You have to love Mother Nature.

Some of our favourite fragrant old garden roses are the following:

- ✔ **'Alfred de Dalmas':** Light pink moss
- ✔ **'Ispahan':** Medium pink damask
- ✔ **'Madame Hardy':** White damask
- ✔ *Rosa gallica officinalis*: Light crimson gallica
- ✔ **'Bishop Darlington':** Pink blend hybrid musk

But don't for one moment believe that there aren't a whole bunch of newer roses that are fragrant and great plants, too. The following varieties are readily available and wonderfully fragrant:

- ✔ **'Dolly Parton':** Orange-red hybrid tea
- ✔ **'Especially for You':** Medium yellow hybrid tea
- ✔ **'Sheila's Perfume':** Apricot blend floribunda
- ✔ **'Sweet Chariot':** Mauve miniature
- ✔ **'Royal William':** Medium red hybrid tea

Chapter 4

The Climates of the Rose

●●

●●

*T*here's virtually no place in the world where you can't grow nearly any type of rose you want. Of course, you may have to turn yourself inside out to keep it alive and thriving, but you can do so if you're masochistically inclined.

Finding roses that are naturally suitable for the climate in which you live, however, is a much better idea (not to mention easier and more satisfying). The rose family is a diverse group of plants that thrive in a wide range of conditions. For nearly every climate, the list of roses you have to choose from is a long one.

Like all plants, each classification of rose, and even specific varieties within a classification, have their own tolerances to high or low temperatures, wind, and other climate factors that can affect its performance, if not its very survival.

And equally important, your climate dictates how you care for your roses — how often you need to water, which diseases you should watch out for, when to fertilize, and other stuff gardeners do.

So that's what this chapter is all about — getting to know the climate you live in and how it affects the roses you choose and the way you care for them. To start out, we brief you on the climate basics, but we often have to refer you to other parts of this book for more specifics on *cultural* (growing) practices. To finish up, we give you a list of rose types that are recommended for specific climate regions.

Cold Winters — Canadian Climate Conditions

The general climate of your region (we talk about localized climates around your home later in this chapter) — that is, the city or county you live in — is determined by a complex mix of factors: how cold the winters are, how warm the summers are, how sunny or cloudy it is, how humid or dry it is, and a whole bunch of other things you can probably guess. And most of these factors affect how different types of roses grow or perform. The more you know about climate factors, the better rose gardener you'll be. So here's the scoop on how different climate factors affect roses.

Getting to know your hardiness zone

Different types of roses have different tolerances to winter cold temperatures. The lowest temperature a rose can withstand without injury is called its *winter hardiness*. Hardiness is not as cut and dried as it sounds, because several things can influence whether a plant reaches its full hardiness. Consequently, a plant's hardiness is generally given in a range. For example, most popular hybrid teas, floribundas, climbers, and grandifloras can be hardy to –12° to –6° C (10° to 20° F) without any type of winter protection. Miniatures are a lot hardier. Many species and shrub roses are hardier still. For example, rugosa roses are said to be hardy to about –37° C (–35° F). But even within groups of roses, different varieties can be hardier than others. For example, the lovely white hybrid tea 'Pristine' doesn't seem to like temperatures much below –1° C (30° F). Rosarians in Canada who can't live without 'Pristine' treat it like an annual and replant it each year.

Miniatures are a lot hardier in the cold because they grow on their own roots and don't have that vulnerable bud union. However, in most parts of Canada, they still require winter protection.

So because we mostly live in a cold-winter area, we want to make sure that you choose roses that can survive the winter with a minimum of injury. But how do you know how cold it usually gets in your area? Living in Canada, the easiest way is to look at the Plant Hardiness Zone Map, as shown in the colour section. (The Quick Reference Card right inside the front cover of this book includes a zone and temperature conversion chart.)

This system of plant hardiness zones divides Canada into nine regions based on average winter minimum temperatures. The warmest, Zone 9, has an average winter minimum above 4° C (40° F) , while zone 1 is something short of tundra frozen solid. Zones 1 through 9 are further divided into a and b regions to distinguish zones where minimum winter temperatures differ by five degrees.

Making some Canadian distinctions

The confusing thing for many Canadian gardeners is that the United States Department of Agriculture (USDA) system is also widely used in gardening literature. And although it appears there is only a one-zone difference between the Canadian and U.S. systems, it is unfortunately not so simple. While your garden in Eastern Ontario may be Canadian zone 5b and USDA zone 4b, subtracting or adding one zone will not work in all parts of the country. Calgary, for example, is a Canadian zone 3a but a USDA zone 3b. The difference can range from half a zone up to two full zones depending on where you live.

You should also be aware that the more recently modified USDA zone map lumps many areas of Canada together under a single zone. Southern Ontario has many different zones, as does the Vancouver area, but on the USDA maps, they tend to appear as single zones. Even the Canadian hardiness zone map, developed in 1967, does not reflect many of the climate changes we are experiencing today. What's a gardener to do?

There is a bottom line here and it is quite simple. Unless you live in the coastal areas of British Columbia or the warmer zones of Southern Ontario, you had better protect your roses for the winter in a serious way. Or, you have to grow those roses that are cast iron when it comes to winter hardiness. See Chapter 21 for information on protecting roses.

Most rose books and some catalogues list hybrid tea roses as being hardy to between –23° to –29° C (–10° to –20° F), but that's with some type of winter protection, such as mounding soil over the base of the plant. Without protection, modern roses, like hybrid teas, floribundas, and most climbers, are damaged or killed by temperatures of –12° C (10° F) and colder. When you think about it, there aren't too many areas of Canada that don't see –12° C winter temperatures at some point in the season.

Rose hardiness isn't at all precise. In fact, sometimes it's downright confounding. Early cold snaps in fall, or late ones in spring, can damage plants that you normally think of as hardy. And different types of cold damage exist. Sometimes just the tips of the canes die; other times everything above the ground dies; and occasionally the whole plant ends up deader than a doornail. To further complicate things, rootstock choice, dry winter winds, bright sunshine, and even how you care for a rose prior to cold weather affects its capability to withstand winter weather.

Here are some strategies to make sure that your roses survive the winter:

   ✔ **Plant hardy types.** Many roses, including the ones listed near the end of this chapter, have good cold hardiness. You may also want to check out mail-order catalogues that specialize in hardy roses. See Appendix B for listings.

✔ **Grow own-root roses.** They are hardier than budded roses. Roses that grow on their own roots, like most miniatures, many old garden roses, and some of the more recent introductions like the 'Dream' series, don't have that vulnerable bud union that most modern roses have. If winter kills your own-root rose to the ground (but not *below* the ground), it is more likely to resprout in the spring.

✔ **Plant deep.** If you don't buy own-root roses, plant deeper than normal so that the bud union is well below the soil surface and protected by the layer of soil above it. For more information about bud unions and planting, see Chapter 17.

✔ **Use winter protection.** For various techniques, see Chapter 21.

A New Meaning for Red Hot

Hot weather during the day and at night has some surprising effects on how roses perform and how you should care for them.

Probably most interesting is how temperature affects the colour and character of roses. Red roses with many petals (more than 45 to 50), like 'Mister Lincoln', need heat, especially at night, to open properly. When grown in cooler areas, (zone 5a or below) or if the summer nights are cool one season, the flower petals tend to stay in a ball and don't unfurl completely. This can be really frustrating for Canadian gardeners in zones 5 or colder, and sooner or later, Mr. Lincoln will wind up in the compost pile.

If you find your favourite novelty or bicoloured variety performs poorly out in the hot sun, you may want to move the plant so that it receives a very little bit of midday shade. Remember, though, that roses require at least six full hours of full, hot sun every day to bloom well. Only the very hottest of Canadian gardens will find it necessary to protect heat-sensitive roses from the sun. We simply do not have Texas weather. Also, before you blame poor performance on temperature, ensure your feeding and watering are adequate. Most growth problems are cultural, not temperature related.

The temperature will influence the flower pattern of bicoloured roses. When summers are warm, their colours meld together and it is hard to tell where one colour starts and the other ends. When it is cool, their colour patterns are more distinct with clear divisions between the colours.

Heat can affect your roses in other ways, too. While this has traditionally been a problem in the southern United States, the last few years have seen very high and prolonged temperatures in Canada; gardeners might consider the following information if they are having trouble with some tender roses.

Rose growth (indeed all plant growth) really slows down when the temperature climbs over 32° C (90° F). Flowers are smaller than they are in the cooler temperatures of early spring or late fall, and flower production, or reblooming, takes longer. As well, the petals on some varieties, like the wonderful new 'Scentimental', a striped floribunda, may scorch or wilt in super-hot sun. Varieties like it are definitely worth the extra effort, but they benefit from being planted where they get partial shade during the hottest hours of the afternoon.

How hot it is also dictates how you care for your roses. The hotter it is, the more often you have to water. The soil in which roses are planted should never dry out, but in hot weather, roses really take a beating if they don't have plenty of water. If the heat combines with summer rainfall or high humidity . . . well, that's a horse of a different colour.

Sultry Summers and Sweaty Roses

We can't say it often enough, and it's certainly worth pounding into your head: The drier or hotter it is, the more often you have to water.

That said, the level of atmospheric humidity in summer, which is often related to the amount of rainfall or fog (or just plain mugginess), has an important impact on the diseases, and sometimes the insects, that attack roses. For example:

- Where it's hot, humid, and rainy in summer (Hello, Victoria B.C.!), or where days are hot and nights are cool, black spot, a fungus that makes round black spots on rose leaves, will be a problem.

- Where nights are humid and cool (Take a bow, Halifax), powdery mildew, a fungus that causes twisting shoots and silvery fuzz on rose leaves, may show up.

- Where humidity is low and summers are hot and dry (Can you say *Saskatoon*?), rust, another fungus that looks like orange spots on leaves and stems, can be troublesome. And red spider mite, a microscopic spider that sucks the life out of rose leaves, will be more of a problem.

So you need to know which pests and diseases are likely to show up in your area. When you're in the know, you can choose varieties that are resistant to those problems or know when to expect to have to do battle. For more information, see Chapter 22, "Outsmarting Rose Pests and Diseases."

Tiny Climates Not Just for Tiny Roses

This chapter should give you a pretty good idea of how climate factors such as low winter temperatures, summer heat and humidity, and the amount of sunshine can affect the roses you want to grow. But take things a step further. You know that big block of wood, nails, bricks, and cement that sits in the middle of your property and you call home? Well, its overwhelming size affects small areas of your garden and makes their climate just a little different from the overall climates of your neighbourhood. These little areas are called *microclimates*. Microclimates are localized climates that, because of their proximity to large buildings or trees, or because of the way the land slopes, differ from the overall climate of an area.

If you walk around your home in the morning and again in the afternoon on a summer day, you'll probably see the following microclimates, illustrated in Figure 4-1:

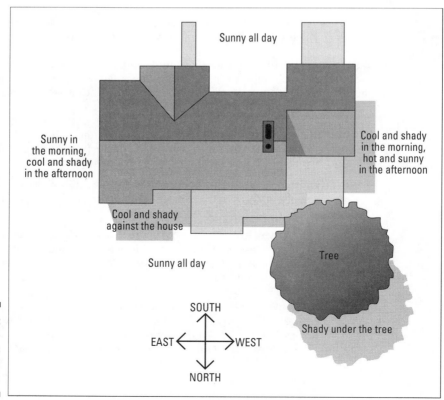

Sunny all day

Sunny in the morning, cool and shady in the afternoon

Cool and shady in the morning, hot and sunny in the afternoon

Cool and shady against the house

Sunny all day

Tree

Shady under the tree

SOUTH

EAST ← → WEST

NORTH

Figure 4-1: Micro-climates vary around your home.

- ✔ **The south side** is mostly sunny and warm all day.
- ✔ **The west side** is shady and cool in the morning and hot and sunny in the afternoon.
- ✔ **The east side** is nice and sunny in the morning and cool and shady in the afternoon.
- ✔ **The north side** is shady almost all day. It's not the best place for roses.

As you walk, you may also notice that other large objects, especially trees, create microclimates that change from morning to afternoon. Even a south-facing slope is warmer than other parts of the garden, simply because it bathes in sun almost all day. Figure 4-2 shows the ideal planting situation.

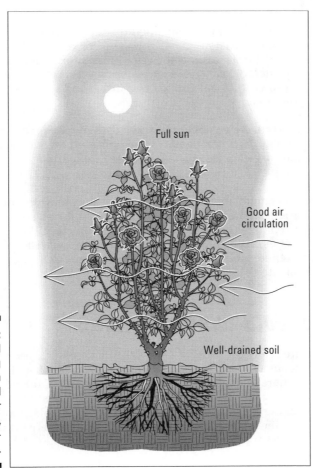

Full sun

Good air circulation

Well-drained soil

Figure 4-2:
The ideal planting situation includes full sun, good air circulation, and well-drained soil.

Once you identify the microclimates around your home, you can choose just the right spot for planting roses. In general, roses want sun all day, as shown in Figure 4-2. And, if you happen to live in a cooler area, you can use the extra heat generated by the south- or west-facing walls of your house to protect your roses. At the other extreme, in urban areas the reflections and reflected heat from absorbed sun on concrete and asphalt creates gardens so hot that plants are stressed and some rose colours will bleach. That said, plant your roses where you want them and hope they grow well. If not, move them about like furniture until they do grow well. See Chapter 17 for planting and moving advice.

Roses for All

The world is rich with lists of recommended roses for specific areas, and you should be able to find a variety that can thrive where you live. Most of these lists are published by local rose societies (for more information about rose societies, see Appendix A). Many retail nurseries offer lists of recommendations as well. You can also visit a local public rose garden and see for yourself how a rose does in your area.

But to get you started, we've compiled some lists of roses recommended for their hardiness in Canadian climates. We collected them from local rose societies and rose experts who have years of experience in growing great roses.

One thing to keep in mind about these lists is that they may not include some of the newest varieties. The newer varieties were introduced so recently that there hasn't been enough time to evaluate them completely. However, many of the newer varieties, especially the award winners, grow well in nearly all climates. Some of them look so great that you may want to throw caution to the wind and evaluate them for yourself. What a novel idea.

Roses for cold-winter climates

Where winters are really brutal (–34° C or –30° F and colder), you're best off with the hardiest shrub roses, particularly any of the Morden and Explorer series, bred right here in Canada for our winters, and any of the rugosas. Table 4-1 lists a few of these as well as some other hardy roses that not only survive winters in Canadian zone 3 without protection but also bloom the following season, even when canes that died in the winter were pruned almost to the ground in the spring.

Table 4-1	Really Hardy Roses for the North	
Name	*Type*	*Flower Colour*
'Applejack'	Shrub	Rose spotted with crimson
'Carefree Beauty'	Shrub	Pink
'Champlain'	Shrub	Dark red
'Eutin'	Floribunda	Red
'Golden Wings'	Shrub	Yellow
'John Cabot'	Shrub	Red
'John Franklin'	Shrub	Red
'Morden Amorette'	Shrub	Pink
'Morden Centennial'	Shrub	Pink
'Prairie Dawn'	Shrub	Pink
'Prairie Princess'	Shrub	Pink

Some modern roses are hardier than others. We compiled the lists of plants in Tables 4-2 through 4-7 from recommended lists from cold-winter regions. We don't list *all* the hardy roses recommended for each area, but only ones that showed up on two or more lists.

Please understand that although Tables 4-2 through 4-4 list the hardiest of the tender roses, the sad reality is that they all require winter protection in any area of Canada other than the mildest of British Columbia's favourite gardens. Hardiness is a question of degree. Having said that, these will help you push the boundaries if you live where overwintering roses is borderline at the best of times. Some of these roses will be difficult to find, while others are common fare in garden centres. Check out the mail-order resources in Appendix B.

If you're looking for some reasonably hardy hybrid teas, here you are. We think you can make a go of these. Check Chapter 8 for more information.

Table 4-2	Hybrid Tea Roses That Are Hardier Than Most
Name	*Flower Colour*
'American Spirit'	Red
'Chicago Peace'	Pink and yellow
'Chrysler Imperial'	Red
'Dainty Bess'	Pink
'Double Delight'	White and red
'Fragrant Cloud'	Coral-orange
'Garden Party'	White
'Granada'	Pink and yellow
'Medallion'	Apricot-orange
'Midas Touch'	Yellow
'Mister Lincoln'	Red
'Olympiad'	Red
'Pascali'	White
'Peace'	Yellow and pink
'Secret'	White and pink
'Sheer Bliss'	White and pink
'Summer Dream'	Apricot-pink
'Swarthmore'	Red
'Tiffany'	Pink
'Touch of Class'	Pink
'Tropicana'	Coral-orange

Floribundas and polyanthas are presented in detail in Chapter 10. Consider these varieties for their good survival rates.

Table 4-3   Floribunda Roses That Are Hardier Than Most

Name	Flower Colour
'Betty Prior'	Pink
'China Doll'*	Pink
'Class Act'	White
'Europeana'	Red
'Eye Paint'	Red and white
'The Fairy'*	Pink
'Gene Boerner'	Pink
'Iceberg'	White
'Impatient'	Orange-red
'Ivory Fashion'	White
'Little Darling'	Salmon-pink and yellow
'Pleasure'	Salmon-pink
'Regensberg'	Red and white
'Sexy Rexy'	Pink
'Showbiz'	Red
'Simplicity'	Pink
'Singin' in the Rain'	Orange
'Sunsprite'	Yellow

*'China Doll' and 'The Fairy' are actually polyanthas.

Tall and vigorous, grandifloras (Chapter 9) make a good alternative to the popular hybrid teas. Try these if you're looking for the tougher ones in the bunch.

Table 4-4	Grandiflora Roses That Are Hardier Than Most
Name	**Flower Colour**
'Aquarius'	Pink
'Gold Medal'	Yellow
'Love'	Red
'Pink Parfait'	Pink
'Queen Elizabeth'	Pink
'Tournament of Roses'	Pink
'White Lightnin''	White

Just because they're little doesn't mean they're wimps. Miniature roses (featured in Chapter 11) grow on their own roots and take less work than you may be thinking — give these guys a shot.

Table 4-5	Miniature Roses That Are Hardier Than Most
Name	**Flower Colour**
'Black Jade'	Red
'Child's Play'	White and pink
'Figurine'	White and pink
'Jean Kenneally'	Apricot
'Judy Fischer'	Pink
'Magic Carrousel'	White and red
'Minnie Pearl'	Pink
'Party Girl'	Yellow
'Rise 'n' Shine'	Apricot-yellow and pink
'Snow Bride'	White
'Starina'	Red

Climbing roses need winter protection in most parts of Canada. Anyone in zone 6 and warmer can use Table 4-6 as a guideline for hardy climbers. Colder-area gardeners — zone 5 and colder — should use Table 4-7 as their guide since the roses in the Explorer series make decent climbing displays and have better hardiness.

Table 4-6	Climbing Roses That Are Hardier Than Most
Name	**Flower Colour**
'Altissimo'	Red
'America'	Pink
'Don Juan'	Red
'Dortmund'	Red and white
'Golden Showers'	Yellow
'Handel'	Pink and white
'Improved Blaze'	Red
'New Dawn'	Pink

If you're looking to improve your odds of keeping a climbing rose alive, you might want to consider some of the roses in the Explorer series. With a bit of coaxing the following roses may be just the ticket. See Chapter 12 for methods of pruning and training Explorer roses into climbers.

Table 4-7	Explorer Roses That Make Good Climbers
Name	**Flower Colour**
'Captain Samuel Holland'	Medium red
'Henry Kelsey'	Medium red
'John Cabot'	Medium cherry red
'John Davis'	Medium pink
'William Baffin'	Deep pink

Most shrub or landscape roses are very hardy, including the entire Meidiland series. But the ones in Table 4-8 come up again and again.

Table 4-8	Landscape Roses That Are Hardier Than Most
Name	**Flower Colour**
'All That Jazz'	Salmon-orange
'Bonica'	Pink
'Carefree Beauty'	Pink
'Carefree Delight'	Pink and white
'Carefree Wonder' Pink and white	

Roses for areas with cool summers

Roses in Tables 4-9 through 4-14 are recommended for areas with cooler summers. Varieties marked with an asterisk (*) have exceptional disease resistance where summers are cool and foggy.

Like most roses, hybrid teas like some good hot sun, but we think you can make these ones work for you even if you live where summers aren't so sweltering.

Table 4-9	Hybrid Teas
Name	**Flower Colour**
'Colour Magic'	Pink
'Dainty Bess'	Pink
'Double Delight'	Red and white
'Folklore'	Orange
'Fragrant Cloud'*	Coral-orange
'Honor'	White
'Just Joey'*	Orange
'Las Vegas'	Orange, red, and yellow
'Medallion'	Apricot-pink
'New Day'	Yellow
'Olympiad'*	Red
'Paradise'	Lavender

Name	Flower Colour
'Pascali'*	White
'Peace'*	Yellow and pink
'Precious Platinum'	Red
'Pristine'	White
'Sheer Elegance'	Pink
'Tiffany'	Pink
'Touch of Class'	Pink
'Voodoo'*	Orange, yellow, and red

You just can't live without a big-blooming floribunda in your yard? Neither can we. They're easy to care for and prolific bloomers. See Chapter 10 for the whole scoop on floribundas and polyanthas. Meanwhile, see how these ones fare in your coolish summer climate.

Table 4-10	Floribundas
Name	Flower Colour
'Amber Queen'	Apricot-gold
'Betty Prior'	Pink
'Class Act'*	White
'Europeana'*	Red
'Eye Paint'*	Red and white
'French Lace'*	White
'Iceberg'*	White
'Little Darling'	Yellow
'Marina'	Orange
'Playboy'*	Red-orange
'Playgirl'*	Magenta-pink
'Redgold'	Yellow-red

(continued)

Table 4-10 *(continued)*	Floribundas
Name	*Flower Colour*
'Regensberg'	Pink and white
'Sarabande'*	Orange-red
'Sexy Rexy'	Pink
'Showbiz'*	Red
'Simplicity'	Pink
'Sun Flare'	Yellow
'Sunsprite'	Yellow
'Trumpeter'*	Orange-red

So many shapes and sizes — your grandiflora options are endless — well, not quite. But Table 4-11 shows a number of varieties that should prove their worthiness in mildly warm summer conditions.

Table 4-11	Grandifloras
Name	*Flower Colour*
'Caribbean'	Orange
'Gold Medal'	Yellow
'Love'*	Red
'Prima Donna'	Pink
'Prominent'	Orange
'Queen Elizabeth'*	Pink
'Sonia'	Pink
'Tournament of Roses'	Pink

A good climbing rose is invaluable in every climate. (See the landscaping ideas in Chapter 5.) If your summers are temperate and misty, the roses in Table 4-12 may be perfect for your arbour or trellis.

Table 4-12	Climbers
Name	*Flower Colour*
'America'	Coral-pink
'Altissimo'	Red
'Dortmund'*	Red and white
'Dublin Bay'*	Red
'Golden Showers'	Yellow
'Handel'*	Pink and white
'Joseph's Coat'	Yellow and red

Diminutive but hard working, the miniature roses in Table 4-13 may be the most versatile plants you put in your garden. (Chapter 11 sings their praises.)

Table 4-13	Miniatures
Name	*Flower Colour*
'Beauty Secret'	Red
'Cinderella'	White
'Holy Toledo'*	Orange and yellow
'Little Artist'*	Red and white
'Little Jackie'	Orange
'Magic Carrousel'	White and red
'Minnie Pearl'	Pink
'New Beginning'	Orange and yellow
'Party Girl'	Yellow and pink
'Rainbow's End'	Yellow and red
'Rise 'n' Shine'	Yellow
'Simplex'*	White and orange
'Starina'*	Red-orange

Any Canadian garden will benefit from adding a shrub rose. Read Chapter 13 to find out all the possibilities.

Table 4-14	Shrubs
Name	**Flower Colour**
'All That Jazz'	Orange
'Bonica'	Pink
'Carefree Wonder'	Pink and white
'Golden Wings'	Yellow
'Graham Thomas'	Yellow
'Sally Holmes'	White

Part II
Using Roses in Your Garden

The 5th Wave — By Rich Tennant

"WELL NO, THEY'RE NOT EXACTLY AWARD WINNING ROSES, BUT MAYBE THEY'D WIN SOMETHING IN THE MUSHROOM CATEGORY."

In this part . . .

This is probably the most useful part of this book. Many people overlook the fact that roses not only are hard-working garden plants but also are one of the most colourful flowering shrubs.

Next time you do some landscaping, think of roses instead of, say, junipers or cotoneaster. When you want summer colour, use roses along with your marigolds and petunias. When you want some colour on your front porch, put roses in a container. Roses work in fantastically colourful ways.

Chapter 5

Landscaping with Roses

· ·

In This Chapter

▶ Using roses as versatile landscape shrubs

▶ Using colour in the garden

▶ Mixing and matching plant textures

▶ Putting roses to work as hedges, edgings, and ground covers

▶ Growing roses on fences, walls, trellises, and arbours

· ·

*H*ave you ever walked into a garden or yard and thought, "Wow, this is beautiful — every plant in its place, just the right mix of colours and textures, and everything so well organized. Someone planned this garden perfectly!"

Good landscaping does take planning and organization. You can find some basic landscape techniques, such as drawing plans and laying paths and patios, described in *Gardening For Canadians For Dummies*. But when dealing with roses, we hope that you really take one piece of advice to heart: Before you plant any rose, think carefully about where you want to plant it and the impact it will have on your garden or landscape. Of course, you have to provide the plant with the requirements for healthy growth in terms of sunshine, soil, and the like, and that's covered in Part IV of this book. But also think about how roses can work for you, how they might fill basic landscape roles as hedges, screens, ground covers, barriers, and more. Even more important, how will their colours blend with the plants in the rest of your garden? How will they affect your emotions when you look at them? Will they add excitement or serenity to your garden?

You may think that we've gone over the edge, but don't be so sure. Roses can fill traditional landscape roles that you may not have considered. And the colours they bring to a garden are bright and dramatic — they have an impact on the look of your yard. Unless you give those colours a little thought, your garden may end up looking like a box of crayons that's been left out in the sun on a hot summer day.

This chapter can help you avoid melted crayon syndrome and show you not only how to use colours and plant texture wisely, but also how to make roses work hard as hedges, screens, ground covers, and more.

Painting the Landscape with Colourful Roses

Taste in colours is a personal thing. If your favourite colour is red and you want a red rose, who can argue with that? Go for it! But if you want to create a harmonious display of colour throughout your garden, you want to think carefully about the colours you choose and how they blend with other plants, and even with the colour of your home.

Different colours have different effects on people's emotions. Red and orange are warm colours that can actually create excitement for viewers. These are great colours for gardens primarily used for entertaining. Blue and pink have the opposite effect. They feel cool and soothing and lend a relaxed mood to the garden. So, if your garden is for relaxing in after the day's work, emphasize blues and pinks with the odd accent of yellow, orange, or red. Having said all that, the best thing to do is choose colours you like. You can't grow wrong that way.

In cool climates, you may want to warm things up with red roses. If you want to attract attention to a certain area of the garden, use bright colours in that spot — they're sure to attract the eye. Bright colours can also lead the eye away from sore spots in the garden.

Choosing Colour Schemes

There are two ways to choose your colour scheme. You can stay with one or two basic colours and only add plants that flower in shades of those colours; this is the artistic method of garden colouring. The normal way that most of us work is to add the plants we like regardless of whether the artists approve or not. Take it from us, either way works if you like the effect.

Basically, colours combine in two ways:

 ✔ **Harmonious colours** blend together smoothly and have a soothing effect. They are usually *shades* of one of the primary colours — red, yellow, and blue. Pink and red are harmonious colours, as are yellow and orange, and blue and green.

✔ **Contrasting colours** highlight each other, making each colour appear brighter and stronger than it would by itself. You create the strongest colour contrasts by putting one primary colour next to another, such as blue next to red or yellow next to blue. In a garden, contrasting colours tend to attract the eye and stand out. They also make things appear closer when viewed from a distance. If used too much, they can be overpowering and dominate a garden.

If you feel a little uneasy about picking colours, keep your choices simple. Fewer colours often work better than more. Some of the most stunning gardens use just one flower colour, such as yellow, or pink. Particularly where you have a good background of green foliage, a single-colour garden offers a rare beauty. Stay away from white gardens, though, as they are one of the most difficult gardens to successfully create. You might even go to a hardware store and pick up some paint chips and use them to experiment with different colour combinations. After you find a combination you like, you can go to Part III and find roses to match.

Often you can get clues about good colours to use from the colour of your house, from existing plants, or from landscape features. For example, using roses that combine well with the trim or siding colour of your house can tie your whole landscape together into one harmonious picture. Or take a cue from your patio, walks, or walls. Pink 'Simplicity' roses around a brick patio are drop-dead gorgeous, as are red 'John Cabot' roses on a brick or wooden fence.

You can also find potential colour combinations in flowers themselves. For example, say your favourite rose is the pink and white hybrid tea 'Secret'. If you combine that rose with other flowers that bloom in shades of white and pink, such as petunias or hardy geraniums, you have a guaranteed winner.

Mixing Plant Texture and Form

After you have an idea of how to work with colour, think for a minute about plant growth habit and texture. Basically, a plant's *habit* is determined by how it grows — stiff and upright, low and spreading, rounded, grasslike, and on and on. You can describe a plant's growth habit in a million ways.

A plant's *texture* is usually described as fine or bold, soft or coarse, or somewhere in between. Texture is most often related to the size and density of the foliage. Plants with many small or finely divided leaves, such as ferns, have fine, or soft, texture. Plants with larger or stiff leaves, such as rhododendrons, are said to have bold, or coarse, texture. Bold plants tend to stand out and appear closer. Soft-textured plants tend to recede and look like they're farther away.

Flowers also vary in texture and form. Most larger roses have to be considered bold flowers, especially when compared with more diminutive blooms like those of the annual lobelia or a perennial salvia. But some roses with smaller flowers are more finely textured. Many roses, especially the crinkly-leafed rugosas and the ferny moss roses (see Chapter 14), have foliage or stems with unique texture. They look good even when they're not in bloom.

Don't worry about exactly what texture or growth habit a plant has. Just realize that plants look different. What a news flash! When you're mixing roses with other plants, which is the topic of Chapter 6, you can create more natural and interesting situations by blending plants with different habits and textures, or even by using roses with different textures. For example, the soft foliage of miniature roses would get lost among other fine-textured plants. But when mixed with bolder plants, miniatures stand out and show their real character.

Roses require a higher soil pH than some evergreens, such as rhododendrons and kalmia. Avoid planting roses in the same beds with such plants if you expect both to thrive.

Creating a Style All Your Own

On a very basic level, gardens can be described as formal or informal in style. *Formal gardens* have a lot of straight lines and geometric shapes and seem very well organized. *Informal gardens* are less rigid and more natural, with plants growing the way they want, without severe pruning or shaping.

Even though distinguishing between formal and informal gardens is difficult (and who cares, anyway?), you should know that you can use roses to create either style. If you think that your garden needs a little more formality or organization, surround your cutting garden of hybrid teas with a low-growing, neatly clipped boxwood or dwarf alpine currant hedge. Voilà! — the formality of kings. Planting long rows of floribundas, shrub roses, or miniature roses as hedges also creates formality, especially if you put a clipped hedge behind them.

If informality is more your style, plant some old garden or Explorer roses way in the back of your yard and just let them have their way. They create a mounding, rolling background with a wonderfully wild look. Mixing shrub and floribunda roses in perennial borders or combining them with other blooming plants (the subject of Chapter 6) also results in a more informal style.

Here are some other tips to remember when landscaping with roses:

- ✓ **Keep short in the front, tall in the back.** Seems obvious, but people always forget. Keep shorter plants in front, adding gradually taller plants, with the very tallest ones in the back. That way, nothing is obscured.

- ✓ **Stick to odd-numbered groupings.** Roses, or any plants, for that matter, look more natural when grouped in odd numbers. Don't ask why this technique works; it just does.

- ✓ **Use soft colours in small spaces.** Lighter colours tend to recede and make a small garden look bigger. Darker or contrasting colours can make a small garden appear even more cramped.

- ✓ **Use repetition to provide continuity.** Even though mixing plants of different texture or form adds interest to a garden, repeating certain plants or groups of plants throughout a garden adds rhythm and order. So try to do a little bit of both.

Putting Roses to Work

Using roses in traditional landscape situations (that is, a landscape with hedges, ground covers, edgings, and so on) is becoming increasingly popular. And it's easy to see why. Roses offer one of the longest seasons of bloom of any flowering shrub, and newer varieties have been almost custom designed for landscape uses such as hedges, ground covers, edgings, and borders.

In the following sections, we list our favourite roses for using in traditional landscape situations. We include the type of rose and its colour so that you can easily find that plant in the appropriate section of Part III of this book.

Using roses for hedges

You can plant roses close together to create a continuous hedge. You won't get a formal hedge with neatly clipped edges; instead, the hedge has an informal style — less pruning enables the plants to bloom more. (For more information about pruning, see Chapter 20.) With the exception of warmer areas in British Columbia, tender roses used for hedging will have to be well protected over the winter. Unless the rose used is quite hardy, such as an Explorer, Parkland, or hardy shrub rose, the rose canes will be severely shortened by winter damage. Note that floribundas, which are often recommended for hedge use, require winter protection in most parts of Canada and will have to be pruned down to 30 to 45 centimetres (12 to 18 inches) tall in the spring. The Explorer rose 'John Cabot' makes one of the most spectacular hedges for a Canadian garden.

Most of these roses can also be used for continuous borders or for backgrounds to other plantings. A *border* differs slightly from a hedge in that a border can be viewed from only one side — for example, a row of roses planted at the base of a fence or wall. A hedge usually separates two areas and is attractive from both sides.

These plants create hedges that vary in height according to the variety you use and how often you prune it. But most are in the 1- to 1.8-metre (3- to 6-foot) range, depending on the climate you live in. Some of our favourite hedge roses and their heights are listed below.

Explorer roses that require little or no winter protection to zone 3 are good choices:

- ✔ **'Champlain':** Red, 0.9–1.2 m (3–4 ft.)
- ✔ **'Jens Munk':** Light pink, 1.5–1.8 m (5–6 ft.)
- ✔ **'John Cabot':** Red, 1.8–2.1 m (6–7 ft.)
- ✔ **'Frontenac':** Deep pink, 0.9–1.2 m (3–4 ft.)
- ✔ **'John Franklin':** Medium red, 1.2–1.8 m (4–6 ft.)

These shrub and rugosa (old garden roses), needing little or no winter protection to zone 4, also make fine hedges:

- ✔ **'F.J. Grootendorst':** Light red, 0.9–1.2 m (3–4 ft.)
- ✔ **'Autumn Bouquet':** Deep pink, 0.9–1.2 m (3–4 ft.)
- ✔ **'Carefree Beauty':** Medium pink, 0.9–1.2 m (3–4 ft.)
- ✔ **'Country Dancer':** Deep pink, 0.9–1.2 m (3–4 ft.)
- ✔ **'Golden Wings':** Medium yellow, 0.9–1.2 m (3–4 ft.)
- ✔ **'Henry Hudson':** White, 0.5–1 m (1.5–3 ft.)
- ✔ **'Hansa':** Purple-red, 1.8–2 m (6–7 ft.)
- ✔ **'Pink Grootendorst':** Medium pink, 1.2–1.5 m (4–5 ft.)

Using roses for edgings

An *edging* is a continuous planting of low-growing plants at the base of taller plants, or along a walkway, patio, or other garden surface. Edgings are one of the best ways to use miniature roses, which have a strong presence in the following list. To create a continuous edging, plant 30 to 45 centimetres (12 to 18 inches) apart so when they grow, the branches intertwine to create an edging. All of these will require winter protection in all but the warmest, zone 8 to 9 parts of Canada.

- ✔ **'Antique Rose':** Medium pink, miniature
- ✔ **'Black Jade':** Dark red, miniature
- ✔ **'Dee Bennett':** Blended rose — shades of orange and yellow, miniature
- ✔ **'Cuddles':** Deep coral-pink, miniature
- ✔ **'Gourmet Popcorn':** White, miniature
- ✔ **'International Herald Tribune':** Mauve, very bushy growth
- ✔ **'Lavender Jewel':** Mauve, hybrid tea type, continuous blooms, miniature
- ✔ **'Loving Touch':** Apricot-orange, miniature
- ✔ **'Ricky':** Coral-pink, heavy bloomer, short
- ✔ **'Save the Children':** Scarlet semi-double blooms, compact grower
- ✔ **'Top Marks':** Orange, heavy bloomer, award winning, compact growth

Using roses for ground covers

Although many rose books written for gardeners in warmer climates describe how to use roses for ground covers, here in Canada most of the hardy roses are taller, upright forms. Everything else dies back to the ground in zone 5 or colder, including the otherwise wonderful 'Flower Carpet' roses. Roses *can* however, make an excellent spreading plant that blooms all summer. (See Chapter 18 for mulching and weed control suggestions.)

Roses that hug the ground

Please don't consider roses as a weed barrier the way gardeners normally use the term "ground cover." Because they die back, roses really don't stop weeds. We've had the best results with using some unnamed climbing roses obtained at a plant sale. These roses are planted deeply (see Chapters 17 and 21) and die back to the ground every winter. In the spring, they produce a half-dozen, ground-hugging shoots that are 1.2 to 1.8 metres (4 to 6 feet) long. The rose gives a magnificent series of blooms repeating for most of the summer. This could be done with any climbing rose that blooms on new wood.

You can create an interesting effect if you secure the ends of long canes to the ground with wire pegs. This process, called *pegging*, is initially done when the plants are dormant, but you generally have to reinforce and repeat the pegging with new growth throughout the growing season. The long, arching canes bloom along their entire length and stay close to the ground. You can make your own pegs by cutting up wire coat hangers into 30-centimetre (12-inch) pieces and shaping each one into a U shape. Just put a peg over the end of each cane and push it into the ground. The taller Explorer roses normally used for climbers are excellent candidates for pegging if you peg the canes while they are young and soft.

For those of you who live in Canada's equivalent of the tropics (zones 8 or 9), there are a few roses that will do a good job as a ground cover. For the most part, rose varieties that make good ground covers are vigorous, spreading plants. However, many shrubby roses, such as low-growing floribundas, shrubs, and miniatures, can be planted en masse to cover a large area.

The following are some of the best spreading roses for use as ground covers. Most should be planted 90 centimetres (3 feet) apart, depending on the vigour of the variety. Leave the most space between vigorous roses.

- ✔ **'Alba Meidiland':** White shrub
- ✔ **'Dortmund':** Red and white climber
- ✔ **'Flower Carpet' series:** Pink, white, and the brand-new 'Appleblossom' low shrub
- ✔ **'Lavender Dream':** Deep pink, shrub
- ✔ **'New Dawn':** Pink climber
- ✔ **'Pearl Meidiland':** White shrub
- ✔ **'Red Cascade':** Red miniature
- ✔ **'Red Meidiland':** Red shrub
- ✔ **'Red Ribbons':** Red shrub
- ✔ **'Scarlet Meidiland':** Red shrub
- ✔ **'Seafoam':** White shrub
- ✔ **'The Fairy':** Pink polyantha
- ✔ **'White Meidiland':** White shrub

Using roses for barriers

The thorny nature of most roses makes them formidable barriers for keeping people and animals from going where you don't want them to. Planting near windows to deter intruders from approaching your home is a great example. Although any thorny rose works, some types are nastier than others. 'Jens Munk', one of the Explorer series, is a miserable plant to prune and work with due to its abundant thorns; it has "bitten" more gardeners more times than we care to mention. This is an excellent barrier plant! Other good barriers include many of the species and old garden roses, shrubs, and climbers.

Using roses on fences, arbours, and walls

Training a climbing rose to sprawl on a fence, wall, or trellis is one of the most beautiful ways to work roses into the landscape and bring their flowers right up to eye level. (See Chapter 12 for more information about climbers.) However, you must realize that training is the key word here. Climbing roses are not true vines. They don't naturally cling to or wrap around a nearby vertical object like vines do. You must plant them near a support structure, like a fence, post, arbour, wall, or trellis, and regularly tie their canes to that structure to make them stay put.

Following are several types of support structures for climbing roses. In all cases, the structure must be sturdy. A mature climber can be quite heavy and can break any support that's not strong enough to handle the weight.

- **Fences:** Split rail, chain link, even barbed wire — you can turn any sturdy fence into a colourful picture when you use it to support a climbing rose. If you have solid fences with few places to tie to, use a trellis or stretch wire between eye screws as described in the "Walls" section.

- **Walls:** Here you usually have to attach some type of support to the wall. One way is to thread 14- or 16-gauge galvanized wire through eyebolts attached to the wall. If you have masonry walls, you have to use bolts with expanding anchors. But your local hardware store can help you make the right choice. Arrange the wires vertically, horizontally, or in a fan shape — whatever your fancy dictates. You can even attach the rose directly to the bolts and skip the wire altogether.

- **Trellises:** A handsome trellis covered with a climbing rose can be a piece of art, turning a blank wall into a garden focal point. Trellises come in many shapes and sizes and are constructed from a variety of materials, including wood lath, metal, and plastic. They can be free-standing or attached to walls and fences. A trip to a local lumberyard or garden centre or a browse through the sources listed in Appendix B of this book can give you a good idea of the variety that's available. Or if you're handy, you can get a good idea of what you can make yourself.

Lattice, one of the most common types of trellis, is designed for mounting on walls or fences. You can also attach it to fence posts for an inexpensive screen. When securing lattice directly to a solid surface, extend the connecting supports several centimetres beyond the surface so that the trellis doesn't lie directly on the surface. This space improves air circulation around the rose, which helps to reduce pest and disease problems.

To make house painting or other maintenance easier, fasten the lattice-work to hinges at the bottom so that you can lay back the trellis for easy access to the wall. Use sturdy, construction-grade metal hooks and eyes to attach the trellis to the wall at the top.

✔ **Arbours and pergolas:** Arbours and pergolas differ from trellises in that they have a horizontal top and are usually free-standing, supported by posts or trellis-like sides. (See Figure 5-1.) You train a rose up the support and then over the top. Like trellises, you can make arbours and pergolas

Figure 5-1:
You can train a rose to climb over an arbour to create a stunning focal point for your garden.

from a variety of materials, from wood to plastic to metal. They also range in size from small enough to frame the entry to a yard or garden to large enough to cover a patio or entire walkway. Also like trellises, many arbours and pergolas are quite ornate or whimsical and can serve as the focal point of a garden.

You can find many styles of prefabricated arbours in the mail-order rose catalogues listed in Appendix B. Or if you're a handy carpenter, you can build your own. You may want to consult a carpenter or builder for advice, though, especially if you plan to build a large arbour. One other tip: Use pressure-treated lumber, or rot-resistant wood like cedar or redwood, in any part of the structure that comes in contact with the soil.

✓ **Pillars:** A *pillar* is a sturdy, rot-resistant wood or metal post set in the ground. The size and shape of the pillar can vary as long as the pillar itself is firmly embedded. You then plant a climber at the base and tie it to the pillar as it grows.

Chapter 6

Roses and Their Partners in the Garden

· ·

In This Chapter

▶ Combining plants with beautiful results

▶ Putting other plants in front of roses

▶ Combining roses and herbs

▶ Using plants with attractive foliage

▶ Creating a white garden

· ·

Certain plants just seem to belong together. Maybe their shapes are a perfect contrast. Or maybe their flower colours blend together just right. Or possibly the plants share a common history. Whatever the reason, many plants combine with roses, including other roses, resulting in classic beauty.

That's what this chapter is all about: specific plants that form classic combinations with roses — plant combinations that give your garden an artist's touch. We list many plants here, and you'll need more information about heights, habits, and bloom times to combine them effectively. This kind of data is almost always included in garden catalogue descriptions (or should be), or you can find it in books about specific types of plants. Refer to the sources in Appendix B to help you locate the plants you want.

We list just a few of the plants that we know work well as companions for roses, but hundreds of others exist as well. Besides, to paraphrase Duke Ellington, who said music that sounds good is good: If a plant combination looks good, it probably is.

The Basics of Combining Plants

This chapter covers basic principles of combining colours and plant textures, and expands on the landscaping ideas outlined in Chapter 5. We're going to quickly repeat some of those principles and throw in some new suggestions as well:

- **Choose colours wisely.** Select the colours you want to work with, taking clues from the colour of your house, garden structures, other plants, or whatever else you have in your yard, and stick with them.

- **Mix and match plant textures.** Blend bold textures with soft textures, vertical shapes with horizontal ones, and round plants with arching plants. Mix plants the way nature would.

- **Unite the overall.** Repeat some plant combinations to add unity to the garden.

- **Use bright colours to direct the eye.** If you want to create a focal point in your garden, surround the area with bright or contrasting colours. Even one bright red rose draws the eye to a garden feature such as a small fountain or bird bath.

- **Vary heights.** In general, use lower plants in front and taller ones in back. However, you don't have to follow this rule religiously. Mixing things up a bit can be interesting.

- **Match bloom times carefully.** Most roses have a long bloom season, so you want to make sure that the other plantings you use also look good over a long season. Combine plants with a staggered bloom season so that you have colour in spring, summer, and fall. Use flowering perennials, shrubs, and annuals.

- **Don't forget the foliage.** One way to make sure that your garden always looks good is to combine roses with plants that have attractive foliage. We give you some ideas a little later in this chapter.

- **Match cultural requirements.** Roses like full sun, regular water, and close to a neutral pH. The plants you combine with them should, too. Otherwise, one or the other will be unhappy. And so will you.

- **Keep it simple.** Always the best advice. Don't get carried away with too many colours or too many different kinds of plants. Simplify, and everything will be fine.

Okay, now that you're an expert, you're ready to get to the good part: choosing your plants.

Plants That Cover the Bases

Many roses, especially hybrid teas and some tall floribundas, tend to get a bit open and sparsely foliaged at the base of the plant. To alleviate this problem, you can plant low-growing or spreading plants right in front of them.

An obvious first choice if there is adequate sunshine at the base of the rose is to use some of the compact miniature roses listed for use as edgings in Chapter 5. But many other options are available; the following sections list some favourite perennial and annual plants that you can use. See Figure 6-1 for an example of how perennial and annual plants can fill in around the base of roses.

Figure 6-1: A rose with low-spreading plants growing around its base.

Perennials are plants that survive from year to year in your garden, usually at least three years. *Biennials* grow leaves the first year; flower, set seed, and die the second. *Annuals* are plants that complete their entire life cycle from seed to seed in one growing season.

Perennials

Here are some perennial plants — ones that live on in your garden from year to year and combine well with roses.

- **Bellflower** *(Campanula species):* Several low-growing species, blues, pinks, and whites

- **Cornflowers** *(Centaurea species):* Rose flowers in midsummer

- **Clematis** *(Clematis* many species): A variety of colours for climbing through larger roses

- **Threadleaf coreopsis or tickseed** *(Coreopsis verticillata, C. rosea* and their cultivars): Yellow or pink, low mound shape, blooms all summer

- **Delphinium** hybrids: Range of colours, go well with roses

- **Cranesbill** *(Geranium endressi* and others): Blossoms range from white to purple, one of our favourites for colour and foliage

- **Baby's breath** *(Gypsophila species):* White tall form is best to combine with roses

- **Coral bells** *(Heuchera species):* Great foliage and delicate white, pink, or red flower spikes

- **Siberian iris** *(Iris sibirica):* Range of colours for early summer blooms

- **Common** or **English lavender** *(Lavandula angustifolia,* 'Hidcote' & other cultivars): Grey-green foliage with flowers from pink to deep violet, excellent at the base of non-fragrant roses

- **Russian sage** *(Perovskia atriplicifolia):* Violet, likes good drainage so avoid on clay soils

- **Catnip** *(Nepeta grandiflora* or Nepeta 'Six Hills Giant'): Violet masses — wonderful

- **Speedwell** *(Veronica longifolia* and cultivars): Violets and white

- **Wild indigo** *(Baptisia australis):* Blue flowers in early summer

Annuals

Here are some of our favourite annuals to combine with roses.

- **Annual mallow** *(Lavatera trimestris* 'Pink Beauty'): Wonderful pink hollyhock-like blooms

- **Flossflower** *(Ageratum houstonianum):* Great blues

- ✔ **Cosmos** ('Sensation' series and 'Sonata' series): Choose your colour to match the roses

- ✔ **Gazania** ('Dorothy' and 'Silvery Beauty'): Yellow blossoms form on a thick carpet of foliage

- ✔ **Flowering tobacco** *(Nicotiana sylvestris):* Produces white, evening-fragrant flowers. Other hybrids in other colours such as pink can be used as well if the height and colour go well with your rose

- ✔ **Pansies** *(Viola hybrida and species):* Popular standby with many colours to choose from

- ✔ **Sweet alyssum** *(Lobularia maritima):* Covered with pink, purple, or white flowers

- ✔ **Sweet peas** *(Lathyrus odoratus):* Pink, white, and purple — grow them as vines through the rose

- ✔ **Zinnias** *(Zinnia elegans):* Many colours — use the compact varieties like the Peter Pan series

Roses and Herbs

Roses share many things with aromatic herb plants — their fragrant flowers are used to make potpourri (see Chapter 24 for information about making potpourri), their hips can be used to make aromatic tea, and the fragrance of the flower can be extracted for perfumes. Hey, maybe roses *are* herbs!

In fact, roses and herbs are closely linked and have been planted together for centuries. Many of the very fragrant old garden roses like the 'Old Blush' China rose and the autumn damask rose, *Rosa damascena,* share a long bond with herbs. But using any fragrant rose variety makes sense.

The family of plants called *herbs* is huge and includes many attractive species, so you have much to choose from. Here are some of our favourites:

- ✔ **Basil** *(Ocimum basilicum):* Variety of foliage colours and fragrances

- ✔ **Chamomile** *(Chamaemelum nobile):* Low growing with yellow flowers

- ✔ **Fennel** *(Foeniculum vulgare):* Airy foliage, especially the variety with bronze foliage

- ✔ **Lavender** *(Lavandula):* Blue flowers and aromatic foliage. We've listed it twice because some retailers sell it as a herb and some as a flower. It doesn't matter what you call it, it is wonderful with roses

- ✔ **Parsley** *(Petroselinum crispum):* Bright green, ferny foliage

- **Rosemary** *(Rosmarinus):* Many shrubby types with blue flowers

- **Sage** *(Salvia officinalis):* Look out especially for the varieties with yellow, purple, or tricoloured foliage

- **Santolina** *(Santolina):* Silvery leaves and yellow flowers

- **Scented geraniums** *(Pelargonium):* Many to choose from with wonderfully fragrant, good-looking leaves and pretty flowers

- **Southernwood** *(Artemisia abrotanum):* Beautiful silvery foliage provides unusual backdrop

- **Thyme** *(Thymus):* Of the many to choose from, we especially like yellow-foliaged creeping thyme and silver thyme

Going for Leaves

Plants with attractive foliage can carry a garden through down times when little is in bloom. But when roses are in bloom, surrounding foliage plants can really show them off and light up their colours.

Silver-dusted leaves

To start, consider any plant with grey or silver foliage. These colours tie everything together and combine especially well with white, pink, red, and blue flowers. Try one of the following plants, for example:

- ***Artemisia ludoviciana* 'Valerie Finnis':** Wide silver leaves

- ***Artemisia* 'Powis Castle':** Great texture and colour

- ***Artemisia stelleriana* 'Silver Brocade':** Low, compact perennial

- **Bush germander** *(Teucrium):* Airy shrub with blue flowers

- **Dusty Miller** *(Centaurea cineraria* or *Senecio cineraria):* Great annuals with purple or yellow flowers

- **Lamb's ears** *(Stachys byzantina):* Silver foliage has wonderfully soft texture

- **Lavender cotton** *(Santolina):* Silvery leaves and yellow flowers, annual

- **Silver sage** *(Salvia argentea):* Huge, woolly silver leaves, biennial

- **Silver thyme** *(Thymus vulgaris* 'Argenteus'*):* Low and aromatic

- **Yarrow** *(Achillea):* Silver foliage and colourful flowers

Grassy and spiky leaves

Here's a list of rose companions that are interesting mostly for their grass or grasslike leaves. In addition, these plants produce flowers in late summer and fall — just when roses are putting on their last show of the season.

- **Blue fescue** *(Festuca glauca):* Silver-blue leaves on a low, mounding grass
- **Daylily** *(Hemerocallis* hybrids): Grassy leaves and mostly orange and yellow trumpet-shaped flowers
- **Feather grass** *(Stipa):* Graceful grasses and soft-textured plumes
- **Iris** *(Iris* species): Strap-like leaves and classic flowers in many shades
- **Lily** *(Lilium species):* Upright plants and colourful trumpet-shaped blooms
- **Lily-of-the-Nile** *(Agapanthus africanus):* Strap-like leaves and bright blue flower balls, tender in zone 6
- **Purple fountain grass** *(Pennisetum setaceum* 'Rubrum'*):* Purplish bronze leaves and soft plumes
- **Spiderwort** *(Tradescantia):* Purple, rose, or white blossoms

White for When the Night Is Bright

Remember that whole thing about there being beauty in simplicity? Well, how about a garden with nothing but white flowers? While this can be a difficult garden to design, good white gardens are stunning during the day (especially if you have a lot of green background), and at night with a full moon. With good outdoor lighting, the garden comes alive. If done poorly, they are hot and uncomfortable gardens.

If you want to take your best shot at it (and we all do, sooner or later), many white roses are available to help you on your way. The best are described in Part III and pictured in the colour section of this book. But do you want the real truth? Our favourite white rose is 'Iceberg', a floribunda. It gives more bloom for your buck than nearly any other white rose.

Following are other white flowering plants that you can use with roses in a moonlit garden. Some come in colours other than white, so make sure to choose the white-flowering varieties. Throw in some of the silvery or grey-foliaged plants mentioned earlier, too. They also reflect light.

- **Snapdragon** *(Antirrhinum majus):* Tall spikes of flowers
- **Jupiter's beard** *(Centranthus ruber):* Tall flower spikes

Ten of our favourite combinations

Some plant combinations just work — who cares why. These do.

- Yellow 'Sunsprite' floribunda combined with blue *Tradescantia* and *Veronica longifolia*

- In a container, violet pansies planted as close as possible to the stems of pink roses and encouraged to climb through the branches. A blue clematis in the same pot climbing through the pink rose

- Any red or pink rose on a white fence or arbour

- 'Simplicity' pink floribunda fronted by blue flowering salvia, *Salvia patens*, and silvery lamb's ears, *Stachys byzantina*

- 'Champlain' Explorer rose with *Pulmonaria* 'David Ward' and *Brunnera macrophylla* 'variegata' tucked under its edges

- Any pink floribunda or miniature rose planted around a red brick patio

- Pink and red roses with pink and red geraniums, *Pelargonium*, fronted by light blue lobelia, *Lobelia erinus*

- 'City of London' pink floribunda, grey-foliaged *Artemisia* 'Powis Castle', and annual blue flowering *Salvia* 'Victoria' fronted by candytuft, *Iberis sempervirens*

- Reddish purple hardy geraniums, *Geranium* species, with pink 'Carefree Wonder' shrub rose and white 'Iceberg' floribunda

Combining different types of plants with beautiful, or even just interesting, results is what gives a garden its personality. The plants you choose are what make the garden uniquely yours. Experiment! This is where gardening gets fun and rewarding.

- **Mums** *(Chrysanthemum):* Beautiful fall flowers

- **Cosmos** *(Cosmos bipinnatus):* Airy foliage and daisy-like flowers

- **Daisies:** Many different species with bright white flowers

- **Dianthus** *(Dianthus):* Many to choose from, some fragrant

- **Candytuft** *(Iberis sempervirens):* Whitest of white on a compact plant

- **Sweet alyssum** *(Lobularia maritima):* Ground-hugging carpet of white

- **Geraniums** *(Pelargonium):* Great balls of white

- **Datura** or **Angel's Trumpets** *(Datura species* and *Brugmansia species):* Large white or pink trumpets on plants that are 90 to 180 centimetres (3 to 6 feet) tall

When combining any plants, don't forget to consider their height, habit, and growing requirements, as mentioned earlier in this chapter.

Chapter 7

Growing Roses in Containers

● ●

In This Chapter

▶ Knowing which roses are best in pots
▶ Using a variety of containers
▶ Deciding how big your containers should be
▶ Uncovering the truth about potting soil
▶ Planting in containers
▶ Caring for roses grown in pots

● ●

*R*oses are great plants for growing in containers. Choose the right pot, and you turn any rose into a garden feature. Not only that, but growing roses in containers also makes the plants mobile — you can move them out front when they're in bloom and then put them out of the way when they're not. And you can cart them off to a protected location when winters get cold.

Growing roses in containers can also solve problems. If you have bad soil, for example, you can fill a pot with a perfect soil mix purchased from a nursery and plant in that. And you always have room for a pot or two even if you have a very small garden, and especially if your "garden" is just a patio, porch, or balcony.

So gardening in containers really adds a wonderful new dimension to growing roses. But this kind of gardening is not quite the same as growing roses in open ground. You need to choose the right rose, the right pot, and the right soil. And after you plant the rose in a container, you need to care for it properly, which also has its nuances. That's what this chapter's about: turning you into an expert container gardener.

Putting the Right Rose in the Right Pot

If you really set your mind to it, you can grow any rose in any pot, but after a while, some of the large types get very hard to care for and keep in bounds. Smaller, compact roses are really best for growing in containers. These include miniatures, polyanthas and floribundas, and some shrub roses. You also can grow any hybrid tea in a container, but to look their best, they usually need to be combined with other low-growing plants. For suggestions, see the lists of plants in Chapter 5. We particularly like growing dark blue violas and pansies with pink rose varieties.

Still, some floribundas and polyanthas (Chapter 10) and shrub roses (Chapter 13) just fit in a pot better than others. The following are some of our favourites. Add to the list any miniature rose you like.

- ✔ **'Bonica':** Pink shrub
- ✔ **'Carefree Delight':** Pink shrub
- ✔ **'Carefree Wonder':** Pink and white shrub
- ✔ **'China Doll':** Pink polyantha
- ✔ **'Dream' series:** Pink, yellow, red, and orange small shrubs
- ✔ **'Europeana':** Red floribunda
- ✔ **'Flower Carpet':** Pink shrub
- ✔ **'Iceberg':** White floribunda
- ✔ **'Margaret Merrill':** White floribunda
- ✔ **'Margo Koster':** Coral floribunda
- ✔ **'Regensberg':** White and pink floribunda
- ✔ **'Sun Flare':** Yellow floribunda
- ✔ **'The Fairy':** Pink polyantha

Containing the Roots

You may not realize it yet, but an amazing variety of plant containers exists. If you don't believe us, go to a large nursery or garden centre and compare sizes, shapes, and materials.

The first criterion in choosing a container is whether you like how it looks. If you want to grow roses in old coffee cans, fine; just don't invite us over to take pictures. A nice-looking pot can really turn a healthy rose into something special. A pretty pot also makes everything else around it look better. A few nice pots can turn a patio into a perfectly ornamented garden room. Or they can turn a front porch into an entry that elegantly says, "Welcome."

After you decide what looks good, you should be aware of some other characteristics of various types of containers. They may or may not sway your decision on what you buy, but some kinds of containers last longer than others; some are heavy, some are light; and some dry out faster than others.

Here are characteristics of some common types of containers:

 ✔ **Clay pots** (shown in Figure 7-1) are attractive, relatively inexpensive, and come in a variety of styles. They break easily, and the larger ones can be quite heavy. The most common type is the familiar terra cotta pot, which is porous and allows the soil to dry out quickly. However, you can get glazed clay or ceramic pots, which are not only colourful but also hold water longer. They are more expensive, too. The more expensive ones (hot-fired) do not flake apart if you let them freeze.

 ✔ **Plastic pots** come in many styles, colours, and sizes. Some are even made to look like wood or clay pots. They're lightweight, inexpensive, and keep soil moist longer than clay pots. Some kinds become brittle after being in the sun for a year or two, and after they break, about all you can do with them is to ship them off to a landfill, where they stay for eternity.

Figure 7-1:
A rose plant
in a clay pot.

✔ **Wooden pots** are attractive, relatively inexpensive, and come in many styles, sizes, weights, and shapes. They include the very popular and inexpensive half wine and whiskey barrels (shown in Figure 7-2). With a little carpentry skill, you can even build your own wooden container.

✔ **Hanging baskets** are what they sound like — pots that hang in the air (see Figure 7-3). Some gardeners build or buy hanging baskets lined with long-fibre sphagnum moss (the natural state of sphagnum moss before it is ground up and put into bags to be sold) or coco-liners (you can ask at your garden centre — good ones will have this material). If you use the larger moss baskets, use this old Parks Department trick. Line the basket on the inside of the moss with plastic. That way they don't dry out too fast. We use an old garbage bag and poke a single hole in the bottom of it for drainage.

There are other types of containers, including heavy ones made of concrete and very inexpensive but short-lived ones made of pressed fibres. But those detailed in the preceding list are the most common and are the best choices for roses.

Figure 7-2:
A rose plant in a half-barrel.

Figure 7-3:
A rose plant in a hanging basket.

TIP

Rottin' to the core

The one downside of wood containers is that they tend to be short-lived — the wood often rots quickly from being in constant contact with wet soil. But you can do a few things to prolong the life of wooden containers:

✓ **Buy containers made of a rot-resistant wood like redwood or cedar.** If you're building your own containers, use these rot-resistant woods or look into pressure-treated woods. Pressure-treated woods have preservatives forced into them and are quite long-lived. However, before you buy them, ask someone at the lumberyard about safety techniques that you must follow when handling pressure-treated wood. Although generally safe if handled properly, the materials used to preserve wood are often toxic.

✓ **Treat the inside of the container.** You can really prolong the life of a wooden container by painting the inside with the black asphalt-like goop used to patch roofs. Ask your hardware guy; he'll know the stuff. Use the goop liberally and let it dry out well before filling the pot with soil. The roof patch is safer for you and the plants and is much longer-lasting than other wood preservatives.

✓ **Keep the containers raised off the ground.** Set wood containers on small pieces of wood or bricks to create an air space under the pot. This space helps the barrels dry out and slows the rotting process of the wood.

Bigger is (usually) better

Obviously, containers come in many sizes. Their sizes are usually described by their diameter at the top — 15-centimetre (6-inch), 25-centimetre (10-inch), 30-centimetre (12-inch), and on up; or by how much soil they hold — 4-litre (1-gallon), 23-litre (5-gallon), and so on. Even though we've switched to metric, most nurseries in Canada still use either the gallon or inch size for pots.

As a general rule, bigger is better. The more soil a container holds, the more root space your rose has and the easier the rose is to care for. But bigger also means heavier and more expensive, so you often have to compromise. Small roses like miniatures need at least a 30-centimetre (12-inch) or 8-litre (2-gallon) container. Large plants like shrubs, floribundas, polyanthas, and hybrid teas can go for a year or two in a 20-litre (5-gallon) or 35-centimetre (14-inch) pot, but a 60-litre (15-gallon) container or half-barrel is much better. In fact, half a wine or whiskey barrel is great for growing roses, especially if you want to include other flowers or more than one rose plant.

Accessories for your pots

You need to consider two other accessories when shopping for pots:

- **A saucer for underneath the pot:** Saucers are always a good idea. They collect water that runs out the holes in the bottom of the pot and prevent the pot from staining whatever it's sitting on. You can find saucers made of the same or similar material as your pot, or get invisible ones made of clear plastic. Plastic saucers are least likely to stain. Saucers can also help you water your pots, but we'll get to that in a bit. Just make sure that you don't let water stand too long in the saucer; water can rot roots and wooden pots.

- **Wheels for mobility:** Most nurseries and garden centres sell wheeled platforms on top of which you can set pots. These are great if your landscape is paved, but they're hard to push on gravel or grass. Mobility is freedom, so take a close look at these accessories. Otherwise, you'll have to lift heavy pots or cart them around on a dolly. We use a kid's old wagon to move our larger pots around.

Potting Soil Simplified

No nonsense here. Rule one and only: Don't fill your pots with soil from your garden. It's too heavy and too dirty (you know, weed seeds, bugs, bacteria — stuff you don't want in your pots), and it will not drain properly after it's in a pot. After a few waterings, it starts to compact, and compacted soil is hard on young feeder roots.

Instead, you need potting soil. Now, we could tell you a lot about potting soils: how they're supposed to be well aerated, sterile, lightweight, and made of a good balance of organic matter and mineral particles like sand or perlite. We could even give you a recipe to make your own. But you'd nod off in a second. Either that or you'd hurt your back mixing up a batch.

Go down to the local nursery or garden centre and buy whichever packaged artificial potting soil is cheapest or comes in the prettiest bag. If you need a lot, many nurseries sell soil in bulk quantities.

Yes, many potting soils are out there, and they have different qualities. So you may want to try different brands over time to see which one you like best in terms of ease of wetting and moisture-holding capacity. But don't have a personal crisis over which one to buy. Caring for a rose properly after you plant it is more important than choosing the perfect potting soil.

Planting Properly in Pots

Piece of cake. Just a few things to remember: Plant 2 to 3 centimetres (1 inch) deeper than you normally would, because potting soil settles quite a bit, and don't fill the container to the very top with soil. Leave at least 5 centimetres (2 inches) of space at the top of the pot (more in large containers) for easy watering.

Here are the basic steps:

1. **Check for drainage holes.**

   Your pots must, and we mean *must,* have holes in the bottom so that water can drain out. Otherwise, the roots will drown. Most pots come with holes in the bottom. But if you build your own wooden container or buy half a wine or whiskey barrel, you will probably have to drill holes in the bottom. Use a 1.25-centimetre to 2.5-centimetre (½- to 1-inch) drill bit. Five to seven evenly spaced holes are usually enough for a half-barrel, but more are better than fewer.

2. **Fill the container halfway with potting soil and then thoroughly wet the soil.**

3. **Place the rose plant in the pot on top of the soil.**

   See Chapter 17 for instructions for planting a rose. Plant in the barrel as you would in the garden. The depth of the rose bud union (Chapter 1) is not as important in a container as it is in the ground because you'll be protecting the pot for the winter.

4. **Fill the container with soil so that the rose bud union is roughly at the soil line.**

Do make sure there is about 5 centimetres (2 inches) of depth between the pot rim and the soil line. When you water, you want the water to stay in the pot — not run out. This is not rocket science. If the bud union is a tad higher or lower than ideal, relax. It will grow anyway.

5. **Water and check for settling.**

Wet the soil thoroughly, let the pot drain, and then repeat. Now check the planting depth. If you need to, add or remove soil around the base of the plant so that it's not planted too high or too deep. Remember to leave some space between the top of the soil and the top rim of the container so that it has plenty of room to hold water.

Caring for Roses Growing in Containers

Roses grown in containers differ from roses grown in the ground in a few important ways:

- **They need more frequent watering.** Potting soils dry out faster than regular garden soil, so roses growing in potting soil must be watered more often. In really hot weather, your roses may need water more than once a day.

  You can check to see whether a container is dry in several ways. First, you can stick your finger in the soil. If your finger comes away dry, you should water. You can also check soil moisture by lifting or tipping a container on its side. If the container is dry, it will be lighter than when wet. When you're really experienced, you can tap the side of the pot and hear the difference between a water-filled "thunk" and a dry "thonk."

- **They need more thorough watering.** Wetting really dry potting soil can be tricky. Soils that are composed of peat moss shrink and pull away from the side of the pot when they are really dry, so when you water, all the water rushes down the space along the side of the pot without wetting the soil. To overcome this problem, make sure that you fill the top of the pot with water more than once so that the rootball can absorb water and expand. In fact, you should do so anyway to be sure that the rootball is thoroughly wet with each watering. If you still have trouble wetting the rootball, place the pot in a saucer and fill it repeatedly with water. The water soaks up into the rootball and slowly wets all the soil.

A good general rule for watering roses in a pot is to water so that 15 percent of the water applied to the top runs out the bottom. It is important to thoroughly soak the entire pot, not just the top 15 centimetres (6 inches). Every time you water, do not stop until water is pouring out the bottom of the pot.

✓ **They need more frequent fertilizing.** The frequent watering that container-grown roses need leaches the nutrients from the soil, so the plants need to be fertilized more often, at least every week, to maintain blooming. Liquid or water-soluble fertilizers are easiest to use and get the nutrients right down to the roots. A complete fertilizer, including chelated iron and other micronutrients, is best. For more on fertilizing roses, see Chapter 19. As a last note, we use fish emulsion on potted roses to keep them blooming heavily all summer long.

Part III
All the Roses You Need to Know

The 5th Wave   By Rich Tennant

"FRANK SPENDS MOST OF HIS TIME HYBRIDIZING BOURBON ROSES.
I THINK OF HIM NOT SO MUCH AS A ROSARIAN BUT MORE AS A
FRUSTRATED BARTENDER."

In this part . . .

A big, wide, wonderful world of roses is out there with more to choose from than you can imagine. In this part, we tell you about the best rose varieties, organizing them by type and flower colour. Everything you need to know about each bloom and plant is here. We also note varieties that have been designated as All-America Rose Selections (AARS). These varieties were evaluated at test gardens and judged to be the best of the new introductions for a particular year.

If you can't find a rose you like here, you'd better check your pulse.

One other bit of information provided for every rose variety described in this part is the year the rose was introduced — but don't bet your life on the accuracy of these dates. Published information on that topic is inconsistent, to say the least. Sometimes, for example, it's unclear whether the date given is when the rose was created or when it was formally introduced for sale. All you really need is an idea of when a rose was introduced. If it's a new variety, it probably possesses all the latest trendy characteristics, such as disease resistance. If the variety is old and still around, it has probably stood the test of time and deserves consideration.

Chapter 8

Hybrid Teas

*H*ybrid teas are the royalty of the rose family — by far the most popular type of rose, as well as being the most popular flower in the world, period. Millions of hybrid tea rose plants are purchased and planted every year by gardeners everywhere. And sales of hybrid teas as cut flowers are a very important part of the florist's business. Can you say "Valentine's Day"?

Their popularity is well earned. The blossoms are exquisite, slowly rolling open petal by petal from beautifully formed buds. Each flower may have as many as 60 petals and is often more than 10 centimetres (5 inches) wide. Supported by long, strong stems, hybrid teas are unmatched as cut flowers, whether you buy them in the dead of winter or grow them in your own backyard. And the fragrance, oh the fragrance — always present but, in some varieties, strong enough to carry you away.

Making Distinctions: Unique Qualities of the Hybrid Teas

A hybrid tea is distinguished from other roses by the way it grows. Hybrid teas produce their flowers one bloom to a long stem, as shown in Figure 8-1, not in clusters like floribunda or shrub roses. Most hybrid tea plants grow about 0.9 to 1.5 metres (3 to 5 feet) high and tend to be open rather than bushy, with long, straight, upright canes. Virtually all hybrid teas are repeat bloomers, producing flowers throughout the growing season.

Figure 8-1:
Hybrid tea
flowers are
typically
borne one
to a stem
and have
more than
25 petals.
The buds
are pointed
and the
petals unfurl
in a spiral
around a
high centre.

The hybrid tea rose plants available for purchase are always budded onto
hardy *rootstock*. (See Chapters 1 and 16 for more information on rootstock.)
Commercial rose growers have found that these plants are more vigorous and
reliable to propagate when they are budded. The point at which they are
budded is called the *bud union*. This bud union is the magic place where new
canes sprout and grow from the base of the plant.

Although the bud union is a truly amazing part of the rose plant, it's also the
most vulnerable. If grown without winter protection where winter temperatures reach –12° C (10° F) or lower, the bud union is the first part of the plant
to be damaged or killed by cold and wind. People who don't grow roses think
that hybrid teas require mysterious culture practices. But the truth is that
although hybrid tea roses may require a little extra work, especially in our
cold climates, nothing is really difficult or mysterious about them.

Hybrid teas are no more or less pest or disease resistant than any other
classification of roses. And every variety of hybrid tea is an individual, demon-
strating a character all its own. Any given hybrid tea may be more or less
floriferous, more or less disease resistant, or more or less winter hardy than
other varieties of hybrid teas.

Hybrid teas are available in almost every colour but true green and blue. Some red varieties are so dark that they're almost black. And the mauves are the closest any rose gets to blue. Many of the loveliest hybrid teas are bicolours or blends. See the section "Knowing Their Namesakes: Hybrid Tea Types by Colour" for a colour-by-colour breakdown of the different varieties of hybrid tea roses.

Although gardeners may grow hybrid teas for their fragrance or their colour, the characteristic that makes rose growers' hearts sing is the form. A hybrid tea's perfection of form, or *exhibition form,* is a trait that must be present in the variety's genetic makeup to begin with, but excellent culture is required to encourage the form to reach its pinnacle of perfection.

Hybrid tea flowers with excellent form have long, pointed buds that unfurl in a perfect spiral around a high, pointed centre. When viewed from the side, the flowers have a triangular shape, with the outside, or lowest petals, remaining horizontal rather than falling below the horizontal plane. Because great form is always associated with the hybrid teas, other classifications of roses that have really good form are often described as having *hybrid tea form.*

Flowers with great form usually have substance as well. *Substance* is the thickness, or leathery rigidity, of the petals. Roses with substance are usually better able to withstand the vagaries of weather and last longer in the vase after being cut. A rose's capability to maintain its beauty for a length of time after it's cut is called *vase life.* Generally, a rose variety's vase life is more important to commercial cut flower growers than to rosarians.

For more information about rose flowers, see Chapter 2.

Some royal tea history

The first hybrid tea, 'La France', was born in 1867 when a French nurseryman, M. Guillot, cross-bred two old garden roses and came up with a whole new kind of rose. Because one of the roses M. Guillot used for crossbreeding, or hybridizing, was an old garden rose of the tea subclass, the classification "hybrid tea" was christened. 'La France' and several of the early hybrid teas have survived and can be found at nurseries specializing in old garden roses. But as wonderful as the first hybrid teas were at the time, they have been improved by judicious hybridizing over the years. Today's modern hybrids bear little resemblance to their forebears.

Some hybrid tea varieties have become so popular that they are synonymous with an era. For example, the 'Peace' rose, hybridized in France just prior to World War II, was sent to the United States to be nurtured and propagated by the Conard Pyle Company during the war years. 'Peace' was introduced to the world in 1945 and is still a favourite symbol of hope for the future. Called 'Gloria Dei' in Europe, 'Peace' celebrated its 50th anniversary in 1995.

Lining 'Em Up: How to Plant Your Hybrid Teas

Hybrid teas are often grown in rows in a traditional rose cutting garden because, well, because that's the way Bonaparte's Josephine grew her rose garden. Some gardeners think they are easier to care for when planted by themselves, but they look and grow very well when integrated into a perennial border and in landscape plantings with other shrubs and flowers. They should be planted 45 to 90 centimetres (18 to 36 inches) apart, depending on growth habit.

Because hybrid teas have little foliage near the base of the plants (see Figure 8-2) and spindly growth in that area should be removed, they may look a little more naked than other types of roses when used in the landscape. However, if you plant low-growing perennials or herbs at their base, hybrid teas can be attractive in flower beds (see Chapter 5 for more information about landscaping with roses). Hybrid teas also combine beautifully with other plants in containers.

Figure 8-2:
Hybrid tea rose plants usually grow between 0.9 and 1.5 metres (3 and 5 feet) high with upright stems.

Shearing Brutality: Pruning Your Hybrid Teas

 Growing hybrid teas takes practically no more effort on your part than most other kinds of roses. They need water, fertilizer, and possibly a spray with a good fungicide. They are, however, usually pruned more severely (see Chapter 20 for pruning information) in spring than are other classifications of roses. Pruning hybrid teas involves cutting out spindly canes and leaving only four or five strong canes to grow. With traditional overwintering methods, the strong canes should be pruned to about 30 to 45 centimetres (12 to 18 inches) in height in the fall and then any winter damage can be further removed in the spring. Drastic pruning encourages the plant to produce larger flowers, while less severe spring pruning results in more but smaller flowers.

Knowing Their Namesakes: Hybrid Tea Types by Colour

You can choose among hundreds of hybrid tea roses. You can go for colour, fragrance, cut flowers, or even a wacky name. Roses are named after places ('Las Vegas', 'Tower Bridge') people ('Elizabeth Taylor', 'Uncle Joe') dreams ('Lady X', 'Perfect Moment') and even somebody's old car ('Chrysler Imperial'). But most people choose by colour, so that's how we break them down.

Red hybrid teas

Every garden needs at least one good red hybrid tea. Trust us: You need them in vases, you need them for their form and fragrance, and besides, what are you going to give that special someone when you want to say, "I love you"?

Red roses are by far the most popular, but no single variety today can be considered the "perfect" red rose. Some red roses turn bluish as the flowers age, some have so many petals that they don't want to open properly when the weather is cool (see Chapter 4 for more on the effects of climate), and some are too small to be considered perfect. If you want to make your everlasting fortune, read Chapter 23 on propagating roses and hybridize a red rose that's big, fragrant, has perfect form, great substance, and is disease resistant.

You can't miss with these favourites: 'Mister Lincoln' and 'Chrysler Imperial' for their fragrance, and 'Olympiad' for its pure energy and all-weather performance. Each of these roses has won the coveted All-America Rose Selection (AARS) award.

Here are red roses you should consider:

- **'Alabama':** Beautifully formed with 25 to 30 petals, deep pinkish red blossoms have a creamy white reverse. Nice fragrance. Tall, upright plant produces an abundance of bloom, ideal for cutting. Best colour with cool temperatures. Introduced in 1977.

- **'American Spirit':** Large, double (30 to 35 petals), bright velvety red blooms open from nicely formed, pointed buds. Long stems. Makes a great cut flower. Reblooms well. Light fragrance. Vigorous, upright habit with dark green leaves. Prone to mildew. Introduced in 1988.

- **'Christian Dior':** AARS 1962. Handsome, deep red buds open into large, double (50 to 55 petals), long-lasting, medium red blooms. Very little fragrance. Leathery, glossy green leaves. Vigorous, upright bush.

- **'Chrysler Imperial':** AARS 1953. A prize-winning hybrid tea much loved for its classic flower form, deep red colour, and intense, spicy fragrance. Beautifully formed buds open into large, double (40 to 50 petals), velvety red blooms. Winner of the James Alexander Gamble Rose Fragrance Award in 1965. Long, strong stems are excellent for cutting. Bushy, medium-sized plant with dark green leaves. A breeding parent for many modern red roses. Performs best in warm-summer climates. Also available in a climbing form.

- **'Crimson Glory':** Probably the first great red hybrid tea, prized for its intense colour and powerful fragrance. Winner of the James Alexander Gamble Rose Fragrance Award in 1961. Pointed blackish red buds open into large, double (30 to 35 petals), velvety red blooms. Vigorous, spreading growth with leathery, dark green leaves. Breeding parent for many modern red roses, including 'Chrysler Imperial'. Performs best in areas with hot summers. Introduced in 1935.

- **'Hoagy Carmichael':** A strong grower, producing well-proportioned velvety red blooms (30 to 40 petals) on very sturdy canes. Very fragrant, although flattish, blossom. Good dark green foliage, quite mildew resistant.

- **'Ingrid Bergman':** Large, bright red, double blooms (35 to 40 petals) with a velvety texture. Long stems, good for cutting. Light fragrance. Medium-sized plant with a bushy habit. Disease-resistant, dark green foliage. Introduced in 1985.

- **'Legend':** Large, wine red, double flowers (30 petals) with especially long stems that are ideal for cutting. Moderately fragrant. Tall, upright plant. Introduced in 1993.

- **'Mister Lincoln':** AARS 1965. One of the truly great fragrant red roses. Lovely deep red buds open into large, velvety red, double blossoms (30 to 35 petals) with a heady rose fragrance. Excellent cut flower. Tall, vigorous plant with deep green leaves. Performs well in all climates.

- **'Oklahoma':** One of the deepest, darkest, almost blackish red roses available. Nicely formed buds of the darkest red open into large, blackish-red, double blooms (40 to 55 petals). Strong musky aroma. Good cut flower. Vigorous, bushy plant with dull green leaves that are prone to mildew. Best in areas with warm summers. Introduced in 1964.

- **'Olympiad':** AARS 1994. One of the best red roses for gardeners in areas with cool summers. Large, brilliant red, double flowers (30 to 35 petals) with a light, fruity fragrance. Excellent cut flower. Tall, compact plant with good disease resistance and hardiness.

- **'Royal William':** Deep crimson, well-formed blooms have 35 petals and a high, very pointed centre section. Makes an excellent cut flower with moderate fragrance. A very vigorous, free-flowering plant. Introduced in 1984.

- **'Taboo':** Large, deep, dark velvety red, double flowers (30 petals) on long, strong stems. Moderately fragrant. Tall, vigorous plant with glossy, deep green leaves. Also known as 'Barkarole' and 'Grand Chateau'. Introduced in 1995.

- **'Tower Bridge':** An exhibition-quality medium red rose with a high pointed centre, excellent for cutting. Extremely fragrant with sweet qualities. Medium height and growth vigour, it should reach 0.9 to 1.5 metres (3 to 5 feet) in height.

Pink hybrid teas

You need pink roses, if for no other reason than they go so well with red roses in a garden and in a vase.

Need a hint on what to plant? You can't miss with 'Dainty Bess', or any of the pink roses whose name includes the words *sheer* or *perfume*. 'Tiffany' and 'Touch of Class' are also proven pink roses in our gardens.

The "can't-miss" pink roses include the following:

- **'Belami':** Also known as 'Woods of Windsor', this soft pink rose with a distinct darker pink edge on each petal has moderate fragrance. A good grower, very free bloomer. Very dark green foliage complements the 40-petalled blooms.

- **'Dainty Bess':** An elegant, free-blooming rose with clusters of single (5 petals) pink blossoms centred with deep red stamens. Flowers resemble the blooms of a dogwood. Light fragrance. Distinctive cut flower. Dense, medium-sized plant with dark green leaves. Good disease resistance but prone to rust in some regions (see Chapter 22 for more on rose pests and diseases). Also available in a climbing form. Introduced in 1925.

- **'Duet':** AARS 1961. A beautiful, two-toned hybrid tea with petals that are light pink on top and darker pink on the bottom. Blossoms are large, double (25 to 30 petals), and sometimes ruffled. Light fragrance. Good cut flower. Vigorous, dense, upright plant with deep green, disease-resistant foliage. One of the better hybrid teas for landscape use, especially as a hedge.

- **'First Prize':** AARS 1970. With lovely shades of silvery pink and perfectly formed flowers, this flower is one of the top exhibition roses among rose society members. The large blooms are double (25 to 30 petals) and mildly scented. The plant is medium-sized, and slightly spreading. The dark green, leathery foliage is susceptible to black spot and mildew. The best colour develops in cooler weather. Also available in climbing form.

- **'Fragrant Memory':** Also known as 'Jadis', this hybrid tea has light rose-pink, double flowers (25 to 35 petals) with a strong old-rose fragrance. Vigorous, medium-sized plant. Introduced in 1988.

- **'Friendship':** AARS 1979. Large, double (25 to 30 petals), deep pink blooms with a touch of red at the petals' edges. Sweetly fragrant. Vigorous, upright plant performs well in a variety of climates and has good disease resistance.

- **'Heaven':** Large, creamy-pink, double flowers (30 petals) are suffused and brushed with darker pink. Moderately fragrant. Medium-sized plant. Introduced in 1995.

- **'Helen Traubel':** AARS 1952. An old-time favourite, peachy-pink rose with a touch of orange in the bud. The large flowers are double (25 to 30 petals) and have a moderately strong, fruity fragrance. The plant is vigorous and upright with abundant bloom, but the flowers are weak-stemmed and often droop. Best colour in cool weather.

- **'Keepsake':** Usually a beautiful blend of dark and light pinks, but often has peach and yellow tones. The large flowers are double with 35 to 40 petals and have moderate, sweet fragrance. The plant is upright, vigorous, and has dark green foliage. Blooms well in all climates. Introduced in 1981.

- **'Miss All-American Beauty':** AARS 1968. Large, rich deep pink, double flowers (50 to 55 petals) have a strong rose fragrance. Large, deep green leaves on a bushy plant. Performs best in areas with hot summers.

- **'New Zealand':** A lovely, soft pink rose with a wonderful honeysuckle-like fragrance. Blossoms are large and double (30 to 35 petals) with strong stems ideal for cutting. Good-looking, glossy, deep green leaves on a medium-sized, upright plant. Disease resistant. Bigger flowers in cooler weather. Introduced in 1995.

'Paul Shirville': A delightful soft pink bloom with blends of salmon. Moderate fragrance on each 30-petalled blossom. This is one of the heaviest blooming pink roses — the plant is literally covered with blooms. Combine heavy blooming with extremely disease-resistant foliage and you have a winner. Introduced in 1983.

'Perfume Delight': AARS 1974. Large, deep rose-pink, double blooms (about 30 petals) with a wonderfully intense fragrance. Strong stems are ideal for cutting. Full-foliaged, upright plant with good disease resistance.

'Pink Peace': A deep pink, double rose (50 to 60 petals) with a strong rose fragrance. Developed from 'Peace' but never as popular. Medium-sized, upright plant is prone to rust. Introduced in 1959.

'Royal Highness': AARS 1963. A delicate pastel pink rose with exceptional flower form and a sweet fragrance. The large, double blooms (45 to 50 petals) are produced in abundance with strong stems, ideal for cutting. Bright green foliage on a medium-sized, upright plant. Best colour in cool weather. Subject to rust and mildew.

'Seashell': AARS 1976. A clean-looking blend of salmon-pink, pinkish cream, and soft orange. The flowers are large and double (45 to 50 petals) with a soft, fruity fragrance. Free-blooming. Good cut flower. Vigorous, upright plant with glossy, dark green leaves.

'Secret': Pink blush blossoms abound on this favourite. A very strong spicy fragrance makes this 30- to 35-petalled rose a strong seller. Good disease resistance on the medium green, glossy foliage makes it easy to grow. Oh, the fragrance!

'Sheer Elegance': AARS 1991. Light but rich pink, double blooms (30 to 35 petals) are lightly dusted with creamy pink. Light fragrance. Great cut flower. Glossy, dark green leaves on a medium-sized, upright plant. Excellent disease resistance.

'Signature': Beautifully formed, deep pink, double blossoms (30 to 35 petals) with swirls of cream and darker pink dancing on the petals. Light fragrance. Strong stems, ideal for cutting. Vigorous, upright plant with deep green, disease-resistant foliage. Introduced in 1996.

'Sweet Surrender': AARS 1983. Large, silvery pink, double blossoms (45 to 50 petals) that have that full-petalled, old cabbage rose appearance (for more specifics on old roses, including the "cabbage" rose, see Chapter 14). Heady fragrance. Long stems, ideal for cutting. Medium-sized, upright plant with dark green leaves. Best performance in warm summer areas.

'Tiffany': AARS 1955. A long-time favourite hybrid tea with large, soft pink, double blooms (25 to 30 petals) touched with yellow at the base of the petals. Wonderfully strong, fruity fragrance. Winner of the James Alexander Gamble Rose Fragrance Award in 1962. Outstanding cut flower. Dark green foliage on a medium to tall plant. Good disease resistance. Best colour in areas with hot summers.

⊛ **'Timeless':** AARS 1997. Long-lasting, deep pink, double blooms (25 to 30 petals). Slight fragrance. Long stems, ideal for cutting. Medium-sized plant with shiny, dark green leaves. Good disease resistance.

⊛ **'Touch of Class':** AARS 1987. Beautifully formed, coral-pink, double blossoms (about 30 petals) with hints of cream and orange. Slight fragrance. Beautiful cut flower. Medium-sized plant with dark green leaves.

⊛ **'Unforgettable':** Large, clear pink, double blooms (about 35 petals). Light fragrance. Tall, vigorous plant produces an abundance of flowers. Introduced in 1992.

Orange hybrid teas

Orange is a strong colour; if you're not careful, it can really mess up the mix of other colours you choose for your garden or bouquets. Mix orange with reds, whites, and yellows or use it by itself, but watch out if orange gets around pink or lavender. Yuck!

Our favourite orange roses include 'Artistry', 'Fragrant Cloud', 'Just Joey', 'Medallion', and 'Tropicana'. Here are more orange (or almost orange) hybrid teas that you'll find at the nursery or in catalogues.

⊛ **'Artistry':** AARS 1997. Brilliant coral-pink, double blossoms (30 to 35 petals) have a touch of cream on the back sides of the petals. Light fragrance. Long stems, ideal as cut flowers. Tall, vigorous, attractive plant produces an abundance of bloom. Best colour in areas with hot summers. Good disease resistance.

⊛ **'Bing Crosby':** AARS 1981. Deep, clean orange, double blooms (40 to 45 petals) with a light, spicy fragrance. Beautiful cut flower. Tall, upright to slightly spreading plant with glossy, dark green leaves. Best bloom in the cool months of fall.

⊛ **'Brandy':** AARS 1982. Beautifully formed, double blossoms (25 to 30 petals) in rich shades of light apricot-orange. Mildly sweet fragrance. Fine cut flower. Medium-tall, upright plant with semi-glossy, bright green leaves.

⊛ **'Command Performance':** AARS 1971. Orange-red buds open into bright orange, double flowers (25 to 30 petals) with an intense, spicy fragrance. Fine cut flower. Free-blooming, vigorous plant with a tall, slightly spreading habit. Best colour in areas with warm summers.

⊛ **'Dolly Parton':** Bright, coppery reddish orange, double blossoms (35 to 40 petals) with an alluring, spicy clove fragrance. Long-lasting cut flower. Bushy, medium-sized plant. Best colour where the nights are warm. Introduced in 1994.

- ❀ **'Fragrant Cloud':** Large, rich coral-orange flowers with an intoxicating, spicy aroma. Winner of the James Alexander Gamble Rose Fragrance Award in 1969. Excellent cut flower. Vigorous, medium-sized plant with glossy, deep green foliage. Deepest colour in areas with cool summers. Prone to mildew. Introduced in 1968.

- ❀ **'Just Joey':** Rich apricot, double flowers (25 to 30 petals) with a strong, fruity fragrance. Free-blooming, medium-sized plant with glossy green leaves. Best colour in areas with hot summers. Good disease resistance. Introduced in 1972.

- ❀ **'Liverpool Remembers':** Also known as 'Frystar' and 'Beauty Star'. Coppery orange blossoms (30 to 35 petals) with a wonderful silvery orange reverse make this a standout in the garden. Light fragrance. Tall plant, growing over 1.8 metres (6 feet) in a season. Extremely disease resistant, glossy foliage rounds out the package. Introduced in 1990.

- ❀ **'Medallion':** AARS 1973. Huge, light creamy apricot, double flowers (30 to 35 petals) with a strong, sweet licorice fragrance. Excellent cut flower. Medium to tall plant with deep green leaves. Picks up some pink hues in cooler climates.

- ❀ **'Spice Twice':** Perfectly formed, bright coral-orange, double blossoms (about 30 petals) with a lighter cream-orange on the back side of the petals. Slight fragrance. Excellent cut flower. Tall, upright plant with good vigour and disease resistance. Introduced in 1997.

- ❀ **'Tropicana':** AARS 1963. One of the most popular hybrid teas, with rich coral-orange, double flowers (30 to 35 petals). Strong, fruity fragrance. Excellent cut flower. Vigorous, tall plant with glossy, dark green leaves. Prone to mildew.

- ❀ **'Voodoo':** AARS 1987. A blend of orange and yellow with a touch of scarlet. Large, double flowers (30 to 35 petals) have a strong, fruity fragrance. Very vigorous, tall plant with glossy, deep green leaves. Good disease resistance. Best colour in areas with warm summers.

Yellow hybrid teas

Yellow roses are about as sunny as you can get — and they look so good with green foliage plants. Our favourite yellow hybrid teas include 'Celebrity', 'Graceland', 'Midas Touch', and almost anything in this list after that. Yellow roses don't seem to grow as well as other colours in northern climates (sigh), so the choice in garden centres and catalogues is not as great as other hybrid tea colours.

- ❀ **'Celebrity':** Beautifully formed, deep yellow, double blossoms (30 to 35 petals) borne in abundance. Flowers sometimes pick up a slight reddish blush. Light, fruity fragrance. Widely adapted to many climates. Vigorous, medium-sized plant with deep green leaves. Introduced in 1989.

'Elina': A soft pastel yellow, double flower (30 to 35 petals) with a light fragrance. Excellent cut flower. Full-foliaged, tall rose producing a lot of blossoms. Grows well in many climates. Dark green, disease-resistant foliage. Introduced in 1984.

'Golden Masterpiece': Huge, golden yellow, double flowers (30 to 35 petals) with a strong licorice-like fragrance. Fine cut flower. Vigorous, bushy plant with shiny, deep green leaves. Performs well in a variety of climates. Introduced in 1954.

'Graceland': Glowing bright yellow, double blossoms (30 to 35 petals) with wavy-edged petals. Lightly fragrant. Fine cut flower. Vigorous, tall plant with glossy, deep green leaves. Good disease resistance. Introduced in 1989.

'Helmut Schmidt': Moderately fragrant, clear golden blossoms (35 petals). Outstanding form and heavy blooming ensure its place in good gardens. Disease resistant foliage and decent hardiness. Introduced in 1979, from Germany.

'Houston': Large, intense yellow, double blooms (35 to 40 petals) with a nice, fruity fragrance. Strong-growing, bushy plant with leathery, dark green leaves. Deepest colour in cool climates; colour fades when exposed to intense sun and heat. Introduced in 1980.

'King's Ransom': AARS 1962. Large, deep golden yellow, double blooms (35 to 40 petals) with a sweet, fruity fragrance. Great cut flower. Medium to tall plant with an upright habit. Glossy, dark green leaves. Performs well in a variety of climates but is prone to mildew.

'Midas Touch': AARS 1994. A fine plant deserving of the first AARS award for a yellow rose in 19 years. Bright yellow, double flowers (25 to 30 petals) produced in abundance. Moderate fruity fragrance. Excellent cut flower. Vigorous, medium to tall plant with dark green leaves. Performs well in a variety of climates, but best size occurs in areas with cool summers.

'New Day': Sunny yellow, double blossoms (30 to 35 petals) with a slight spicy fragrance. Good cut flower. Vigorous, medium to tall, upright plant with unusual grey-green foliage. Introduced in 1977.

'Oregold': AARS 1975. Large, deep golden yellow, double flowers with exceptional form. Slight fruity fragrance. Fine cut flower. Medium-sized, upright plant with glossy, dark green leaves.

'St. Patrick': AARS 1996. An unusual light yellow, double rose (30 to 35 petals) with hints of green when grown in areas with hot summers. Slight fragrance. Interesting cut flower. Vigorous, medium to tall plant with grey-green foliage. Best colour in areas with hot summers. Only the second AARS winner to be developed by an amateur.

◎ **'Shining Hour':** A soft yellow bloom (20 to 25 petals) on vigorous, disease-resistant canes. Fragrance is moderate. The dark green foliage ensures that the blooms stand out. Introduced in 1991.

◎ **'Summer Sunshine':** Bright deep yellow, double flowers (24 to 30 petals) with a light, fruity fragrance. Medium-sized, rounded plant with deep grey-green foliage. Performs best in areas with cool summers. Introduced in 1987.

◎ **'Sunbright':** Glowing light yellow, double flowers (25 to 30 petals) with a light, fruity fragrance. Bushy, medium-sized plant with glossy, deep green leaves. Cooler weather results in large, brighter flowers. Introduced in 1984.

◎ **'Sun Goddess':** Beautifully formed, deep yellow, double blossoms (about 35 petals) with a light fragrance. Excellent cut flower. Vigorous, tall plant with dark green leaves. Introduced in 1994.

White hybrid teas

White hybrid teas light up the garden or a bouquet, making every other colour look brighter. Our favourites include 'Honor', 'John F. Kennedy', and 'Pascali', but all the varieties in the following list are good choices.

◎ **'Crystalline':** Pure white, double flowers (30 to 35 petals) with classic form. Moderately strong, sweet fragrance. Excellent cut flower. Vigorous, tall plant with dark green foliage. Introduced in 1987.

◎ **'Garden Party':** AARS 1960. Creamy white, double blooms (25 to 30 petals) with a touch of pink on the outside petals. Light fragrance. Fine cut flower with excellent form. Medium-sized, slightly spreading plant with semi-glossy green leaves. Best performance in areas with hot summers.

◎ **'Honor':** AARS 1970. Large, clear white, double flowers with exquisite form and substance. Light fragrance. Great cut flower. Tall, upright plant with dark green, disease-resistant foliage. Best form in areas with cool summers.

◎ **'Ivory Tower':** Large, shapely blossoms are clear white, often with a touch of yellow or pink. 35 petals. Fragrant. Upright, bushy plant with medium green leaves. Introduced in 1979.

◎ **'John F. Kennedy':** Interesting double rose (40 to 45 petals) that starts out greenish white in the bud and gradually turns clean white as the flower opens. Moderate to strong fragrance. Medium-sized plant with leathery green leaves. Best in areas with hot summers. Introduced in 1978.

- ☺ **'Louisiana':** Medium to large, double blossoms (35 to 40 petals) are greenish in the bud, opening to creamy white with a touch of green in the centre. Interesting cut flower. Light fragrance. Tall, slightly spreading plant with dark green leaves. Performs best in warm-summer climates. Introduced in 1975.

- ☺ **'Pascali':** AARS 1969. A long-time favourite white rose, loved for its generous production of well-formed, double flowers (30 to 35 petals). Light fragrance. Vigorous, upright plant with dark green leaves. Good disease resistance. Introduced in 1968, this rose was granted the World's Favourite Rose Award in 1991.

- ☺ **'Sheer Bliss':** AARS 1987. Soft, creamy white with a blush of pink. Double flowers (about 35 petals) with a strong, sweet fragrance. Dark green, glossy foliage on a medium-sized, upright plant.

Lavender hybrid teas

As much as people want to call these roses blue, they are really lavender or purple. Of these, we especially like 'Blue Moon', 'Lady X', and 'Paradise'. Each rose in the following list can add a delicate colour accent to your garden.

- ☺ **'Blue Girl':** Large, light lavender, double blooms (30 to 35 petals) with a moderate spicy fragrance. Medium-sized, rounded bush with dark green foliage. Introduced in 1965.

- ☺ **'Blue Moon':** Good form in the fragrant lavender blooms. Superior cutting rose and one of the easiest and most successful to grow. Dark green foliage. Introduced in 1965.

- ☺ **'Heirloom':** Deep lilac, double blooms (30 to 35 petals) that are darker purple on the edges of the petals. Strong, sweet fragrance. Medium-sized plant with dark green leaves. Introduced in 1972.

- ☺ **'Lady X':** Well-formed, lavender-pink, double flowers (35 to 40 petals) with a mild fragrance. Nice cut flower. Tall, vigorous plant with medium green leaves. Best colour in areas with cool summers. Introduced in 1966.

- ☺ **'Moon Shadow':** Nicely formed, deep lavender, double blooms (30 to 35 petals) borne in clusters. Strong fragrance. Tall, upright plant with glossy, deep green leaves.

- ☺ **'Paradise':** AARS 1979. Large, lavender, double flowers (25 to 30 petals) edged with deep red along the outside of the petals. Moderately fruity fragrance. Produces many blossoms; excellent for cutting. Medium-sized, vigorous plant with glossy, deep green leaves. Good disease resistance.

- **'Stainless Steel':** An improved version of 'Sterling Silver' with paler silvery lavender, double blooms (25 to 30 petals). This plant produces more flowers and is easier to care for. Strong fragrance. Good cut flower. Tall, upright plant with dark green leaves. Best colour where summers are cool. Introduced in 1997.

- **'Sterling Silver':** Silvery lavender, double blooms (about 30 petals) with a fruity fragrance. Nice cut flower. Medium-sized plant with dark green leaves. Best colour in areas with cool summers. Add extra winter protection. Introduced in 1957.

Multicoloured hybrid teas

These whirlwinds of colour change complexion on a daily basis. How distinct their colours are usually depends on where they're grown. Before you buy a variety, check it out at a local rose garden to make sure that you're getting what you want.

Of these roses, several stand out. Our favourites include 'Double Delight', 'Granada', 'Peace', 'Secret', and 'Sutter's Gold'. Each selection in the following list will make a splash in your garden.

- **'Brigadoon':** AARS 1992. Nicely formed, double blossoms (25 to 30 petals) that start out creamy white to pink in the bud and then darken to pinkish red around the edges, with a creamy pink centre. Light fragrance. Excellent cut flower. Best colour in warm-summer areas. Medium to tall with a slightly spreading habit. Dark green, disease-resistant foliage.

- **'Broadway':** AARS 1987. Large orange-yellow, double blossoms (30 to 35 petals) edged with red. Strong, spicy fragrance. Medium-sized plant with dark green, leathery leaves. Good disease resistance. Best colour in cool weather.

- **'Chicago Peace':** A mutation of 'Peace' with darker pink edging set off by a bright yellow centre. Double flower (40 to 45 petals) with a light, fruity fragrance. Medium-sized, bushy plant with dark green leaves. Very susceptible to black spot. Introduced in 1962.

- **'Double Delight':** AARS 1977. One of the most popular bicoloured roses. Large, creamy white, double flowers (30 to 35 petals) are edged with bright red. Strong, spicy fragrance. Winner of the James Alexander Gamble Rose Fragrance Award in 1986. Excellent cut flower. Medium-sized, rounded bush with dark green leaves. Best colour with warm days and cool nights. Also available in a climbing form.

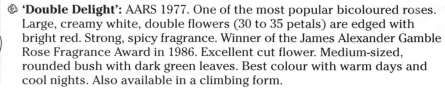

'Granada': AARS 1963. Swirling, ever-changing shades of gold, yellow, pink, and red. Double blossoms (18 to 25 petals) with a strong, spicy fragrance. Long-lasting cut flower. Medium to tall, upright plant with crinkled, dark green leaves. Best colour in cool climates.

'Las Vegas': Glowing orange-red, double blooms (about 25 petals) with a golden-yellow reverse. Light fragrance. Medium to tall plant with glossy, dark green leaves. Introduced in 1981.

'Lynn Anderson': Large, creamy white, double blossoms (25 to 30 petals) are edged with bright pink. Light fragrance. Tall, upright plant with dark green, disease-resistant leaves. Best colour in cool climates. Introduced in 1995.

'Mikado': AARS 1988. Deep scarlet red, double blooms (25 petals) with yellow at the base of the petals. Light, spicy fragrance. Excellent cut flower. Medium-sized, upright plant with glossy, dark green leaves. Good disease resistance. Colours intensify in cool weather.

'Monet': Huge, double rose (30 to 35 petals) in blended shades of pink, yellow, peach, and apricot. Moderate fragrance. Good cut flower. Vigorous, medium-sized plant with medium green leaves. Disease resistant. Introduced in 1996.

'Party Time': A hot blend of bright yellow edged with red. Double flower (30 to 35 petals) with a licorice-like fragrance. Fine cut flower. Medium-sized, round plant with medium green leaves. Best where summers are warm. Introduced in 1987.

'Peace': AARS 1945. Award-winning rose that is one of the most popular flowers of all time. Large, perfectly formed, double blossoms (40 to 45 petals) are bright yellow edged with pink. Best colour where summer temperatures are mild. Light, fruity fragrance. Medium-sized plant with glossy, dark green leaves. Prone to black spot.

'Perfect Moment': AARS 1991. Large, deep yellow, double flowers (25 to 30 petals) are heavily edged with red. Best colour in mild-summer areas. Light, fruity fragrance. Good cut flower. Medium-sized, upright plant with dark green leaves. Good disease resistance.

'Rio Samba': AARS 1993. Bright yellow, double flowers (about 25 petals) are edged with orangish red. Light fragrance. Medium-sized, bushy plant with dark green leaves. Good disease resistance. Best colour in cool weather.

'Secret': AARS 1994. Lovely, creamy white, double flowers (30 to 35 petals) edged with soft pink. Strong, spicy fragrance. Excellent cut flower. Larger flowers in cool weather. Medium-sized plant with dark green leaves. Good disease resistance.

🌹 **'Sutter's Gold':** AARS 1950. A much-loved, beautifully formed golden-yellow rose blushed with orangish red. Large, double flowers (25 to 30 petals) have an intense, spicy fragrance. Winner of the James Alexander Gamble Rose Fragrance Award in 1966. Best colour where summers are mild. Excellent cut flower. Medium-sized, bushy plant with leathery, dark green leaves. Good disease resistance.

Strolling through the worldwide rose garden

One way to whet your appetite for rose growing and get your imagination off and running is to see roses in person. In the summertime, you can visit rose gardens in almost every province to get a sense of which rose you absolutely need in your garden.

On the Web, go to the Canadian Rose Society site and follow the links to other rose sites and pictures. Start at www.mirror.org/groups/crs/index.html.

You'll likely wind up at the American Rose Society pages at www.ars.org/ as well, and they too have a large selection of rose links. If you know you're travelling south, you can check out the rose gardens to visit on your route. Is there a better way to go on a holiday than to combine travelling with fragrance breaks?

If you're interested in European gardens, the Web offers you a way to see gorgeous plants and landscapes overseas too. Visit www.ostavizn.com/site/15newgardenF/Garden.html for some lovely garden photographs and tour information on English rose gardens.

From these Web sites, the world is at your doorstep for information and pictures to dream on.

Chapter 9

Grandifloras

In This Chapter

▶ Treating grandifloras right

▶ Placing your grandifloras in a good location

▶ Taking advantage of the grandiflora palette of colours

*A*s a class, grandifloras bear large, long-stemmed, hybrid tea-like flowers, either in clusters or one to a stem. Grandifloras often grow taller than hybrid teas, having lengthy stems, so they're excellent producers of cut roses. Generally, grandiflora plants are tall, hardy, and vigorous. In this chapter we point out how to care for, and landscape with grandifloras, as well as listing some great varieties in each of the colours available.

Treat Them Like Hybrid Teas: Looking After Grandifloras

As you can see in Figure 9-1, grandifloras have peaked blossoms similar to hybrid tea roses. Figure 9-2 shows the tall growth habit of grandifloras. Care for grandifloras as you would hybrid teas — watering, fertilizing, winter protection, pruning practices, and so on are pretty much the same. (Part IV, "Growing Healthy Roses," fully describes all that.)

Grandifloras are often used like hybrid teas and planted in rows for cut flowers. However, they tend to put on a better show of colour than many hybrid teas do, so don't hesitate to use them in the landscape. Tall varieties, especially 'Queen Elizabeth', make useful hedges or background plants. Lower-growing types can be mixed with other flowers in perennial borders or grown in containers. You can find more on landscaping with roses in Chapter 5.

Figure 9-1:
A grandiflora flower resembles a hybrid tea.

Figure 9-2:
Grandiflora bushes grow tall and vigorously.

The *grand* controversy

Grandiflora roses always seem to be having some type of identity crisis. The class was created in the U.S.A. around 1954 to accommodate 'Queen Elizabeth', a tall, vigorous hybrid that has large flowers on long stems like a hybrid tea, but the long stems grow in clusters like a floribunda. 'Queen Elizabeth' was named for the young Queen of England and won nearly every international award for roses. In 1980, the World Federation of Rose Societies declared it the world's favourite rose.

Although 'Queen Elizabeth' is still very popular, grandifloras as a class never really made the big time in the rose world. In fact, England doesn't even recognize grandifloras as a true class of roses. Instead, they are called floribundas with hybrid tea-type flowers or *cluster-flowered* roses.

Anyway, North Americans are going to keep calling them grandifloras, so don't worry about all the international debate, just enjoy the flowers.

Grandifloras by Colour

Grandifloras come in many colours and sizes. The following sections list some of our favourites.

Red grandifloras

Unfortunately, there are only a few red grandifloras to choose from. We particularly like 'Love', but check the other varieties in this list and pick your own favourite.

- **'Carrousel':** Bright red, velvety blossoms with 15 to 20 petals generally grow in small clusters and singly on long stems. Long-lasting flowers with colour that does not fade as the bloom ages. Sweet fragrance. Very tall, bushy, and upright. Leaves are bright green. Likes summer heat. Introduced in 1950.

- **'Love':** All-America Rose Selection (AARS) 1980. Part of a trio of roses introduced in 1980: 'Love', 'Honor', and 'Cherish' ('Love' and 'Honor' are great; 'Cherish' is sort of blah). True to the name, the flowers are bright red with a silvery reverse. 35 petals. Slight, spicy fragrance. Good cut flower. Medium height and compact bush.

- **'San Antonio':** Long-stemmed, pointed buds open to display cardinal-red blossoms with mild fragrance. 30 to 35 petals. This tall, upright bush with glossy, dark green leaves produces flowers continuously. Easy to grow. Prefers warmer summers. Introduced in 1967.

Pink grandifloras

If you can't make up your mind on a pink grandiflora, go with 'Queen Elizabeth' or 'Tournament of Roses', but all of these varieties can be delightful in your garden.

- ❀ **'Aquarius':** AARS 1971. Light pink flowers with deep pink edges (30 to 40 petals) grow singly on long stems. Long-lasting when cut. Moderate fragrance. Free-blooming. Long-lasting, even in hot weather. Medium to tall, slender, upright bush. Large, reddish green leaves. Disease resistant and hardy.

- ❀ **'Camelot':** AARS 1965. The largest of the grandiflora flowers, up to 13 centimetres (5 inches) across. Blooms are pale salmon in colour with 50 to 55 petals, opening in a cup shape. The colour changes with the weather from salmon when it's cooler to orange when it warms. Light to moderate fragrance. Tall and spreading bush. Vigorous grower; likes hot weather. Leaves are large, heavy, and glossy.

- ❀ **'Pink Parfait':** AARS 1961. Petite buds open into well-formed flowers, coloured with a blend of deep pink and cream. 20 to 25 petals. Grow singly on narrow stems. Slight fragrance. Good cut flower. Profuse bloomer. Colour may fade in hot weather. Medium, upright, and bushy with lots of branches. Leathery, semi-glossy green leaves. Disease resistant.

- ❀ **'Prima Donna':** AARS 1988. Deep, fuschia-pink flowers with 27 petals and a light fragrance. Foliage is large, glossy, and medium green. Spreading growth. Plant disease resistance. Introduced in 1984.

- ❀ **'Queen Elizabeth':** AARS 1955. The first grandiflora, and still the finest, has received top honours in many countries over the years. Clear pink, ruffled blooms adorn the stately, tall bush in long-stemmed clusters. Abundant and ever-blooming. Blossoms are high-centred or cup-shaped. Moderately fragrant, vigorous, and bushy. Leaves are dark green and glossy. Easy to grow. Disease resistant.

- ❀ **'Sonia':** A popular florist's rose in the United States and Europe, but grows pretty well in the garden, too. Delicate, long buds give way to shapely, pastel pink flowers on long stems. 30 to 35 petals. Sweet, fruity fragrance. Glossy green leaves. Medium height and bushy. Disease resistant. Introduced in 1974.

- ❀ **'Tournament of Roses':** AARS 1989. Flowers profusely in clusters. Two-toned pink blooms. 25 to 30 petals. Medium, upright bush with glossy green leaves. Light fragrance. Highly disease resistant and easy to grow.

Orange grandifloras

Our favourite orange grandiflora? We like 'Caribbean', but try any of the roses in this list — all have fragrance and tall vigorous growth.

- **'Caribbean':** AARS 1994. Luscious, bright orange-yellow blend. Spiral-shaped flowers grow on long stems with bright green foliage. 30 to 35 petals. Mild fragrance. Medium, upright bush. Vigorous and productive. Best form and colour in the fall.

- **'Montezuma':** Produces loads of long-stemmed, reddened coral-orange flowers. 30 to 35 petals. The plant is tall, bushy, and slightly spreading with dark green, leathery foliage. Light fragrance. Disease resistant and winter hardy. Does well in cool climates. Warm night temperatures help flower colour remain stable. Introduced in 1955.

- **'New Year':** AARS 1987. A colourful blend of yellow and orange with hints of gold. 20 petals. Light, fruity fragrance. Upright plant with deep green, glossy foliage. Excellent disease resistance.

- **'Prominent':** AARS 1977. Star-shaped, hot orange blooms with 25 to 30 stiff petals that curve under. Flowers are small (6 to 9 centimetres; 2½ to 3½ inches) compared to most grandifloras. Blooms continuously, and the colour does not fade. Light fragrance. Stately, upright, tall plant. Foliage is matte green. Disease resistant. Introduced in 1971.

- **'Shreveport':** AARS 1982. Named for the city in Louisiana that is home to the American Rose Center. Full flowers (45 to 50 petals) of warm, blended salmon and yellow tones bloom all season. Mild scent. Cut flowers have a long vase life. Tall, upright plant is covered with dark green, shiny foliage. Fall conditions bring out the best colour. Easy to grow.

- **'Solitude':** AARS 1993. Brilliant bright orange blooms with hints of yellow and gold. Best colour with heat. 30 to 35 petals. Mild, spicy fragrance. Upright plant with bright green leaves. Good disease resistance.

- **'Sundowner':** AARS 1979. Distinctive, warm apricot colour. Extremely fragrant. Blooms well all season in clusters and singly. Flowers are cup-shaped with 35 petals. Plant is tall, upright, and vigorous. Leaves are large, leathery, and medium green. Disease resistant, but susceptible to mildew in cool, wet climates.

Yellow grandifloras

We particularly like the following yellow grandiflora roses.

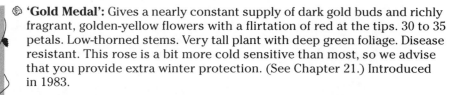

⚙ **'Gold Medal':** Gives a nearly constant supply of dark gold buds and richly fragrant, golden-yellow flowers with a flirtation of red at the tips. 30 to 35 petals. Low-thorned stems. Very tall plant with deep green foliage. Disease resistant. This rose is a bit more cold sensitive than most, so we advise that you provide extra winter protection. (See Chapter 21.) Introduced in 1983.

⚙ **'Shining Hour':** AARS 1991. Deep yellow, cup-shaped flowers grow singly and in clusters or sprays. 33 petals. Moderate fragrance. Upright, bushy, medium-height plant with shiny, dark green leaves. Introduced in 1989.

White grandifloras

Both of these white grandifloras have won the coveted All America Rose Society Award and you'll love either one.

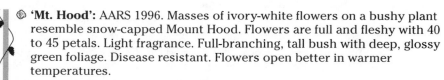

⚙ **'Mt. Hood':** AARS 1996. Masses of ivory-white flowers on a bushy plant resemble snow-capped Mount Hood. Flowers are full and fleshy with 40 to 45 petals. Light fragrance. Full-branching, tall bush with deep, glossy green foliage. Disease resistant. Flowers open better in warmer temperatures.

⚙ **'White Lightnin':** AARS 1981. Small, white clusters of cupped, very fragrant flowers burst forth all season on the tall, robust bush. 26 to 32 petals. Disease resistant. Dark green, glossy leaves.

Lavender grandifloras

Here are our picks for the two top lavender (or mauve) grandifloras.

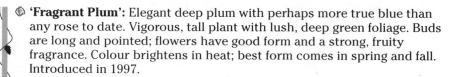

⚙ **'Fragrant Plum':** Elegant deep plum with perhaps more true blue than any rose to date. Vigorous, tall plant with lush, deep green foliage. Buds are long and pointed; flowers have good form and a strong, fruity fragrance. Colour brightens in heat; best form comes in spring and fall. Introduced in 1997.

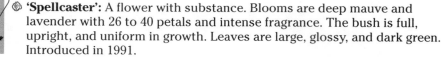

⚙ **'Spellcaster':** A flower with substance. Blooms are deep mauve and lavender with 26 to 40 petals and intense fragrance. The bush is full, upright, and uniform in growth. Leaves are large, glossy, and dark green. Introduced in 1991.

Multicoloured grandifloras

Either of these grandifloras makes a great choice for a spot of zingy colour in your garden.

- 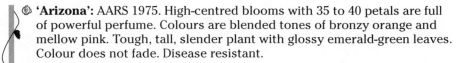 **'Arizona':** AARS 1975. High-centred blooms with 35 to 40 petals are full of powerful perfume. Colours are blended tones of bronzy orange and mellow pink. Tough, tall, slender plant with glossy emerald-green leaves. Colour does not fade. Disease resistant.

- **'Charisma':** Hard to believe that this rose is real as it throws so many blossoms. Arriving in changing hues of orange, yellow, and red, each 40-petalled blossom has a light fragrance. A tough, bushy, compact rose with glossy, dark green leathery leaves.

Chapter 10

Polyanthas and Floribundas

. . . .

In This Chapter

▶ Revealing the origins of polyantha and floribunda roses

▶ Using polyanthas and floribundas in the landscape

▶ Caring for polyanthas and floribundas

▶ Recognizing great polyantha and floribunda varieties

. . . .

*P*olyanthas and floribundas are the workhorses of the rose garden. They are the most prolific bloomers of all the different kinds of roses, and they are useful in the landscape, in perennial borders, and in large groups or mass plantings. If you can't find a floribunda you love, you'd better get your eyesight checked! Treat them exactly like hybrid teas when it comes to watering, feeding, and winter protection.

Polyanthas were discovered in France in the late 1800s, and only a few varieties are still widely grown. But polyanthas are important not only because they are excellent roses but also because they are the forerunners of the very popular and useful floribundas. For that reason, we group the two together in this chapter.

To France, Late 19th Century

The origin of polyantha roses is credited to M. Guillot in 1875 — about the same time as the first hybrid tea. They can probably claim *Rosa multiflora* and *Rosa chinensis* as their parents, but some kind of hanky-panky must have been going on somewhere, because no one really knows who mom or dad is.

Anyway, polyanthas are compact plants that usually grow about 60 to 90 centimetres (2 to 3 feet high). And do they ever bloom! They virtually cover themselves in large, flat clusters of small flowers (usually about 2.5 centimetres, or 1 inch wide) in shades of white, pink, red, orange, and yellow. (See Figure 10-1.) And they bloom and bloom again, all season long. Polyantha leaves are small and narrow and the plants are fairly hardy, at least more so than hybrid teas. The most common polyantha, 'The Fairy', is one of the hardiest and most reliable, thriving without winter protection even to –31° C (–25° F).

Figure 10-1:
Polyanthas bear small flowers in large clusters.

Floribundas: Workaholics of the Rose Garden

Early in the 20th century, someone got the bright idea to cross the generous-blooming polyanthas with the larger-flowering hybrid teas. The results are what we now call the *floribundas*, which, as their name suggests, offer *flo*wers in a*bunda*nce.

Today, floribundas are one of the most useful types of roses. The flowers are borne in large clusters like polyanthas (see Figure 10-2), but the individual blooms are bigger, often with that beautiful hybrid tea form, and most are great cut flowers. In the landscape, where they can brighten a dreary corner of the yard, highlight a garden ornament, or keep a perennial border wonderfully colourful all season, is where they really shine.

Floribundas come in all the hybrid tea colours, which is probably almost any flower colour you can think of except blue and black. The plants grow from 0.9 to 1.5 metres (3 to 5 feet) high and can be anything from upright to low and spreading, as shown in Figure 10-3. Their range in plant shape makes them versatile landscape plants.

Some floribunda varieties have compact growth habits and are very "tuckable" into small areas of the garden or for creating a generous show in a container. Others grow tall and wide and exhibit many of the characteristics of modern shrubs. "Grow as shrub" is a common description in rose catalogues. Choose varieties that suit the area in which you want to plant them.

Figure 10-2:
Floribundas
bear flowers
in clusters.
Individual
blooms are
smaller than
hybrid teas,
but the
overall show
of colour
is more
dramatic.

Figure 10-3:
Floribundas
are generally
compact,
shrubby
plants about
0.9 to 1.5
metres (3 to
5 feet) high.
They are
top-notch
landscape
plants with
a long
season of
bloom.

But the amount and persistence of bloom are what really make floribundas so great. Some varieties, like 'Iceberg' and 'Simplicity', have almost cult-like followings because of their generosity of bloom.

Try 'em; you'll like 'em.

All This and Easy to Grow, Too

Floribundas and polyanthas are among the easiest roses to grow. Most have good disease resistance and need little care other than water and fertilizer.

Removing spent flowers during the growing season is important if you want a bush to keep producing flowers. You can just get out your hedge shears to cut off faded flowers. Spring pruning is equally simple — cut off any part of the plant that was damaged over the winter. See Chapter 20 for pruning information and how to recognize winter damage.

Today's rose hybridizers are working very hard to breed disease resistance into new varieties of roses. Therefore, many of the newer varieties of floribundas are naturally resistant to the diseases that attack our favourite flower. Rose culture, especially for the new floribundas, is getting simpler every year. If a floribunda variety excels in the disease resistance department, you can bet that the rose catalogues will say so. So if you don't care much about spraying for black spot and powdery mildew, choose disease-resistant varieties. On the other hand, as is always the case, many of the most unique and desirable varieties are susceptible to disease but respond nicely to disease-control measures. It just goes to show you: If it's not one thing . . .

Even though floribunda and polyantha rose plants tend to be slightly hardier than hybrid teas, you will need to provide winter protection for most of them. But protecting roses in winter is no big deal; see Chapter 21. If in doubt, protect!

Don't Plant Just One!

If you haven't already guessed, we really like polyantha and floribunda roses. The reason is simple: The amount of bloom, clean-looking foliage, and ease of care make these roses exceptional landscape plants.

Using specific varieties for specific landscape purposes is covered in Chapter 5, but one piece of advice is worth repeating here: Polyanthas and floribundas are best used in mass plantings. Don't buy just one or two plants; get a bunch and line them up as hedges or edgings for other plants. Or plant several of them in a bed all by themselves. Season-long colour will knock your neighbours' socks off! Some of the lower-growing varieties, such as 'Red Ribbons', can even be grouped as ground covers. Or you can spread them throughout your garden to tie everything else together. These babies are real troopers; they can carry an entire garden.

There's another reason to buy these roses in quantity: Many of the mail-order catalogues listed in Appendix B offer discounts when you buy more than one of any variety.

Oh yeah, floribundas, and especially polyanthas, are also great planted in containers.

A Few of Our Favourite Things

The following sections list our favourite floribunda varieties. Also described is our favourite pink polyantha, 'Cécile Brünner'.

Red roses

Here are four great red floribundas. You can't lose with any of them, especially the first three:

- ☺ **'Europeana':** All-America Rose Selection (AARS) 1968. Produces large clusters of dark crimson, long-lasting blossoms with 15 to 20 petals. Blooms abundantly midseason and repeats blooming. Young, red leaves mature to a dark, glossy green. Slight fragrance. Disease resistant and reasonably winter hardy. Top exhibition rose. Introduced in 1963.

- ☺ **'Frensham':** A glorious red rose that bursts open to reveal feathery, golden stamens. Excellent midseason and a repeat bloomer. Vigorous, bushy, spreading plant with dark green, semi-glossy leaves. Disease resistant. Light fragrance. Winner of the American Rose Society Gold Medal in 1955, awarded to roses that show the best performance over a five-year period. Introduced in 1946.

- ☺ **'Red Ribbons':** New England Rose Trials Award 1996. Flowers are dark red, semi-double, and appear in huge quantities. An excellent ground cover floribunda, it grows well in difficult spots. Very winter hardy for a floribunda.

- ☺ **'Showbiz':** AARS 1985. A fire-engine red workhorse that is rarely out of bloom. 28 to 30 petals. Makes an excellent ever-blooming mass of colour on dark green, glossy leaves. Disease resistant with good winter hardiness. Introduced in 1981.

Pink roses

There's not a bad rose in this batch of pink floribundas and polyanthas:

- **'Betty Prior':** Charming, old-fashioned rose that blooms profusely and continuously. The exuberant, five-petalled flowers are carmine pink. When in full bloom, the plant resembles a flowering dogwood. Moderate fragrance. Vigorous, tall plant with glossy leaves. Excellent resistance to black spot and mildew. Introduced in 1935.

- **'Bridal Pink':** A florist's favourite. Long, elegant buds and creamy pink, luxurious flowers with 30 to 35 petals grow abundantly in spring and fall. Moderately spicy fragrance. Dark green foliage. Medium to low bush. Introduced in 1967.

- **'Cécile Brünner':** This polyantha is the original sweetheart rose. Little pink buds and small, perfectly formed blooms that resemble diminutive hybrid teas blanket the plant throughout the growing season. 30 petals. Light fragrance. Compact, long-lived, and healthy. Can even tolerate poor soil and partial shade. Introduced in 1881.

- **'Cherish':** AARS 1980. Large — 8 centimetres (3 inches) across — coral-pink flowers open flat from a high centre. 28 petals. Slightly fragrant. Compact, spreading bush with large, dark green leaves.

- **'Columbus':** Egg-shaped, pointed buds unfurl into deep, rose-pink blooms carried singly or in sprays of three to five. These flowers hold their colour with little fading and make good exhibition roses. 28 petals. Medium-sized, bushy plant with large, dull green leaves. Introduced in 1990.

- **'Gene Boerner':** AARS 1969. Blossoms of unflinchingly true pink grow in clusters or singly on long, strong stems — upright for all to see. 30 to 35 petals. Slightly fragrant. A super-vigorous, tall bush (up to 1.5 metres; 5 feet) with light green, glossy leaves. Disease resistant with good winter hardiness. Makes a good cut flower.

- **'Neon Lights':** Large, fragrant blooms displayed in small clusters are hot magenta-pink. 15 to 25 petals. The plant is medium and bushy with shiny green leaves. Introduced in 1991.

- **'Pleasure':** AARS 1990. Established plants give lots of bloom, though colour often fades quickly. The warm pink flowers with 30 to 35 petals are beautifully formed and frilly when fully opened. Fragrance is slight. Compact, rounded bush. Dark green foliage.

- **'Rose Parade':** AARS 1975. Lovely coral-pink blooms, often with a hint of peach, are large and fragrant. 25 to 35 petals. Large, glossy green leaves on a compact, bushy plant. Good disease resistance.

◉ **'Sea Pearl':** Stylish, long, pointed buds are part of 'Sea Pearl's' charm. They unfurl with free-blooming intensity, revealing pink blooms with creamy yellow reverses. Blooms tend to occur early to midseason in clusters. 24 petals. Light fragrance. Upright, vigorous grower with dark green leaves. Introduced in 1964.

The *reverse* is the underside of a petal. A different colour on the reverse makes for visual interest both coming and going.

◉ **'Sexy Rexy':** Rarely out of bloom. Large clusters of rose-pink flowers that are lightly scented. Vigorous, low-growing bush with small, glossy, leathery leaves. Excellent plant in groups, as a hedge, or in a container. Resistant to mildew and black spot. Introduced in 1984.

◉ **'Simplicity':** Tall, dense, and free-flowering, 'Simplicity' is an excellent landscape or hedge rose. Medium pink blossoms (18 to 24 petals) appear in clusters all season long. Little to no fragrance. Medium green, semi-glossy leaves. Disease resistant with good winter hardiness. Introduced in 1983.

◉ **'Sweet Inspiration':** AARS 1993. Large blossoms are a gentle pink with cream tones at the base on both sides of the petals. Borne in big clusters. The plant is upright and bushy with medium green leaves.

◉ **'The Fairy':** One of the all-time favourite roses, this very heavy-blooming light pink rose can be used anywhere in the garden. Good disease resistance and massive clusters of blooms mark it as a must-have. Good shiny, dark-green leaves. Introduced in 1932.

Orange roses

These floribundas make a stunning statement in bright orange and apricot:

◉ **'Apricot Nectar':** AARS 1966. Tight clusters sometimes obscure the beauty of this rose. Removing some of the buds enhances the large, pure apricot blooms. 35 to 40 petals. Very fragrant. Good repeat bloomer. Does well as a cut flower. Upright and bushy. Glossy, dark green leaves. Disease-resistant and hardy for a floribunda.

◉ **'Brass Band':** AARS 1995. A band of colours plays on the petals of these well-formed blooms, mixing bright shades of melon with subtle apricot and lemon reverses. Gives the best performances in cool weather. Large blooms of 25 to 30 petals. Moderately fragrant. Medium-sized, rounded bush with bright green foliage.

◉ **'Cathedral':** AARS 1976. Elegant, long-lasting flower clusters and excellent disease resistance make this flower a top exhibition rose. Wavy petals of deep salmon tinted with scarlet create a stained-glass window effect. 15 to 18 petals. Light to moderate, sweet scent. Compact, low, bushy, glossy olive-green leaves. Not as winter hardy as others. Introduced in 1975.

'First Edition': AARS 1977. Shimmering coral-orange. Long-lasting blooms with 20 to 30 petals and a light scent. Medium-sized, rounded bush has waxy, glossy green leaves with good disease resistance. Continually produces flowers in showy clusters. Moderate temperatures enhance the colours. Makes an excellent low hedge.

'Impatient': AARS 1984. If you are an impatient gardener, this plant is for you, because it is an easy-care rose. 'Impatient' is one of the best orange floribundas and is rarely out of bloom. Produces lots of deep orange blossoms continuously from late spring until frost. 25 petals. Blooms are displayed in large clusters held high on the plant for all to see. Light fragrance. Tall, upright shrub with dark green foliage and bronzy new growth. Heat brings out the brightest colour.

'Livin' Easy': AARS 1996. The rose for the hammock gardener, 'Livin' Easy' practically grows itself. The foliage on this rounded, medium-sized bush is so glossy and green that the bush looks good without flowers. But the flowers come and come and keep coming. Large apricot-orange blooms with 25 to 30 petals and a moderately fruity scent. Very consistent performer in all climates, but a bit cold-tender compared to other floribundas.

'Marina': AARS 1981. Well-known as a greenhouse rose, but also does very well in the garden. Produces orange blooms with red and gold overtones in clusters on long stems. 30 to 40 petals. The plant is disease-resistant, vigorous, and very bushy.

'Sarabande': AARS 1960. A spectacular rose that has garnered numerous awards since its introduction in 1957. Orange-red flowers with 10 to 15 petals opening to reveal bright yellow stamens. Blooms continuously in flashy clusters on low, spreading shrubs with glossy foliage. Makes an excellent low hedge or container plant. One of the most disease-resistant floribundas. Grows best in cool climates.

'Trumpeter': Produces abundant and continuous brilliant orange-red flowers with 35 to 40 wavy petals. Dark green, glossy leaves. Slight fragrance. Disease resistant. Introduced in 1977.

Yellow roses

These yellow floribundas are as clear and bright as a sunny day:

'Allgold': Brilliant, buttercup-yellow flowers grow singly or in large clusters. 15 to 22 petals. Nicely set off by the glossy, dark green leaves. Slightly fragrant. Grows vigorously. Introduced in 1958.

'Amber Queen': AARS 1988. The combination of the soft apricot colour, sweet scent, and glossy green foliage make this rose a winner. 25 to 30 petals. The plant is low, bushy, and compact with a high degree of disease resistance, making it an ideal choice for the landscape. Best colour in cool temperatures. Introduced in 1983.

'Mirabella': A sunny yellow rose with 40 to 50 frilled petals and a moderate, musky fragrance. The flower has an old garden rose character, but the plant is disease resistant and has good vigour. Fine cut flower. Compact, medium-sized plant with glossy, dark green leaves. Colourful hips. Introduced in 1996.

'Singin' in the Rain': AARS and New England Rose Trials Award 1995. A moody rose with many hues, depending on the weather. Colours can change from shades of brown and cinnamon pink to apricot gold and russet orange. 25 to 30 petals. Rounded, bushy plant. Glossy, dark leaves. Sweet fragrance.

'Sunbonnet': This yellow rose is truly cheerful. Flowers have 40 to 45 ruffled petals. Blooms in abundant clusters and fills the air with a sweet scent. Leathery, dark green leaves. Low, rounded bush. Likes heat. Introduced in 1967.

'Sun Flare': AARS 1983. One of the few yellow roses that makes an excellent landscape planting. The low, mounded, bushy plant is covered with bright lemon-yellow blossoms in large clusters. 25 to 30 petals. Blooms all season. Light fragrance. Polished green leaves are highly disease resistant. Good winter hardiness.

'Sunsprite': The best of the yellow floribundas has every quality you could ask for — nonstop bloom, fragrance, vigour, and disease resistance. The flowers are a glowing lemon-yellow with 25 to 30 petals. Glossy, dark green leaves. Performs best in cooler temperatures. Introduced in 1977.

White roses

Two of our all-time favourite roses, 'Class Act' and 'Iceberg', are among these white floribundas. Both are top-of-the-line landscape plants, but these are all good performers:

'Class Act': AARS 1989. One of the most generous-blooming and easy-to-care-for white floribundas on the market. Produces continuous clusters of pure white blooms that have a mild fragrance. Semi-double flowers open flat and bloom continuously on vigorous bushes with glossy leaves. Effective as a mass planting, but equally nice mixed in a perennial garden. Excellent disease resistance.

⊛ **'French Lace':** AARS 1982. Large, full blossoms with 35 creamy white petals bloom on cutting-length stems. Mild, fruity scent. Upright, tall plant with dark, glossy leaves. Performs best in cooler temperatures. Disease resistant but not winter hardy compared to other floribundas.

⊛ **'Iceberg':** One of the best white roses for landscape planting, and probably the best-known rose in the world. Though the name varies by country, wherever you go you're likely to see it. Not only is it robust, beautiful, and delightful to smell, but it also flowers freely and profusely with little care. The bush is medium to tall with dark green foliage. Introduced in 1958.

⊛ **'Ivory Fashion':** AARS 1959. Clear ivory blooms with 15 to 20 petals open wide, showing decorative yellow stamens. Flowers freely in clusters. Medium-sized, sturdy, hardy bush, and a vigorous grower. Leathery, semi-glossy leaves. Disease resistant.

⊛ **'Margaret Merril':** This extremely fragrant rose won the Edland Fragrance Medal in 1978 for its perfume. The blossoms are soft white and large with a hybrid tea-type shape. 28 petals. Introduced in 1977.

Lavender roses

You can count the great lavender floribundas on one hand, and here they are:

⊛ **'Angel Face':** AARS 1969. A bit of heaven for the garden. The unusual, deep mauve flowers send out an ambrosial fragrance that permeates the air throughout the summer. 35 to 40 ruffled petals. Vigorous, disease resistant, good winter hardiness with leathery, semi-glossy leaves.

⊛ **'Blueberry Hill':** Clear lilac with a sweet fragrance. Flowers grow in clusters on long stems, perfect for cutting. 8 to 15 petals. Displays all summer long. Rounded, upright plant. Disease resistant and decently hardy. Introduced in 1997.

⊛ **'Intrigue':** AARS 1984. Absolutely intriguing — red-purple buds give way to velvety, plum flowers with an intense perfume. 25 to 30 petals. Blooms midseason with good repeat blooms. Bushy, medium-sized plant. Disease resistant but quite tender, it will require excellent winter protection. (See Chapter 21 for more information).

Multicoloured roses

Here's a dazzling collection of multicoloured floribundas:

- **'Charisma':** AARS 1978. Ever-changing hues of yellow, orange, and red combine in abundant blooms set against glossy, dark green leaves. At times, the flowers with 40-plus petals totally obscure the compact, bushy plant. Light scent. A little heat brings out the best colour.

- **'Eye Paint':** Buds open into scarlet flowers of five to six petals with white centres and golden stamens. The shrub is tall, spreading, and dense with small, shiny, dark green leaves. Flowers continuously. Slight scent. Can be used as a hedge. Disease resistant with good hardiness for a floribunda. Introduced in 1975.

- **'Judy Garland':** As charming as its namesake, strongly perfumed blossoms with 30 to 35 petals blush from yellow to hot orange to scarlet. Blooms abundantly in clusters. Glossy green leaves on a rounded, bushy plant. Introduced in l978.

- **'Little Darling':** A salmon-pink and yellow duo-tone rose with a hybrid tea shape and a spicy fragrance. 24 to 30 petals. Blooms abundantly in clusters in early to midseason and reblooms well. The plant is bushy and spreading. Leaves are glossy, leathery, and dark green. Long-lasting cut flower. Disease resistant with a good hardiness rating. Introduced in 1956.

- **'Peppermint Twist':** The red-, white-, and pink-striped blossoms look almost like candy canes in flower form. Very full, with over 40 petals, they open flat or slightly cupped. Borne in small clusters on a medium, upright bush with shiny green leaves. Slight fragrance. Introduced in 1992.

- **'Playboy':** A dazzling red-orange flower stamped in the centre with a large, golden eye full of orange stamens. Five to seven petals. Blooms are produced almost continuously in clusters that are excellent for cut flowers. A bushy, spreading shrub with glossy leaves. Introduced in 1976.

- **'Redgold':** AARS 1971. Each of the 25 to 30 petals is deep yellow with a bright scarlet edge. Produces an abundance of long-lasting flowers suitable for cutting. Grows vigorously in all climates. Mild fragrance. Upright, bushy plant. Leaves are dark green with red new growth. Good winter hardiness and disease resistant.

- **'Regensberg':** From a group of roses known as the *hand-painted series,* all of which have flowers that look like they've been splashed with different colours of paint. This one truly looks handcrafted. Bright white flowers with 20 to 25 petals are splashed with hot pink. At times, the low, compact plant can be completely covered with blossoms. Sweet fragrance. Flower size increases in cool weather. Works well as a landscape plant or in a container. Introduced in 1979.

'Scentimental': AARS 1997. Shocking burgundy-red flowers have swirls of creamy white on the petals. Each bloom is different — some are splashed white, others are striped white, and still others are almost all white with red markings. Cup-shaped flowers have 25 to 30 petals and a strong, spicy fragrance. The rounded plant has excellent disease resistance.

Chapter 11

Miniature Roses

· ·

In This Chapter

▶ Understanding miniature roses

▶ Exploring the origin of miniature roses

▶ Caring for miniature roses

▶ Landscaping with miniature roses

▶ Selecting miniature roses

· ·

Few groups of plants, roses or otherwise, are as versatile and useful as miniature roses. Miniatures, as you can probably guess, are perfectly scaled down versions of larger roses, with all the colours, forms, substance, and often fragrance of full-sized roses. Like other types of roses, each variety of miniature rose has different characteristics, with plant size varying between 10 centimetres (4 inches) and 120 centimetres (4 feet) and plant shapes that include bushy, compact, climbing, and cascading.

Looking at Mini Form

Smaller definitely doesn't mean miniature roses are less attractive or less fun to grow. Happily, in most cases, smaller *does* mean easier to grow. Their smaller habit makes miniature roses ideal for growing in containers, and they also make excellent landscape and bedding plants.

No matter what the shape or height, a good miniature rose has flowers and leaves in perfect proportion to each other, as shown in Figure 11-1. The flowers provide bright and constant spots of colour throughout the growing season, and their flowers can be cut for mini-bouquets and arrangements. (See Figure 11-2 for a close-up of a miniature rose flower.) As well, the selection of varieties is awesome, with hundreds of new ones being introduced each year. We've picked some of the best (mostly award winners) for you to start with.

Figure 11-1:
A miniature rose plant with flowers and leaves in perfect proportion.

Figure 11-2:
A miniature flower looks quite similar to a flower on a full-sized plant.

Tracing Their Tiny Origins

Many stories about the origin of miniature roses exist, and it appears that miniatures have come and gone over many centuries at least. Genetically, miniature roses have been traced back to the miniature China rose, *Rosa chinensis minima,* but the forerunner of today's miniature roses was discovered in a window box in Switzerland in 1917. This variety, named 'Rouletii' (for Colonel Roulet, who owned the window box and the rose), was used to hybridize the first of the modern miniatures.

The very first miniature sold in the United States, 'Tom Thumb', was introduced in 1936. Since those days, hybridizers of mini roses have crossed miniature varieties with virtually every other type of rose, creating the huge diversity of colour, form, and·habit that you can find today.

Diminutive but not frail: Protecting and pruning

Miniature roses are actually pretty tough plants. They are almost always propagated and grown on their own roots, which makes them hardier in cold weather than many other types of roses. Like most plants, however, they're not real thrilled with harsh winter winds and the nasty freeze-and-thaw cycles that some winters bring. Your miniature roses will suffer less damage and thrive more readily if you hill them with soil or heavily mulch the base of the plant with leaves — 45 centimetres (18 inches) or more — for winter protection. We have also noted the hardier varieties throughout the chapter. For more information about own-root roses, see Chapter 16.

Smaller plants mean smaller roots. Smaller roots don't grow very deep in the soil. Therefore, your mini rose needs more frequent watering if Mother Nature doesn't comply and provide water in the form of rain. Also, smaller plants require smaller doses of fertilizer. A general rule for fertilizing miniatures is this: half as much, twice as often.

As with full-sized roses, regularly removing faded flowers (called *deadheading*) is pretty much all the pruning you need to do during the growing season. With hilling or mulching, there's no need to cut back minis in the fall, and in spring the minimum pruning necessary is to cut away the dead parts.

If you have lots of minis, a hedge trimmer — you know, that tool that looks like giant paper scissors — does a great job. In any case, shearing plants back about halfway, meaning that 30-centimetre (12-inch) plants should be 15 centimetres (6 inches) tall after pruning, is an excellent spring task that will increase the number of summer blooms.

However, many gardeners like to treat their miniatures with a little more respect, so if you want, you can prune them just like you would hybrid teas. (Check out Chapter 20 for more information.)

Small but not less colourful: Landscaping with miniatures

Miniatures are wonderful landscape plants. Because the plants are so small when you buy them, it seems like they'll take forever to grow and put on a good show. But don't let that small size fool you. Miniature roses reach full size in just a few weeks, and they flower big-time all season long.

Miniatures make beautiful up-front plants. Use them to edge a flower border or walkway, or plant them at the base of taller-growing plants. And don't forget about containers. You'll be hard pressed to beat a good-looking miniature rose growing in a handsome pot. You can find specifics about using miniatures in the landscape in Chapter 5. For more on growing roses in containers, refer to Chapter 7.

Buying Quality Miniature Roses

Miniature roses seem to show up in a lot of places where you don't usually see rose plants for sale, like at supermarkets and florist shops. So you don't have to look far to find them. But if you want varieties that really have proven themselves in garden situations, you're better off buying from a local nursery or a mail-order catalogue that specializes in roses. You can find their addresses in Appendix B.

People may try to convince you that growing miniature roses on a windowsill is easy. *Don't buy it.* Although a miniature may stay in bloom for a week or two inside, eventually the plant needs to go outside where light is sufficient and conditions are better for healthy growth. Many people do have success growing miniatures indoors, but they have a greenhouse or provide some type of supplemental lighting. Like any other rose, a miniature requires at least six hours of full, direct sunshine per day. Get out those grow lamps!

Giving You the Lowdown on Miniature Varieties

Many new miniatures are released every year — possibly more than any other type of rose — so you have many varieties to choose from. The following sections list some of our favourites. Miniatures that receive the American Rose Society Award of Excellence have been judged as outstanding in test gardens and are good plants to start with.

Red miniatures

Here are some of our favourite red miniatures. If we had to pick three to start with, we would choose 'Beauty Secret', 'Red Cascade', and 'Starina'.

- **'Beauty Secret':** American Rose Society Award of Excellence 1975. Pointed, bright red buds open into hybrid tea-type blooms of medium red. 24 to 30 petals. Very fragrant. Prolific and dependable, 26- to 45-centimetre (10- to 18-inch) plants have shiny, medium green leaves. Disease resistant with good winter hardiness. Grows well indoors under lights. Introduced in 1965.

- **'Billie Teas':** American Rose Society Award of Excellence 1993. Full, dark red flowers with 26 to 40 petals. Blooms grow singly with no fragrance. The plant is upright with medium green, matte leaves. Introduced in 1992.

- **'Black Jade':** American Rose Society Award of Excellence 1985. Pointed, near-black buds open to chocolatey red blossoms on long stems. Flowers boast 30 petals each, but only slight fragrance on this 45- to 60-centimetre (18- to 24-inch) bush with glossy, dark green leaves. Best colour in bud stage. Introduced in 1985.

- **'Centerpiece':** American Rose Society Award of Excellence 1985. Deep red, velvety blooms with 35 petals. Lightly fragrant, long-lasting flowers adorn this compact plant. The bush reaches 30 to 40 centimetres (12 to 16 inches) high, covered with deep green leaves. Introduced in 1984.

- **'Debut':** All-America Rose Selection (AARS) 1989. Radiant scarlet blooms change from cream to yellow at the base. Older blossoms turn cherry red and white at base and have 15 to 18 petals. Grow singly. No fragrance. Foliage is shiny and dark green. Introduced in 1988.

- **'Jingle Bells':** American Rose Society Award of Excellence 1995. Bright red blooms with a lighter reverse. Nice round habit, reaching about 52 centimetres (20 inches) high. Glossy, dark green leaves and good disease resistance. Introduced in 1994.

- **'Kathy':** Soft red and fragrant. Hybrid tea form with 24 to 30 petals. Blooms abundantly and has a tendency to spread. 20- to 26-centimetre (8- to 10-inch) bush with leathery, dark green leaves. Vigorous, disease resistant, and as hardy as miniatures come. Introduced in l970.

- **'Old Glory':** American Rose Society Award of Excellence 1988. Large, fire-engine red blossoms grow alone or in small sprays. 23 to 25 petals. No fragrance. The plant is a vigorous grower with medium green, glossy leaves. Introduced in 1988.

- **'Red Cascade':** American Rose Society Award of Excellence 1976. Climbing miniature. Excellent for hanging baskets. Deep red, cup-shaped flowers bloom abundantly. 35 petals. Little or no fragrance. Disease resistant but needs protection from mildew in some climates. Dark green, shiny leaves. Introduced in 1976.

- ⚙ **'Sweet Caroline':** American Rose Society Award of Excellence 1999. A deep red blend of a red rose with white edges (or a white rose with red centres), this is a sweetheart of a flower. Exhibition-quality blooms (17 to 25 petals) that flower constantly all summer give it a place in any garden. A tall plant at 60 to 90 centimetres (24 to 36 inches).

- ⚙ **'Starina':** Pointed buds. Hybrid tea-type blossoms of a deep red-orange. 35 petals. Abundant, continuous bloom. Light fragrance. Plant is 30 to 45 centimetres (12 to 18 inches) tall, bushy, and dense. Dark green, glossy leaves. Disease resistant with good winter hardiness. Easy to grow. Consistent performer. Introduced in 1965.

Pink miniatures

You have many pink miniatures to choose from. Our favourites include 'Baby Betsy McCall', 'Jeanne LaJoie', and 'Judy Fischer'.

- ⚙ **'Angelica Renae':** American Rose Society Award of Excellence 1996. Medium pink blooms with a splash of orange at the base. Free blooming. Forms a nice, rounded, 60-centimetre (2-foot) bush. Dark green foliage. Introduced in 1996.

- ⚙ **'Baby Betsy McCall':** Light pink, fragrant, cup-shaped flowers with 20 to 24 petals. Continuous bloom. 30- to 45-centimetre (12- to 18-inch) bush. Leathery, light green leaves. Excellent winter hardiness and disease resistant. Introduced in 1965.

- ⚙ **'Cuddles':** American Rose Society Award of Excellence 1979. Deep coral-pink petals unfurl evenly into long-lasting blossoms. 55 to 60 petals. Slight fragrance. Abundant bloom. 35- to 41-centimetre (14- to 16-inch) tall bush with glossy green leaves. Easy to grow. Disease resistant with good winter hardiness. Introduced in 1978.

- ⚙ **'Cupcake':** Lots of pastel pink flowers and buds with 45 to 50 petals. Little fragrance. Hybrid tea-shaped flower. Bush is 30 to 45 centimetres (12 to 18 inches) tall with glossy green foliage and a neat, rounded appearance. Disease resistant and reasonably winter hardy. Introduced in 1983.

- ⚙ **'Funny Girl':** The small, light pink flowers deliver a hint of fragrance. 20 petals. Small green leaves. Upright shape. Introduced in 1982.

- ⚙ **'Jeanne Lajoie':** American Rose Society Award of Excellence 1977. Climbing miniature. Medium pink flowers grow in clusters nonstop throughout the season. 35 to 40 petals. Slight fragrance. Vigorous canes reach 120 to 240 centimetres (4 to 8 feet). Foliage is abundant, small, and glossy. Good disease resistance. Introduced in 1975.

'**Judy Fischer**': American Rose Society Award of Excellence 1975. One of the best pink miniatures. Flowers last for weeks and don't fade, even in hot weather. 24 to 30 petals of rose-pink. Hybrid tea-shaped flower. Very low and bushy. Abundant, small, glossy green leaves. Slight fragrance, it grows 45 to 60 centimetres (18 to 24 inches) high. Disease resistant with good winter hardiness. Introduced in 1968.

'**Scentsational**': Flowers are pink, edged with mauve, and have a creamy pink reverse. Nicely fragrant. Makes a good cut flower. Medium green foliage. Easy to grow. Introduced in 1996.

Orange miniatures

Here are five great orange miniatures. You can't miss with any of them.

'**Dee Bennett**': American Rose Society Award of Excellence 1989. Delightful blended rose washed with shades of orange and yellow. The nicely formed flowers are borne singly and in clusters; they have 25 petals and a light fruity fragrance. Medium-sized, bushy growth with dark green, semi-glossy foliage. Introduced in 1988.

'**Loving Touch**': American Rose Society Award of Excellence 1985. Creamy apricot-orange blossoms with 20 to 25 petals are set against abundant medium green leaves. Mild fragrance. Bush is 30 to 45 centimetres (12 to 18 inches) tall and rounded. Moderate temperatures produce the deepest colours. Introduced in 1985.

'**Mary Marshall**': American Rose Society Award of Excellence 1975. Deep coral flowers with a yellow base blossom all season. Hybrid tea-type blooms. Slight fragrance. Bush grows 26 to 35 centimetres (10 to 14 inches) tall; the climbing form can reach 150 centimetres (5 feet). Medium green, glossy leaves. Disease resistant. Introduced in 1970.

'**New Beginning**': AARS 1989. A bright orange-yellow flower with lots and lots of petals (40 to 50) but no fragrance. Glossy green leaves. Compact plant. Introduced in 1988.

'**Sheri Anne**': American Rose Society Award of Excellence 1975. Profuse clusters of bright orange-red flowers bloom continuously on this upright bush. 15 to 18 petals. Light fragrance. Glossy, dark green leaves. Introduced in 1973.

Yellow miniatures

These are all excellent yellow miniatures, but 'Center Gold', 'Rise 'n' Shine', and 'Yellow Doll' always stand out in a crowd.

- **'Bojangles':** Deep yellow and small, these flowers have no fragrance. 20 petals. Small, light green leaves. Upright, bushy growth. Introduced in 1981.

- **'Cal Poly':** American Rose Society Award of Excellence 1992. Blazing yellow, round blooms set against large, rich green leaves look like water lilies. 20 to 25 petals. Mild scent. 35- to 45-centimetre (14- to 18-inch) bush. Blooms best in warm summer climates. Introduced in 1992.

- **'Center Gold':** American Rose Society Award of Excellence 1982. Deep yellow flowers occasionally shade toward white. You may find an all-white bloom among the yellow, or you may see flowers with yellow centres and white outside petals. 25 to 35 petals. Hybrid tea-type blossoms. Little or no fragrance. Glossy, medium green leaves. 35- to 45-centimetre (14- to 18-inch) plant. Vigorous. Disease resistant and winter hardy for a yellow. Introduced in 1981.

- **'Golden Halo':** American Rose Society Award of Excellence 1991. Bright yellow blooms sometimes have a touch of red. Flowers have a slight fragrance and 24 to 26 petals. Vigorous, bushy plant grows about 40 to 52 centimetres (16 to 20 inches) high with dark green leaves. Introduced in 1991.

- **'Little Tommy Tucker':** American Rose Society Award of Excellence 1999. Butter yellow blossoms with slight fragrance cover this plant all summer. Heavy bloom alert! Medium height plant grows 35 to 50 centimetres (14 to 20 inches) in height. Glossy green foliage rounds out the picture.

- **'Rise 'n' Shine':** American Rose Society Award of Excellence 1978. One of the finest yellow miniatures. Delivers abundant and continuous blooms of brilliant yellow flowers set against dark green foliage. 30 to 40 petals. Bushy, compact, and low. Disease resistant with good winter hardiness. Introduced in 1977.

- **'Sequoia Gold':** American Rose Society Award of Excellence 1987. Golden yellow blossoms bloom singly or in clusters. 20 petals. Moderate, fruity fragrance. The bushy, spreading plant has glossy, medium green leaves. Introduced in 1986.

- **'Yellow Doll':** Free-blooming, with large, light yellow flowers. 24 to 30 petals. Slight fragrance. Leathery green leaves. The 20- to 26-centimetre (8- to 10-inch) plant is low, compact, and rounded. Disease resistant with good winter hardiness. Introduced in 1962.

White miniatures

These are all top-notch white miniatures:

- ❀ **'Cinderella':** Round, satiny white blossoms with a blush of pink at the centre grow singly and in clusters. 40 to 60 petals. Prolific bloomer. Spicy fragrance. Small, glossy green leaves. Grows 20 to 26 centimetres (8 to 10 inches) high. Disease resistant and winter hardy for a miniature. Introduced in 1953.

- ❀ **'Figurine':** American Rose Society Award of Excellence 1992. Ivory, dipped in a pastel pink wash. Long, pointed buds and high-centred, hybrid tea-type flowers look almost like fine china. 18 to 25 petals. Blooms abundantly on long stems that are suitable for cutting. Moderate, sweet fragrance, it's a 35- to 50-centimetre (14- to 20-inch) bush. Introduced in 1991.

- ❀ **'Gourmet Popcorn':** Small, flat, bright white blooms explode all over this vigorous plant in cascading clusters. 15 to 20 petals. Extremely fragrant, it grows 50 to 70 centimetres (20 to 28 inches) tall; bushy plant. Disease resistant with good cold tolerance. Easy to grow. Introduced in 1988.

- ❀ **'Simplex':** Five white petals frame a large nucleus of fluffy, golden stamens. Lots of flowers throughout the season on this vigorous, upright bush. Produces pink blossoms in cool, cloudy weather. Light green, shiny leaves on a 40- to 45- centimetre (15- to 18-inch) tall bush. Disease resistant with good winter hardiness. Introduced in 1961.

- ❀ **'Snow Bride':** American Rose Society Award of Excellence 1983. Formal, creamy white buds open to large, full blossoms with 20 to 25 petals. Mild scent. Rounded bush, 30 to 45 centimetres (12 to 18 inches) tall, has deep green leaves. Forms the best flowers in moderate climates. Introduced in l983.

- ❀ **'Starglo':** American Rose Society Award of Excellence 1975. Extremely fragrant, white blossoms with a classic hybrid tea shape. 35 petals. Blooms midseason and repeats blooming. Upright bush, 25 to 35 centimetres (10 to 14 inches) tall, will grow indoors in pots over the winter. Disease resistant and good winter hardiness. Introduced in 1973.

Lavender miniatures

Here are four of our favourite lavender-flowered miniature roses:

- ❀ **'Incognito':** Unusually coloured flowers of dusty light mauve with a yellow reverse. Perfect exhibition form. A vigorous grower, and always covered with flowers. Grows to 75 centimetres (30 inches) tall. Winner of the New England Rose Trials Award, 1996.

⊛ **'Lavender Jewel':** Mauve colour stays true. Produces many blooms throughout the season. 12 to 20 petals. Open, cup-formed flowers. Little fragrance. Dark green, glossy leaves, the bush reaches heights of 25 to 40 centimetres (10 to 15 inches) with long, spreading canes. Disease resistant and winter hardy for a miniature. Introduced in 1978.

⊛ **'Sweet Chariot':** Ruffled, fluffy blossoms seem to burst forth in fragrant, cascading blooms. As the flower ages, the deep purple gives way to lavender, creating a two-toned effect. 45 to 50 petals. Small, deep green leaves on a 30- to 45-centimetre (12- to 18-inch) bushy plant. Highly disease resistant. Introduced in l985.

⊛ **'Winsome':** American Rose Society Award of Excellence 1985. Big, pointed buds and large, shapely, magenta blooms appear freely all season on this vigorous bush. 35 to 40 petals. Little fragrance for this 40- to 55-centimetre (16- to 22-inch) rounded plant with dark green leaves. Disease resistant. Introduced in 1985.

Multicoloured miniatures

These are all popular miniatures, but you have to love the award-winning 'Child's Play'. Otherwise, choose by your favourite colour combinations.

⊛ **'Autumn Splendor':** American Rose Society Award of Excellence 1999. Yellow blend of yellows, golds, and oranges with a touch of red every now and then. Exhibition-quality blooms give this plant a classy look. A large plant, it can grow 60 to 90 centimetres (24 to 36 inches) tall.

⊛ **'Child's Play':** AARS 1993, American Rose Society Award of Excellence 1993. First miniature to win both awards. These blooms are as sweet-smelling as they look. Pink and white blossoms have a classic hybrid tea shape. Foliage is dark green and very disease resistant.

⊛ **'Dreamglo':** Long-lasting, formal flowers are red, blended with white at the base. 50 petals. Slight fragrance. Blooms with abandon midseason. Upright bush, 45 to 60 centimetres (18 to 24 inches) tall, with dark green, glossy leaves. Disease resistant with good winter hardiness. Introduced in 1978.

⊛ **'Heavenly Days':** American Rose Society Award of Excellence 1988. Like a St. Lawrence River landscape, lots of vibrant colour in clusters. Maple red-orange petals with a lemon-yellow reverse. Flowers are cup-shaped and have 28 to 32 petals. No fragrance. The plant is compact and bushy with glossy green leaves. Introduced in 1988.

⊛ **'Holy Toledo':** American Rose Society Award of Excellence 1980. Deep apricot blossoms with yellow at the base burst into bloom throughout the season. Borne singly and in clusters. 25 to 30 petals. Slight fragrance. Medium to tall, vigorous bush has glossy, forest green foliage. Introduced in 1978.

'Little Flame': American Rose Society Award of Excellence 1999. We're talking bright tangerine orange that deepens with age to a burnt orange — you won't miss this one in the garden. Good disease resistance on a mounding 40- to 60-centimetre (16- to 24-inch) plant with glossy foliage. Flowers develop in clusters and tend to drop cleanly from the hip, leaving a clean-looking plant rather than old, dying flowers.

'Kristin': American Rose Society Award of Excellence 1993. Nicely shaped flowers are white with carmine red edges. Blooms often one to a stem with 27 to 30 petals. No fragrance. Upright, bushy plant, 50 to 60 centimetres (20 to 24 inches) high, with glossy, dark green foliage. Introduced in 1992.

'Little Artist': The profuse, long-lasting flowers appear to be painted a glowing red with a white eye and reverse. 10 to 15 petals. The best colours come in the spring and do not fade. The rounded bush has moderate fragrance and ranges 30 to 45 centimetres (12 to 18 inches) in height. Polished green leaves are extremely disease resistant. Introduced in 1984.

'Magic Carrousel': American Rose Society Award of Excellence 1975. Famous for its cheery colours — white with a fine, red edge — this power-house blooms continuously and is easy to grow. Open or cup-shaped flowers with 30 to 35 petals and a mild fragrance. The bush grows 45 to 60 centimetres (18 to 24 inches) high with glossy green leaves. Vigorous and disease resistant. Introduced in 1972.

'Over the Rainbow': American Rose Society Award of Excellence 1975. An eye-catcher — red and yellow blossoms with 28 to 35 pointed petals. Continuous bloom. Little fragrance for this 30- to 35-centimetre (12- to 14-inch) bush, but it has nice glossy, dark green foliage. Disease resistant with good winter hardiness. Introduced in 1972.

'Party Girl': American Rose Society Award of Excellence 1981. Blossoms blended with apricot-yellow and pink are spicily fragrant. Hybrid tea-type form with 25 petals. Repeats blooming all season. Plant is 30 to 35 centimetres (12 to 14 inches) tall and bushy with glossy green leaves. Disease resistant and winter hardy — for a miniature. Introduced in 1979.

'Peaches 'n' Cream': American Rose Society Award of Excellence 1977. A tapering bud gives way to light peach-pink and cream blooms loaded with 52 petals. Slightly fragrant. Dark foliage. Introduced in 1976.

'Pride 'n' Joy': AARS 1992. Urn-shaped blooms are bright orange with an orange and cream reverse. 30 to 35 petals. Fragrant. Dark green, glossy leaves. Spreading, bushy plant.

'Puppy Love': American Rose Society Award of Excellence 1979. Multi-coloured flowers are orange, pink, and yellow with 20 to 25 petals. Blooming freely on long stems, they make excellent cut flowers. Slight fragrance. Medium, upright, compact plant with medium green leaves. Disease resistant. Introduced in 1978.

@ **'Rainbow's End':** American Rose Society Award of Excellence 1986. Golden yellow blossoms blush prettily to their orange-red tips. Shapely, hybrid tea-type flowers (30 to 35 petals) with mild fragrance abound on this repeat bloomer. Plant is 30 to 45 centimetres (12 to 18 inches) tall with glossy green leaves. Disease resistant with good winter hardiness. Introduced in 1984.

@ **'Toy Clown':** American Rose Society Award of Excellence 1975. Beautiful hybrid tea-type blossoms (12 to 20 petals) are white with red or deep pink edges. Free-blooming and attractive bush is 26 to 35 centimetres (10 to 14 inches) tall. The bush has smallish, leathery green leaves and little or no fragrance. It is disease resistant and winter hardy for a miniature. Introduced in 1966.

Chapter 12

Climbing Roses

• •

• •

A pretty amazing variety of climbing roses flourishes throughout the world — including many shrubs and old garden roses. (We describe some of those types in Chapters 13 and 14, respectively.) Usually, rose growers train their climbers' vigorous growth to follow trellises or other structures. Throughout this chapter we discuss the diverse range of climbers, give care and growing suggestions, and list a full range of colourful options to help you select a good climbing rose for your garden.

So Many Climbers, So Little Time

Climbing roses, as shown in Figure 12-1, represent a diverse group of plants that produce long, supple canes that can reach over 6 metres (20 feet) long. The plants are not true vines in that they won't cling to, climb on, or in any way attach themselves to an upright support. Left on their own, they tend to be large, sprawling shrubs.

However, most climbing roses are not left on their own to sprawl shapelessly in the backyard. You usually tie them in an upright fashion to some type of a support, such as a fence, arbour, trellis, or wall. They make a beautiful vertical statement in a garden and are very useful for adding colour to blank walls or narrow planting areas.

Figure 12-1:
You can train climbing rose plants to make a vertical statement in a garden (left). Climbing rose flowers often grow in clusters (right).

Most climbing roses fall into one of four categories for our Canadian gardens:

✔ *Large-flowered climbers* are the most popular and widely used climbing roses. They produce clusters of flowers on long, arching canes that generally reach from 2.4 to 4.2 metres (8 to 14 feet) high. They bloom most heavily in spring but do produce flowers throughout the growing season.

Large-flowered climbers are generally hardy to –10° to –7° C (15° to 20° F) and need serious winter protection wherever temperatures regularly drop lower. (For more information about protecting these plants in winter, see Chapter 21.)

✔ *Climbing sports* result from unusually vigorous canes that grow from popular hybrid teas, grandifloras, and floribundas. They produce the beautiful flowers of their shrubby parent but on a more sprawling plant. Climbing sports don't usually bloom as heavily as large-flowered climbers, but they do produce flowers with excellent size and character throughout the growing season. These plants are generally hardy to –12° to –7° C (10° to 20° F) and need good winter protection.

Climbing sports are generally named after the variety from which they originate. Favourites include 'Climbing First Prize' from the pink and silver hybrid tea, 'Climbing Iceberg' from the generous-blooming white floribunda, 'Climbing Cécile Brünner' from the pink polyantha, and 'Climbing Queen Elizabeth' from the famous pink grandiflora. (You can find descriptions of these flowers in the chapters describing the class of roses from which the climber originates.) Some climbing sports, such as 'High Noon', described later in this chapter, are listed as climbing hybrid teas.

✔ *Ramblers* are less popular than other types of climbing roses, primarily because they bloom only once a year, in spring, and they are not as hardy as other climbers. These plants are very vigorous and can grow up to 6 metres (20 feet) tall. They are hardy to about –12° C (or about –10° F). Their height makes them tough to overwinter where the temperatures are truly Canadian.

✔ *Explorer Roses*, bred in Ottawa and Quebec for our northern conditions, have some varieties that make excellent, and hardy, climbers that require no winter protection in most parts of Canada. Although many of them have a single flush of bloom in early summer with sporadic blooming thereafter, there are some new introductions that promise extended bloom times. See Chapter 15 for varieties.

✔ *Climbing miniatures* are a fifth type of climber. Many are produced by crossing popular miniature varieties with climbing forms of *Rosa wichuraiana*. Favourites include 'Jeanne Lajoie' and 'Climbing Rise 'n' Shine'. (You can find descriptions of their flowers in Chapter 11.) One other climbing miniature, 'King Tut', is described later in this chapter. These require extensive winter protection if they are to survive. See Chapter 21.

Special Needs: Caring for Climbers

Climbing roses need a little different care than most other roses, particularly when it comes to pruning, training, and winter protection. You can find more information about those subjects in Chapter 20, "Pruning Roses," and Chapter 21, "Protecting Roses Where Winters Are Cold."

Otherwise, watering, fertilizing, and controlling pests on climbers are similar to other types of roses. See Part IV of this book for details.

Up Against a Wall: Planting Climbers

As landscape plants, climbing roses present many opportunities. Following are some planting suggestions:

- ✔ Plant climbing roses in a narrow area, where there isn't room for much else.

- ✔ Turn a blank wall into living art with a trellis and a climbing rose plant.

- ✔ Cover up that ugly chain-link fence.

- ✔ Use a climbing rose to increase the shade from your arbour.

You can find more ideas for using climbing roses, including different types of supports and ways to attach climbing roses to them, in Chapter 5.

Climbers in Every Colour of the Rainbow

Climbers are the high risers of the rose world. They can grow up and over whatever you can tie them to and produce flowers in all the rose colours, as you'll see in the following lists.

Note that when we describe a variety as "hardy" we mean hardier than most. But hardy is still a relative term. If you grow any of these plants, you have to protect them in all but the warmest parts of Canada.

Red climbers

All these red varieties are large-flowered climbers. Don't overlook 'Improved Blaze'. It's a stunner and its one of the hardiest of the red climbers.

- **'Crimson Cascade':** Deep red blooms with a medium fragrance cover this 2.4-metre (8-foot) tall climber. The blooms are long lasting and cover the plant — a heavy bloomer! Introduced in 1991, this has good winter hardiness and excellent disease resistance.

- **'Don Juan':** Deep red blossoms with an intense fragrance bloom profusely from midseason on. 35 petals. Dark green, glossy leaves. Climbing canes reach 3.5 to 4.2 metres (12 to 14 feet). Makes an excellent trellis rose. Blooms on new and old wood. Disease resistant, but not dependably winter hardy. Warm night temperatures give the best colour. Introduced in 1958.

- **'Dublin Bay':** Cupped blossoms with 25 true red petals bloom profusely midseason and follow up with good repeat bloom later. Flowers open in cool or hot weather. Moderately fragrant. Lots of dark green leaves. Bush is upright and vigorous. Blooms on old or new wood. Climbing canes reach 2.5 to 3.5 metres (8 to 12 feet). Disease resistant and winter hardy. Introduced in 1975.

- **'Heidelberg':** Medium red blossoms with good fragrance cover this 2.5-metre (8-foot) grower. Good disease resistance and winter hardiness make it a candidate for any garden. Introduced in 1959 from Germany.

- **'Improved Blaze':** The most popular climbing rose. Large, cup-shaped flowers of pure red bloom in clusters all season. 20 to 25 petals. Light scent. Climbing canes reach 3.5 to 4.2 metres (12 to 14 feet). Medium green, shiny leaves. Blooms on old and new wood. Winter hardy and disease resistant. Easy to grow. Introduced in 1932.

- **'Tempo':** Flowers are deep red and full. 35 to 45 petals. Slight fragrance. Foliage is dark green, glossy, and large. Good disease resistance and winter hardiness. Introduced in 1975.

Pink climbers

These are all large-flowered climbers. 'New Dawn' is the hardiest of pink climbers.

- **'America':** All-America Rose Selection (AARS) 1976. Large, well-formed, cup-shaped flowers of coral pink broadcast a spicy fragrance. 40 to 45 petals. Plant is vigorous and bushy with bright green leaves. Climbing canes reach 3 to 3.5 metres (10 to 12 feet). Blooms on old and new wood. Disease resistant and winter hardy.

- **'Dorothy Perkins':** Rambler. Many-petalled, rose-pink flowers. Fragrant. Blooms only in spring. Very vigorous plant can grow 3.0 to 6.0 metres (10 to 20 feet) high. Dark green, glossy foliage. Introduced in 1901. Wonderful if you can overwinter it.

⊕ **'Dr. J. H. Nicolas':** Large, round, rose-pink flowers with 45 to 50 petals are heavily fragrant. Blooms profusely. Upright and slender with leathery, dark green leaves. Climbing canes can reach 2.5 to 3.0 metres (8 to 10 feet). Disease resistant and winter hardy. Introduced in 1940.

⊕ **'New Dawn':** Large, pale pink flowers with sweet perfume and glossy, dark green leaves. 35 to 40 petals. Climbing canes can reach 5.5 to 6.0 metres (18 to 20 feet). Produces continuously throughout the season. Hardiest of the climbing pinks. Introduced in 1930.

⊕ **'Rosarium Uetersen':** Medium-sized, deep pink flowers with an incredible number of petals — well over 100. Fragrant. Vigorous growth with dark green, glossy foliage. Introduced in 1977.

Orange climbers

Some folks can't do without their orange climbers. If you just have to have your dose of orange in the garden, here are a few climbers you might try.

⊕ **'Spectacular':** An orange-red blend with slight fragrance. Also known as 'Danse de Feu', it is a vigorous 2.5-metre (8-foot) grower introduced in 1953 from France.

⊕ **'Rosanna':** A heavy-blooming, repeating orange-pink-toned rose with excellent heavy fragrance. You'll smell this one! Very large blooms last a long time on 2.5-metre (8-foot) canes. Introduced in 1982 from Germany.

Yellow climbers

Here are four great yellow climbers. One of them, 'King Tut', is a climbing miniature. Note that the yellow climbers tend to be more tender than other colours and this means you have to protect them over the winter if you want them to bloom next summer.

⊕ **'Golden Showers':** AARS 1957. Large-flowered climber. Large, bright yellow, ruffled flowers resemble a star burst when in full bloom. Blooms abundantly all season. 20 to 35 petals. Fragrant. Climbing canes reach 3.6 to 4.3 metres (12 to 14 feet). Bright green leaves. Cool temperatures give the best colour and size. Introduced in 1956. Protect well as it is tender.

⊕ **'High Noon':** AARS 1948. Climbing hybrid tea. Large, light yellow flowers with a loosely cupped form bloom all season. 25 to 30 petals. Spicy fragrance. Leathery, glossy green leaves. Climbing canes reach 3 to 3.6 metres (10 to 12 feet). Disease resistant.

- **'King Tut':** Climbing miniature. Golden yellow flowers have a touch of pink. Small blooms have 20 to 25 petals and appear in abundance. Plant grows about 2 to 2.5 metres (7 to 8 feet) high with glossy, dark green foliage. Disease resistant. Great in containers. Introduced in 1995.
- **'Royal Gold':** Large-flowered climber. Yellow buds blossom into lasting, golden flowers with 30 to 40 petals in a hybrid tea-type shape. Borne singly and in clusters on long, strong stems. Moderate to strong fragrance. Glossy green leaves. Flowers do not fade, but flower production is not as prolific as with other climbers. Good cut flower. Climbing canes reach 2.5 to 3 metres (8 to 10 feet). Introduced in 1957.

White climbers

Two good ones to choose from, both large-flowered climbers:

- **'Lace Cascade':** Full, white flowers with 26 to 40 petals grow in small and large clusters amidst large, dark green leaves. Fragrant. Tall with a spreading growth. Disease resistant. Introduced in 1992.
- **'White Dawn':** Free flowering and vigorous, this rose delivers loads of bright white, ruffled flowers and a sweet perfume. 30 to 35 petals. Climbing canes reach 3.6 to 4.3 metres (12 to 14 feet). Glossy green foliage. Disease resistant. Introduced in 1949.

Lavender climbers

Few lavender large-flowered climbers exist, but you might be able to find 'Climbing Blue Girl', a sort of hybrid tea rose described in Chapter 8. 'Veilchenblau' is another lavender climber that blooms on old wood (you have to successfully *winter* it to get blossoms — it only blooms on its second year's growth).

Multicoloured climbers

Following are four favourite multicoloured climbers, of which 'Dortmund', with its beautiful single blooms, always ranks very highly with us.

- **'Dortmund':** Climbing shrub. Nail-polish red blossoms, which have a small, white eye, bloom in clusters. Five to eight petals. Moderate scent. Lacquered, deep green leaves. Climbing canes reach 3 to 3.6 metres (10 to 12 feet). Highly disease resistant and winter hardy. Introduced in 1955.

'**Handel':** Large-flowered climber. Ruffled, pale pink or white blossoms edged with deep pink unfurl singly on cutting-length stems. 20 to 25 petals. The bush is covered with blooms from top to bottom all season. Light scent. Dark, olive-green foliage. Climbing canes reach 3.6 to 4.3 metres (12 to 14 feet). Bloom improves as the plant gets older. Hardy. Introduced in 1965.

'**Joseph's Coat':** Large-flowered climber. Very popular. A kaleidoscope of colours dance on the petals, often in the same cluster — shades of red, pink, orange, and yellow. 23 to 28 petals. Light scent. Vigorous, glossy, bright green foliage. Climbing canes reach 3 to 3.6 metres (10 to 12 feet). Tender and susceptible to mildew. Introduced in 1964.

'**Rosy Mantle':** A large-flowering hybrid tea form with pink blended blossoms. A vigorous grower with good disease resistance. Slight fragrance on the blooms but good repeat blooming all summer long. Introduced in 1968 from Scotland.

Chapter 13

Shrub Roses

- -

In This Chapter

▶ Understanding what a shrub rose is

▶ Appreciating all kinds of shrub roses

▶ Caring for shrub roses

▶ Landscaping with shrub roses

▶ Choosing shrub rose varieties

- -

Shrub roses are a diverse group of plants that don't neatly fit into any of the other rose categories. Shrubs, especially the modern ones, are very popular because of their long season of bloom, pest and disease resistance, and versatility in the landscape. In this chapter we describe all the forms shrub roses are available in and how to raise 'em right.

A Splendid Assortment of Shrub Roses

We really mean it when we say — shrubs are a *diverse* group of plants! In fact, these rose plants are often more different than they are alike. You can find shrubs that are neat, compact little plants staying about 90 centimetres (3 feet) high. (See Figure 13-1.) Others are upright giants that you'd swear would reach the clouds if you didn't whack them back once in a while. Still others are low-growing, sprawling plants able to grow 3 to 3.6 metres (10 to 12 feet) wide in warmer parts of the country.

To further complicate things, many roses that really don't need to be called shrubs, particularly some floribundas and climbers, often are labelled as such. And to add to the confusion, some rose growers call their shrubs *landscape* roses.

Oh well — no matter. Shrubs are great roses with great flowers, as shown in Figure 13-2. Their diversity translates into versatility in the landscape. But we'll get to more examples of growing a bit later in this chapter.

Figure 13-1:
A compact
shrub rose.

Figure 13-2:
Shrub roses
produce
beautiful
flowers in
addition
to being
versatile
in the
landscape.

Shrub roses really come into their own as landscape plants. If you're thinking about planting any flowering shrubs, think hard before you overlook shrub roses. Plants like 'Carefree Beauty', 'Dreams Yellow', and 'Flower Carpet' are tough to top when it comes to amount of bloom and ease of care. And they're versatile in the landscape. You can use sprawling types as ground covers and the upright ones as hedges, and the smaller ones are ideal for pots, perennial borders, or low hedges. Chapter 5 lists specific varieties of shrub roses for various landscape uses.

Even though shrub roses are diverse, some that resulted from the same breeding programs have similarities, such as the following groups:

- ✔ **Hardy shrubs:** Several breeding programs have concentrated on creating hardy shrubs for cold climates. These shrubs include Buck hybrids, such as 'Prairie Princess', which were bred at Iowa State University, and the Morden and Explorer (named after famous explorers) shrub roses from Canada. Most of these hardy shrubs can withstand temperatures down to –26° to –32° C (–15° to –25° F) and lower and have excellent disease resistance. See Chapter 15 for more information on Explorer and Morden roses.

- ✔ **Meidiland roses:** These roses originate in France. Most are sprawling plants that are useful as ground covers or hedges. They are good repeat bloomers, have excellent disease resistance, and are generally hardy to about –23° C (–10° F).

- ✔ **David Austin English roses:** These shrubs are meant to combine the ever-blooming character and disease resistance of modern roses with the flower form and fragrance of old roses. The problem is that they don't always keep their promise. Although many are beautiful roses, some varieties do not rebloom and are prone to disease, especially black spot. But the fragrance! Choose your variety carefully. Most varieties are hardy to about –18° C (0° F), which means they need protection in most parts of Canada. Treat them the same as hybrid teas.

Taking It Easy

Most shrub roses are easy-to-grow roses that can get by on little care, other than regular watering and occasional fertilizer. You can find out more about watering and fertilizing in Chapters 18 and 19, respectively, of this book.

Many shrub roses can get along fine without much pruning, but you still want to *deadhead* them (remove the faded flowers) to keep them blooming over the entire season. Those that do have repeat blooms benefit from normal pruning methods. A new series, the 'Dream' roses, are pruned thoughout the summer with hedge shears; whack them back and they rebound with more flowers. Our kind of rose! Otherwise, prune to keep some of the large varieties in bounds. For more on pruning, see Chapter 20.

Many shrub roses are grown on their own roots (see Chapter 16 for more information) and are pretty hardy, if not extremely so. You still want to mound soil over the base of the more tender ones to protect them from freezing and thawing and to ensure that not all the aboveground parts are killed if the temperature gets really cold.

Shrub Roses by Colour

The following sections list the best of the most widely available shrub roses. Some rugosa roses (considered old garden roses) make useful, very hardy shrubs, too. See Chapter 14 for more information about rugosas — the newer rugosa hybrids are often included in the category of modern shrub roses.

Red shrubs

Here are some useful shrub roses with red flowers:

- **'Dream Red':** Large 10-centimetre (4-inch) bright red blooms smother this low-growing shrub rose. The repeat-blooming nature of this shrub makes up for its lack of fragrance. Classic-shaped bloom with 24 petals. Dark green, glossy foliage and reasonable hardiness; protect in zone 6 and colder. Produced on its own roots. Introduced in 2000.

- **'L. D. Braithwaite':** David Austin English rose. Crimson red, fully double blooms are cupped and open at the centre. Deeply fragrant. Always in bloom during the growing season. Vigorous-growing and slightly spreading plant can reach over 1.5 to 1.8 metres (5 to 6 feet) high and 1.8 to 2 metres (6 to 7 feet) wide. Introduced in 1988.

- **'Prairie Fire':** Pointed buds open into bright red flowers with a white base. Eight to ten wavy, heavily textured petals. Almost always in bloom with enormous clusters — 35 to 50 blooms — on long stems. Fragrant. The bush is vigorous and tall with dark, glossy foliage. Very hardy and disease resistant. Introduced in 1960.

- **'Red Meidiland':** Rich, red blooms with white centres almost hide the bright foliage on this graceful bush. Five petals. Starts blooming in late spring and repeats all season. No fragrance. Orange-red seed hips (rose fruits that form after the flowers) remain in fall. The vigorous bush has a mounded shape and is reasonably winter hardy. Grows 30 to 60 centimetres (1 to 2 feet) high, 1.5 metres to 1.8 metres (5 to 6 feet) wide. Works well as a ground cover. Introduced in 1989. Protect in zone 5 or colder.

- **'Red Ribbons':** A vigorous, spreading ground-cover rose with bright red, single flowers. Good bloomer. Grows 60 to 75 centimetres (2 to 2.5 feet) tall and about 1.2 metres (4 feet) wide. Good disease resistance. Introduced in 1996.

- **'Scarlet Meidiland':** Bright, cherry-red blooms of small, ruffled flowers (15 to 20 petals) grow in huge clusters on a fast-spreading bush that makes an excellent ground cover. Slight fragrance. The plant can spread up to 1.8 metres (6 feet) in the season after planting and attain a height of 0.9 to 1.2 metres (3 to 4 feet). Glossy, disease-resistant leaves. Reasonably winter hardy in zone 5. Introduced in 1985.

- **'Sevilliana':** A profuse-blooming Meidiland rose. Covers itself with fiery red, double blooms all season and red hips into winter. The upright, broad bush, 1.5 metres tall and 1.2 metres wide (5 feet tall and 4 feet wide) makes an excellent traffic barrier or hedge. Bright, bronze-green foliage. Not hardy below –23° C (–10° F). Introduced in 1978.

- **'Wenlock':** David Austin English rose. The dark crimson, cup-shaped flowers with 40 or more petals are strongly fragrant. Constant bloomer. Vigorous, upright, bushy plant with dark green foliage. In warmer areas of the country, this shrub can become quite tall. It requires winter protection in zone 5. Introduced in 1984.

Pink shrubs

So many pink shrubs to choose from. Let the plant's growing habit be your guide.

- **'Autumn Bouquet':** Deep pink blooms that appear continuously all summer long mark this plant as desirable. Add extreme fragrance to the mix and at 1.2 metres (4 feet) tall, it earns a place in many gardens. Introduced in 1948.

- **'Bibi Maizoon':** David Austin English rose. Lovely rose-pink, double blooms are round and cabbage-like in the bud and cup-shaped when fully open. Pleasantly fragrant. Vigorous plant, reaching at least 1.2 metres (4 feet) high and equally wide, with long, arching canes. Introduced in 1986.

- **'Bonica':** All-America Rose Selection (AARS) winner 1987. Meilland rose. Small, ruffled, warm pink blossoms open in clusters all summer. 35 petals. Fragrant and very free-blooming. Produces long, arching canes that reach about 1.2 metres (4 feet) high. Foliage is deep green and glossy. Beautiful hedge or planted in groups. Highly disease resistant. Winter hardy in zone 6, needs protection elsewhere. Introduced in 1985.

- **'Carefree Beauty':** All that the name implies, this rose practically laughs at adversity. Large, pink, mildly fragrant flowers blanket the bushy, full plant all season. 18 to 24 petals. Bright, apple-green foliage. Disease resistant and winter hardy. Introduced in 1977.

- **'Carefree Delight':** AARS 1996. Pink flowers with five petals and a bright white eye open each day of the growing season and disappear after blooming. (Deadheading isn't needed.) Slight fragrance. The bush grows in a spreading mound. Winter hardy and disease resistant. Consistent performer in all climates. Introduced in 1991.

- **'Cymbaline':** David Austin English rose. Light pink blooms with a strong fragrance. 35 petals. Slightly spreading plant with medium green leaves. Introduced in 1983.

'Dream Pink': Soft pink 15-centimetre (6-inch) blooms cover this plant. Very fragrant with a musk scent. Repeats all summer on mounded, disease-resistant shrub. Large, glossy green foliage, grown on its own roots. Requires some winter protection in zone 5 and colder. Introduced in 2000.

'Flower Carpet Pink': Deep pink flowers with a lighter reverse grow in large sprays. Cup-shaped flowers have 15 petals and a light fragrance. Foliage is small, dark green, and glossy. Low, spreading bush has small, dark green, glossy foliage that is disease resistant. Vigorous grower requires protection in zone 5 or colder. Introduced in 1989.

'Flower Carpet Appleblossom': Soft pastel pink flowers with mild fragrance. Foliage is small, dark green, and glossy. Low, spreading bush is disease resistant. Vigorous grower requires protection in zone 5 or colder. Introduced in 1997.

'Fuchsia Meidiland': One of the first roses to bloom in the spring, this plant continues to bloom until frost. Covered with small, semi-double blooms of a startling fuchsia pink. The canes spread to a width of 1.2 metres (4 feet), but the height is only 45 to 60 centimetres (1.5 to 2 feet), making the shrub an ideal ground cover or mass planting. Covered with shiny, bronzy green foliage. Extremely disease resistant. Introduced in 1995.

'Gertrude Jekyll': David Austin English rose. Bright pink blooms gently trail to pale pink edges. Fully double flowers provide strong perfume. Very vigorous plant can easily reach over 2.5 metres (8 feet) high in mild-winter climates. Poor repeat bloom. Introduced in 1986.

'Heritage': David Austin English rose. Clear, shell pink flowers with a cupped form. 40 or more petals. Extremely fragrant. Recurrent bloomer throughout the season. Vigorous, compact plant with small, dark, glossy leaves. Upright, bushy shrub reaches at least 1.5 metres (5 feet) high. Introduced in 1985.

'Lilian Austin': David Austin English rose. Named in honour of the hybridizer's mother, this rose produces cup-shaped, salmon-pink blooms in profusion early in the season with reliable repeat blooms. 33 petals. Very fragrant. Blooms in clusters. Spreading, arching shrub with dark, glossy leaves. Variable disease resistance. Needs winter protection. Introduced in 1981.

'Mary Rose': David Austin English rose. Produces abundant cup-shaped, rose-pink flowers with a gentle fragrance in late spring. Blooms again in autumn. Vigorous and wide, the bush can work as a hedge. Variable disease resistance. Introduced in 1983.

'Pink Meidiland': Single, deep pink blossoms with big, white eyes bloom dependably and freely. Five petals. No fragrance. The plant is bushy and clean looking, reaching 0.6 to 1.2 metres (2 to 4 feet) high. Disease resistant and winter hardy. Introduced in 1983.

- **'Prairie Dawn':** Bright pink flowers. Good repeat bloom. Compact, very hardy plant with excellent disease resistance. Reaches about 1.5 metres (5 feet) high. Introduced in 1957.

- **'Prairie Princess':** Blooms profusely with clusters of large, pastel pink blooms in late spring. Rests awhile and then blooms again. Repeats blooming this way all summer. Light perfume. Upright, vigorous bush with dark, leathery leaves. Highly disease resistant and very hardy. Makes an excellent cut flower. Introduced in 1971.

- **'Royal Bonica':** Meidiland rose. Always in bloom. Clusters of small, long-lasting, rosy-pink double blossoms. Light fragrance. Easy to care for. Winter hardy in zone 6 and disease resistant. Grows about 1.5 metres (5 feet) high and equally wide. Good hedge. Introduced in 1996.

- **'Sharifa Asma':** David Austin English rose. Elegant, cup-shaped blossoms form a perfect rosette of delicate blush pink. Repeats blooming. Strong fragrance. Compact bush reaches about 0.9 metres (3 feet) high. Introduced in 1989.

- **'Sparrieshoop':** A beautiful and popular rose. Fragrant blooms with five to seven petals open into a saucer shape, showing golden stamens. Blooms in clusters in spring and fall. Upright, tall, very vigorous bush with green, leathery leaves. Grows about 1.8 to 2.5 metres (6 to 8 feet) high. Makes a fine hedge. Disease resistant and reasonably winter hardy. Introduced in 1953.

- **'The Reeve':** David Austin English rose. Peony-style blooms with more than 50 petals are a dark, deep pink. Repeat bloomer. Powerful perfume. Arching, spreading plant reaching at least 1.2 metres (4 feet) high. Small, dark foliage — red turning to green. Introduced in 1979.

Orange shrubs

Four to choose from, and all are great, especially the one with the musical name:

- **'Alchymist':** Yellow blooms sometimes shade to orange or red. Large, with many petals and a nice fragrance. Vigorous, upright plant grows to about 1.8 metres (6 feet) high. Deep green leaves tinged bronze. Blooms only in spring. Introduced in 1956.

- **'All That Jazz':** AARS winner 1992. Luminous, poppy-orange flowers are highly visible against the dark, super-glossy leaves. Five to ten petals. Light scent. Bush is upright and tall. Almost impervious to disease and winter weather. Introduced in 1991.

- **'Dream Orange':** Mid-orange 10- to 15-centimetre (4- to 6-inch) blossoms with 32 petals cover this shrub all summer. Very disease-resistant foliage is medium full but dark green and glossy. It is grown on its own roots but needs protection in zone 5 and colder. Introduced in 2000.

- ❀ **'Perdita':** David Austin English rose. Blushing, billowy apricot blooms grow in small clusters among glossy green leaves. At least 40 petals. Blooms continually. Bushy, medium-sized plant is about 90 centimetres (36 inches) high. Won the Harry Edland Medal for fragrance from the English Royal National Rose Society. Introduced in 1992.

- ❀ **'Tamora':** David Austin English rose. Small clusters of medium-sized, apricot-yellow, cup-shaped blossoms with over 40 petals. Very fragrant. Small, dark green leaves on a medium-sized, bushy shrub. Introduced in 1992.

Yellow shrubs

Here are the best shrubs with yellow flowers:

- ❀ **'Abraham Darby':** David Austin English rose. Large, fully double blooms come on like gangbusters all summer long. Delicate apricot tones and a rich fragrance create a delicious effect on the bush or in a vase. Tall, moderately bushy, and vigorous, ideal for training on a fence. Shiny foliage. Introduced in 1985.

- ❀ **'Dream Yellow':** Lemon yellow, 15-centimetre (6-inch) blossoms with 32 petals cover this shrub all summer. Citrus tones and fruity fragrance make each bloom special. Disease-resistant foliage is medium full but dark green and glossy. On its own roots but needs protection in zone 5 and colder. Introduced in 2000.

- ❀ **'English Garden':** David Austin English rose. Double, yellow blooms with a pleasing apricot-yellow centre, tightly packed petals, and intense fragrance. Flowers profusely. Repeat bloomer. Upright, bushy plant grows to at least 90 centimetres (36 inches) high. Pale green leaves. Introduced in 1986.

- ❀ **'Golden Wings':** American Rose Society Award of Excellence 1958. Blooms early and remains in flower longer than most roses. Clusters of five-petalled, light yellow blossoms open into a saucer shape, showing bright gold stamens. Slight fragrance. Upright, vigorous bush reaches 1.2 to 1.8 metres (4 to 6 feet) high. Leaves are dull and light green, prone to black spot. Good winter hardiness. Introduced in 1956.

- ❀ **'Graham Thomas':** David Austin English rose. Large, cupped, deep yellow blooms are richly fragrant. The first bloom in late spring is abundant. Subsequent blooms tend to be fewer in number and sit on top of tall stems that in long-season climates reach over 2.4 metres (8 feet). Ruthless pruning helps to keep the flowers lower. Variable disease resistance. Introduced in 1983.

'Maigold': Cup-shaped, bronzy yellow blossoms with intense fragrance. 14 petals. Bushy, upright growth to about 1.5 metres (5 feet) high. Glossy foliage. Blooms only in spring. Introduced in 1953.

'The Pilgrim': David Austin English rose. Pure yellow blossoms with a delicate softness form a flat flower with abundant small petals. Strong fragrance. Repeat blooming. Grows about 1.5 to 1.8 metres (5 to 6 feet) high. Best colours where nights are cool. Introduced in 1991.

'Windrush': David Austin English rose. Light yellow, semi-double blossoms with golden stamens grow abundantly on a strong, bushy plant. Flowers are large and very fragrant. Medium-sized, light green foliage. Repeat bloomer and one of the earliest to bloom in the spring. Vigorous growth to at least 1.5 metres (5 feet) high and equally wide. Introduced in 1985.

White shrubs

Here's an extremely diverse and useful group of white-flowering shrub roses:

'Alba Meidiland': Large clusters of pure white flowers loaded with ruffled petals (over 40). Blooms profusely throughout the summer. The old petals drop off completely, making deadheading unnecessary. Light scent. The dark, glossy foliage makes a vivid contrast against the white flowers. Low, spreading bush, 60 to 90 centimetres (2 to 3 feet) high and twice as wide, is an excellent ground cover. No pruning required. Disease resistant and winter hardy. Introduced in 1987.

'Fair Bianca': David Austin English rose. Combines the perfume of an antique rose with the repeat bloom of a modern rose. Large, cupped, fully double blooms of pure white, satiny petals open into a saucer shape. Extremely fragrant. The foliage on this bushy, upright plant is shiny and bright green; new growth is reddish. One of the better English roses for a small garden, the shrub rarely exceeds 90 centimetres (3 feet) high and remains about as wide. This rose is an excellent addition to any garden viewed at dusk. Introduced in 1982.

'Pearl Meidiland': Small, double flowers begin as soft pink blooms and then fade to a pearly white. They grow profusely and continuously in large clusters. Abundant dark green, glossy foliage covers the low, spreading plant. Grows about 60 to 90 centimetres (2 to 3 feet) high and twice as wide. Disease resistant and winter hardy. Excellent ground cover. Introduced in 1989.

● **'Seafoam':** Carefree, low-spreading shrub. Double, creamy white flowers grow abundantly and continuously. Slight fragrance. The plant is vigorous and covered with small, shiny, dark leaves. Makes a good ground cover when given plenty of room. Disease resistant. Introduced in 1964.

● **'Flower Carpet White':** White-flowering form of 'Flower Carpet'. Free-blooming plant gets by on a minimum of care. Reaches about 60 centimetres (2 feet) high and equally wide. Hardy in zone 6 and disease resistant. Good ground cover or container plant. Introduced in 1996.

● **'White Meidiland':** Heavily petalled, snow-white blossoms grow in abundant clusters on arching, spreading canes. More than 40 petals. Repeat bloomer. Lightly fragrant. Lots of glossy, rich green foliage. Grows about 30 centimetres (1 foot) high and 1.5 metres (5 feet) wide. Can be used as a ground cover. Disease resistant and winter hardy. Performs best in mild climates. Introduced in 1987.

Lavender shrubs

Shakespeare must have loved lavender roses. Why else would so many of his characters congregate here? Unfortunately, they brought their love of mild winters with them and will require protection in zones 6 and colder.

● **'Lavender Dream':** Dainty, lilac-pink flowers are produced continuously in clusters on smooth stems with small, shiny leaves. No fragrance. The plant is mounded and bushy. Arching canes reach over 1.5 metres (5 feet) long and spread even wider. Excellent disease resistance. Introduced in 1984.

● **'Othello':** David Austin English rose. Large, cupped, fully double blooms begin as crimson and then fade to purple. Extremely fragrant. Strong plant grows upright to at least 1.8 to 2.5 metres (6 to 8 feet) high with stiff canes covered with dark green leaves. Repeat bloomer. Introduced in 1986.

● **'Prospero':** David Austin English rose. Dark red to purple flowers with more than 40 petals are large, flat, and very fragrant. Foliage is dark green on an upright plant, 1.2 to 1.5 metres (4 to 5 feet) high. Excellent in mild-winter climates but needs extra protection elsewhere. Introduced in 1983.

● **'The Prince':** David Austin English rose. Velvety, rich, royal purple flowers with a heady perfume. Fully double blooms have a cupped, rosette form. Compact plant reaches about 60 to 90 centimetres (2 to 3 feet) high. Good choice for smaller gardens. Introduced in 1990.

● **'Wise Portia':** David Austin English rose. Heavy-textured blooms display lovely shades of purple and mauve with golden centres. 40 petals. Blooms abundantly. Repeat bloomer. Rich fragrance. Bushy plant, about 1.2 metres (4 feet) high with dark, glossy leaves. Introduced in 1982.

Multicoloured shrubs

Colour preference should guide your choices among this kaleidoscope of shrub roses, but 'Carefree Wonder' is one fine plant.

- **'Carefree Wonder':** AARS 1991. This rose is amazingly carefree. It has superb disease resistance and hardiness. The large flowers are bright pink with a white eye and a creamy reverse. They practically cover the plant all season long. 25 to 30 petals. Light scent. The 1.2- to 1.8-metre (4- to 6-foot) bush has abundant, bright green leaves and grows in an upright, mounding fashion. Performs well everywhere. Introduced in 1990.

- **'Evelyn':** David Austin English rose. Full flowers with an apricot-pink colour open into a rosette form. Over 40 petals. The roses appear in small clusters and are very fragrant. The plant is upright and bushy with glossy green leaves. Introduced in 1991.

- **'Magic Carpet':** Yellow flowers splashed with orange, scarlet, and rose. The semi-double flowers are borne in clusters on long stems. Spicy fragrance. Small, bronze, leathery leaves. Vigorous bush has a climbing or spreading growth style. Grows less than 60 centimetres (2 feet) high and spreads 0.9 to 1.20 metres (3 to 4 feet). Good ground cover if you can find it. Introduced in 1941.

- **'Oranges 'n' Lemons':** Yellow blossoms are splashed with orange stripes so distinct that it seems as if someone painted them on. 30 to 35 petals. Moderate fragrance. New foliage is mahogany red and ages to a deep green. The plant is a vigorous grower with tall, arching canes that are shaped like a fountain. Produces more blooms in cool weather. Introduced in 1995.

- **'Ralph's Creeper':** Dark orange-red flowers with a bright yellow eye and a yellow or white reverse grow in open clusters on a low, spreading bush. Grows about 80 centimetres (2.5 feet) high and 1.5 metres (5 feet) wide. 15 to 18 petals. Moderate scent. Small, dark green foliage. Introduced in 1988.

- **'Rocking Robin':** Lively blend of pink-, red-, and white-striped flowers with 45 to 50 ruffled petals. Mild apple fragrance. Free-blooming, mounding plant. Glossy green foliage. Good disease resistance. Introduced in 1996.

Chapter 14

Species and Old Garden Roses

*I*n this chapter, we describe mostly old roses and a few species. While these roses make up only a fraction of all roses, they are among the easiest and winter-hardiest to grow. If you can't grow some of these, can we suggest knitting as a hobby?

Species roses and old garden roses are sometimes referred to as *antique roses.* They are an incredibly diverse group of plants, with great variety in plant habit, flower form, and fragrance. Some have historical importance; others were useful to hybridizers, who used them as breeding stock to create modern rose varieties. Still others, such as the rugosas, continue to be bred today to create better new hybrids.

Species and old garden roses enjoy great popularity for many reasons, including the following:

✔ They have a rugged toughness — at least many of them do.

✔ Their flowers are singularly beautiful.

✔ Their fragrance is intense.

✔ They maintain a certain wildness, which sets them apart from the more well-behaved modern roses.

With these great qualities come some caveats, however. You may also encounter the following troubles with your species and old garden roses:

 ✔ Some varieties can be very vigorous plants that literally take over a small garden.

 ✔ Some varieties are shy bloomers.

 ✔ Most varieties bloom only once a season.

 ✔ Some varieties are extremely disease prone.

Choose your species and old garden roses with care, especially if you're just getting into roses. And that's what this chapter is all about — selecting old roses that give you that wonderful antique quality without turning into garden monsters.

What Cabbage Has to Do with Roses

Many old garden roses are a historical botanist's dream, with mixed origins and seemingly untraceable heritages. For the rest of us, their backgrounds and parentage can be very confusing. Suffice it to say that early rose growers loved to create new roses by crossing everything they could get their hands on. The results, although often bewildering, brought about the lovely modern roses that are grown today.

The following sections list the main types of old garden roses. We describe our favourite varieties of each type, grouped by flower colour, later in this chapter.

Alba roses

These roses are thought to be hybrids between *Rosa damascena* and a white-flowering form of the dog rose, *Rosa canina*. Though once popular in Europe, few varieties are widely available today. Flowers are generally white to pink and very fragrant, blooming primarily in spring. Plants are upright to about 1.8 metres (6 feet) and are generally very hardy. These roses are also candidates for gardens with a bit too much shade for modern roses. As a rule, most are hardy into zone 4.

Bourbon roses

Bourbons originated on the island known as L' Isle Bourbon (now Reunion) in the Indian Ocean. They are generally vigorous plants with a compact, shrubby, or slightly climbing habit. Bourbons are useful as hedges. The blooms are pink to red, cupped, and nicely fragrant. Hardiness is quite variable within this class; they are best purchased from a catalogue or nursery that can identify which are hardy. Unfortunately, most of them are very susceptible to black spot.

'Pink Peace': hybrid tea
A granddaughter of 'Peace', this hybrid
tea produces large individual blossoms.

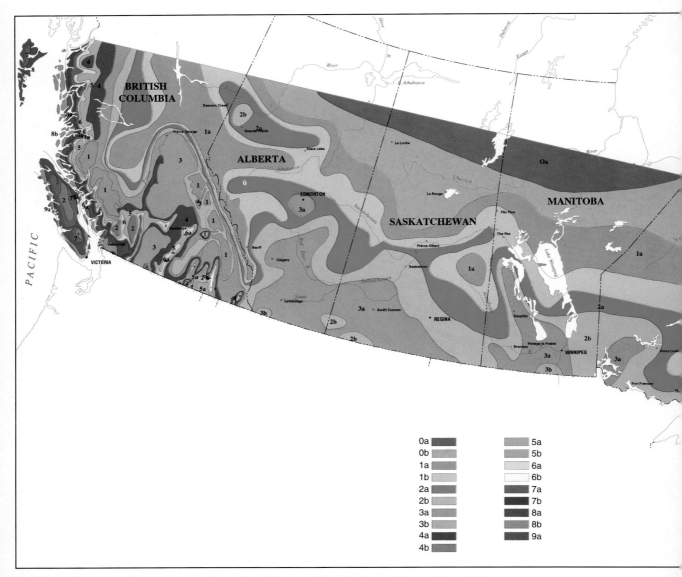

0a	5a
0b	5b
1a	6a
1b	6b
2a	7a
2b	7b
3a	8a
3b	8b
4a	9a
4b	

Reproduced from Agriculture & Agri-Food Canada Publication "Plant Hardiness Zones of Canada"
Reproduced with the permission of the Minister of Public Works and Government Services Canada 1999.
This map is available online at `http://res.agr.ca/CANSIS/SYSTEMS/online_maps.html`

Hardiness areas are divided into 10 zones in the most populated areas of Canada; 0 is the coldest and 9 the mildest. Most zones are divided into dark ("a") and light ("b") sections to represent colder and milder portions.

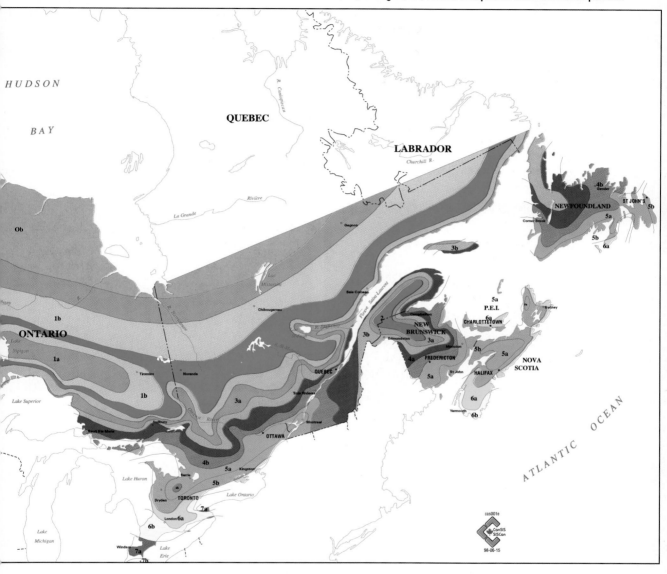

'Dream Red': shrub
Produces constant summer blooms on disease-resistant foliage—no fragrance, though.

'John Cabot': Explorer
One of the hardiest and best climbing Explorer roses.

'Blaze Improved': climber
Clusters of large pure red blossoms make this a very popular climbing rose.

'Champlain': Explorer
A low-growing ever-blooming bush that can easily be in anyone's garden.

'Dublin Bay': climber
An ever-blooming, bright red climber for a protected space.

'Morden Cardinette': Parkland
A hardy, short shrub rose that you cannot kill—we hope!

'Europeana': floribunda
This crimson beauty is an excellent choice to grow in containers.

'Showbiz': floribunda
One of the heaviest-blooming
red floribundas.

Top left, **'Thérèse Bugnet'**: old garden. Extremely hardy and deliciously fragrant—bred in Canada, for Canada.

Centre left, **'Mary Rose'**: shrub. Some say this is the most fragrant Austin rose.

Below left, **'Captain Samuel Holland'**: Explorer. This climbing, hardy Explorer blooms all summer in the full sun.

Top right, **'Konigin von Danemark'**: old garden. Slightly tender but with a fragrance to die for.

Below right, **'Dream Pink'**: shrub. Growing on their own roots, these disease-resistant, very fragrant blooms are the gardener's ideal.

'Morden Amorette':
Parkland
A short, pink rose,
extremely hardy in
any garden.

Rosa gallica officinalis: species
Known as the medieval apothecary's rose, this fragrant
flower has many uses from potpourri to preserves.

Above, **'The Fairy':** polyantha
This heavy-blooming rose is perfect
in containers.

Right, **'William Baffin':** Explorer
The rose is as tough as its
namesake and creates a stunning
archway at Toronto's Casa Loma.

'Dee Bennett': miniature
Colourful blossoms have a light
fruity fragrance.

'Dream Orange': shrub
Another stellar example in the Dream series.

'Livin' Easy': floribunda
A winner in containers; grow with anything blue.

'Brass Band': floribunda
An All-America Rose Selections winner—grow it for the fragrance!

Left, **'Rise 'n' Shine':** miniature
Disease-resistant, as hardy as they come, and one of the best bloomers.

Above, **'Graham Thomas':** shrub
The most popular Austin rose and deservedly so.

Above, **'Sutter's Gold':** hybrid tea
Large, award-winning, fragrant flowers—need we say more?

Left, **'Golden Showers':** climber
A delicate rose, but worth the effort.

'Roberta Bondar': climber
A Canadian-bred rose that deserves a place in your garden.

Rosa hugonis: species
Single blooms cover this shrub.

Rosa harisonii: species
Antique, super-hardy shrub rose with a short bloom time. Grow it anyway.

'Iceberg': floribunda
Simply the best white
floribunda in the world.

'Simplex': miniature
Cool weather turns this
blossom pink. Good disease
resistance and hardiness.

'Madame Hardy': old garden
White, heavy-blooming, and
fragrant to boot.

'Seafoam': shrub
Makes a wonderful hedge and is impervious to all but arctic cold.

'Fair Bianca': shrub
Snow white with deep fragrance and good re-blooming ability.

'Snow Bride': miniature
Pretty, well-formed blossoms adorn this mild-scented rose.

Above, **'Peace':** hybrid tea
Simply the most popular rose in the world.

Above left, **'Brigadoon':** hybrid tea
This rose offers good hardiness, disease resistance, and a light fragrance.

Left, **'Double Delight':** hybrid tea
A charming All-America Rose Selections winner.

'Carefree Wonder': shrub
This pink and white bi-colour lives up to its name.

'Dreamglo': miniature
A very heavy bloomer with good disease resistance and winter hardiness. Gorgeous in any garden.

'Rio Samba': hybrid tea
Its vivid colours make this rose a standout in any garden.

'Dortmund': climber
A bi-coloured single
bloom to win your heart.

Above left, **'Flower Carpet White'**
Every member of the family will enjoy container roses when they're done like this.

Above right, **'New Dawn':** hybrid tea
One of the hardiest of climbing tea roses.

Left, **'Dream Orange'**
Combining other plants with your roses can make a dynamic colour contrast in your garden.

'Dream Yellow'
Combined blues and purples with fragrant yellow roses make a vivid exciting mix.

'Flower Carpet Pink'
If roses are your favourite flower, put them everywhere.

Cabbage roses

Cabbage roses (see Figure 14-1) are varieties of *Rosa centifolia*, which have flowers with very thin, overlapping petals, making them look somewhat like a head of cabbage. The flowers have a spicy fragrance. The plants bloom once in spring in pink to purple shades. Their growing habit varies from shrub-like to spreading. Most are hardy to –26° C (–15° F) without protection.

Figure 14-1:
A cabbage
rose.

China roses

China roses have contributed many of their good characteristics, including a long season of bloom, disease resistance, and a compact habit, to various modern roses. The variety 'Minima', with its dainty leaves and small flowers, is the forerunner of modern miniature roses. Chinas are excellent in pots and as edgings. However, *they lack hardiness* and are tough to grow without a lot of winter protection. Leave these to those who are compulsive about winter protection for roses.

Damask roses

These roses date all the way back to early Greek civilization. Their clustered flowers are intensely fragrant and come in shades of white, pink, and red. The plants are very hardy and don't need winter protection until temperatures drop below –29° C (–20° F). They have thorny stems and are usually not good repeat bloomers.

Gallica roses

Various forms of *Rosa gallica* have been grown for centuries, and some have interesting histories (see the description of *Rosa gallica officinalis* later in this chapter). The red, pink, or purple flowers are intensely fragrant, have showy yellow stamens, and are followed by bright red hips. The foliage turns red in the fall. Plants are stiffly upright but have a neat, shrub-like habit. Gallica roses are candidates for growing in a bit of shade. They are very hardy to at least −29° C (−20° F).

Hybrid musks

Another group with a confusing background, but most can be traced to the musk rose, *Rosa moschata*. The flowers have that strong, musky fragrance that most people call *old rose fragrance*. Most hybrid musks are vigorous, spreading plants that are best treated as climbers, but some are shrubbier. They bloom most heavily in spring and fall. Most varieties bloom in shades of pink, and many produce bright orange hips. Hybrid musks tolerate more shade than many other roses and need winter protection where temperatures drop below −26° C (−15° F).

Hybrid perpetuals

The heritage of these roses is pretty confusing. Hybrid perpetuals were popular in the 19th century prior to the development of the hybrid tea. The fragrant flowers come in shades of pink, purple, red, and sometimes white. They're great in bouquets. The best bloom is in spring, but you often get some flowers throughout the summer. Plants are vigorous with arching canes and are slightly more winter hardy than hybrid tea roses. Protect in zone 6 and colder.

Moss roses

In their true form, moss roses (see Figure 14-2) are naturally occurring mutations — called *sports* — of *Rosa centifolia* and damask roses. They get their name from the small hairs on their stems and bottoms of their flowers. (However, now almost any rose that has mossy hairs is called a moss rose.) The flowers are double, come in shades of white, pink, and red, and are very fragrant. Early moss roses bloom only in spring, but newer hybrids are good repeat bloomers. Hardiness varies and winter protection is recommended from zone 6 and colder.

Figure 14-2:
A moss rose.

Portland roses

These roses have a mixed heritage, with traces of China, damask, and gallica roses in their background. Although few are grown today, they were once loved for their repeat bloom and very fragrant, multipetalled flowers, usually in shades of pink. These are quite variable in hardiness. As a sub-group of the damask rose, you'll often find them listed with the damasks in catalogues.

What's all the noisette about?

Noisettes are historically important old garden roses, having contributed orange and yellow shades to many modern climbing roses. The plants usually are best treated as climbers supported by a trellis or fence. Noisette rose flowers are fragrant and come in shades of white, cream, yellow, orange, and sometimes red. *They are not hardy plants* and suffer damage when temperatures fall below freezing. The canes have a tendency to not harden off quickly enough; this leads to extensive winter injury in most years. Try them only if you live in the warmer parts of Southern Ontario or British Columbia.

Rugosa roses

Rugosas (derived from *Rosa rugosa*) and their many hybrids are tough, extremely useful shrub roses valued for their spicy scent, attractive crinkled foliage, disease resistance, and hardiness. They are among the hardiest roses, able to withstand temperatures down to –37° C (–35° F) with little protection. Actually, some of the newer hybrids can be, and often are, included in the category of modern shrub roses. They are compact plants, 1.2 to 2.5 metres (4 to 8 feet) high, and bloom in spring and fall in shades of white, pink, red, purple, and yellow. Many varieties produce colourful hips. (See Figure 14-3.)

Figure 14-3:
A rugosa
rose.

Scotch roses

Scotch roses are attractive shrubs with white, pink, or yellow, mostly single blooms. Many varieties have handsome, finely cut, or crinkled foliage and colourful hips. These plants may require winter protection in zones 6 or colder. Some are hardier than others, so check your local supplier for hardiness recommendations.

Species roses

Various species of rose (a *species* is a plant that, when crossed with itself, produces seedlings that are identical to themselves and to each other) are native from the North Pole to the Equator. They are a diverse group of plants that have contributed many valuable characteristics to modern roses.

Making a difference

To make the distinction between species roses and old garden roses clear (or at least somewhat more so): A species rose is a rose just as nature made it. You can still find many of them growing naturally in various parts of the world. Species roses have a specific botanical name, such as *Rosa rugosa*.

Exactly what makes an old garden rose an old garden rose is less specific. Usually, these are simply roses that were popular prior to the 20th century.

If you crossed a species rose with itself, the roses that grew from the seed would be identical, or nearly so, to the parents and to each other. Old garden roses are most often descended from a mixed background of natural or man-made hybrids, and if you planted their seeds, the resulting plants would be distinctly different from each other and from the parents.

Tea roses

The original tea rose was a cross between a China rose and *Rosa gigantea*. Remnants of its free-blooming character and shapely flower buds can be found in many modern hybrid teas. Fragrant flowers come in shades of creamy white, pink, and yellow. The bushy plants are best adapted to milder climates, where winter temperatures stay mostly above –9° C (15° F), because they lack hardiness. This lets out most of Canada. On the bright side, if you can grow them (with protection) they do have good disease resistance. (See Figure 14-4.) Note that these are not *hybrid* tea roses.

Figure 14-4:
A tea rose.

Antiques in the Garden

The size and habit of species and old garden roses dictate how you can use them in the landscape. Vigorous types, like the Portlands, can be trained to a fence or arbour like a climbing rose, or they can be left to sprawl over a slope as a ground cover. Shrubbier ones like the rugosas make excellent hedges or can be mixed in with perennial borders. (See *Perennials For Dummies*, published by IDG Books Worldwide, for more information about creating perennial borders.) Even though many bloom only once in spring, they often make up for it by producing colourful hips that last long into winter. Others, like the rugosas and some of the Scotch roses, have attractive foliage that looks good throughout the growing season.

Most antique roses have very interesting flowers. In fact, in many parts of this book, you'll see modern roses, such as the David Austin English roses, described as having "old rose character." The phrase is not very precise, but it usually means that the flower is flat-topped, rounded, and rather cup-shaped, with many petals. That's quite a bit different from the high, pointed, urn-shaped buds and swirling petals of the classic hybrid tea, to which roses are usually compared.

If you like cut flowers, antique roses are tops. Although most don't have the strong, straight stems of modern hybrid teas, their beautiful flower form makes for a unique bouquet. And, oh, the fragrance. It doesn't get any more alluring.

Just remember one thing about many species and old garden roses: They usually grow on their own roots and, as such, often spread like crazy, forming dense thickets. Make sure that you plant these roses where they have plenty of room to grow. If you have any doubts, contact one of the mail-order catalogues that specialize in species and old garden roses, such as Pickering Nurseries, and ask a few questions. (You can find addresses and phone numbers for various suppliers in Appendix B.)

Carefree Antiques

Many species and old garden roses need less care than modern roses do. In fact, many seem to thrive on neglect. However, where summers are dry, regular watering is necessary to keep the plants healthy. And almost anywhere, applying fertilizer regularly keeps the plants growing vigorously.

Prune your plants to keep them within bounds and remove dead branches. Otherwise, less pruning is probably better than more. Roses that bloom just once in spring should be pruned after they bloom. If you prune in winter or late spring prior to blooming, you remove branches that would otherwise produce flowers. Just to confuse the issue, renovation pruning, pruning that restores an old plant, is best undertaken when the plant is dormant so the branches you want to remove are not obscured by leaves. This is for two reasons: The first is that if you can see the plant structure, you can see the dead or rubbing canes to remove them. The second is that you won't get stuck so often by the thorns because no leaves are hiding them.

For more information about caring for species and old garden roses, refer to Part IV of this book.

Few nurseries and garden centres carry a wide selection of species and old garden roses. For the best selection, you have to order plants from one of the catalogues that specialize in antique roses. Several catalogues are listed in Appendix B, including Hortico Nurseries. Even if you don't buy anything, these catalogues make for fun reading.

Roses with Colourful Heritage

The following sections list some of our favourite species and old garden roses by colour.

Red roses

Here are some of the best species and old garden roses with red flowers. Go for the ones with strong fragrance.

- **'Fellenberg':** Noisette. Bright crimson flowers with 35 petals in a cupped form. The bush grows vigorously and tends to spread. Grows 0.9 to 1.5 metres (3 to 5 feet) high. Introduced in 1835.

- **'F. J. Grootendorst':** Hybrid rugosa. Small, red, semi-double flowers resembling carnations grow continuously on mounded shrubs that are 1.2 to 1.5 metres (4 to 5 feet) tall and wide. Slight fragrance. 25 petals. The foliage is bright green and crinkled. Disease resistant, but may develop some black spot by the end of the season. Winter hardy. Introduced in 1918.

- **'Henry Nevard':** Hybrid perpetual. A rugged, hardy bush that produces loads of dark red, aromatic flowers all season. Reaching 1.2 to 1.5 metres (4 to 5 feet) tall, the bush has dark, glossy leaves. 30 petals. Disease resistant. Introduced in 1924.

- **'Hugh Dickson':** Hybrid perpetual. Fragrant, deep crimson, double blossoms are always in bloom until hard frost on this easy-to-grow bush. The plant reaches 1.5 to 1.8 metres (5 to 6 feet) tall and is disease resistant. Introduced in 1905.

‧ **'Linda Campbell':** Hybrid rugosa. Large clusters of deep red, semi-double flowers with contrasting yellow stamens are borne on arching stems that are 1.8 to 2.5 metres (6 to 8 feet) tall. 25 petals. Good repeat bloomer. Foliage is a lovely, textured grey-green. Grows best in heat. Can develop mildew in coastal conditions. Introduced in 1991.

‧ **'Rose du Roi':** Portland. 100 rich, velvet-red petals make for a regal flower. Add the intense fragrance and continuous bloom, and you have a prince of rosedom. The bush is compact and upright with glossy green leaves. Disease resistant. Introduced in 1815.

‧ *Rosa gallica officinalis*: Gallica. This flower is the Red Rose of Lancaster, used as the badge of the Lancasters during the century-long Wars of the Roses in England. The plant has been in cultivation since before 1300. Also known as the apothecary's rose. Used in fine potpourris, preserves, syrups, and powders. We agonized whether to put it under pink roses (the blossom is pretty pinkish) or red (it is after all the Red Rose of Lancaster) but we decided to go with tradition and call it a red rose.

The intensely fragrant flowers are light crimson and have one annual flowering in late spring. 12 to 18 petals. The bush grows 0.9 to 1.2 metres (3 to 4 feet) tall with green, rough foliage. Has a tendency to sport. (*Sports* are shoots that mutate naturally and produce a different rose — so the same bush may have one or more variations.) Disease resistant and winter hardy.

Pink roses

You'll find more pink species and old garden roses than any other colour. If you can't make up your mind, choose by plant habit, capability to repeat bloom, or fragrance.

‧ **'Alfred de Dalmas':** Hybrid moss. Also known as 'Mousseline' because the petals resemble a delicate French muslin. Light blush pink, cupped blooms fade to white. 55 to 65 petals. Blooms repeatedly in clusters. Strong perfume. Compact, spreading bush is 60 to 90 centimetres (2 to 3 feet) tall. Sparse, brownish moss on stems. Disease resistant. Introduced in 1855.

‧ **'Autumn Damask':** Damask. Medium pink, double flowers with rich fragrance bloom in clusters in the spring and then again in autumn. The plant is compact enough to be grown in a container at 0.9 to 1.5 metres (3 to 5 feet) tall and 0.6 to 1.2 metres (2 to 4 feet) wide. Foliage is dull green and rough. Winter hardy. Also known as the Rose of Castille, autumn damasks grow nearly wild in New Mexico and California, where Spanish missionaries first transplanted it. Introduced in the 1600s.

'**Ballerina':** Hybrid musk. Perpetually blooming clusters are covered with masses of small, pale pink flowers with white centres. Five petals. Fragrant. The compact, arching bush with thick foliage achieves the effect of a ballerina's skirt. Gets tiny orange-red hips in the fall. Tolerates filtered light. Grows 1.2 to 1.5 metres (4 to 5 feet) wide and about as tall. Can be trained as a low climber. Disease resistant. Hardy to –23° C (–10° F). Introduced in 1937.

'**Baroness Rothschild':** Hybrid perpetual. Cupped, fragrant blossoms with pale pink outside petals offset by deep pink inside petals bloom profusely in spring and then again in autumn. 40 petals. Usually one flower per stem with lots of foliage surrounding the blossom. Long-lasting bouquets of cut flowers. The plant grows in an upright, bushy manner with light green leaves. Grows 1.2 to 1.8 metres (4 to 6 feet) tall. Introduced in 1868.

'**Baronne Prévost':** Hybrid perpetual. Candy-pink blooms with a silvery reverse flower continually until frost. Classic old-rose shape, big, flat, open flowers with many tightly packed petals — about 100 of them. Rich perfume. Tall, erect plant is 1.2 to 1.8 metres (4 to 6 feet) tall and bushy. Disease resistant. Introduced in 1842.

'**Belle Poitevine':** Rugosa. Lilac-pink flowers with pleated petals bloom continuously on a 1.2- to 1.8-metre (4- to 6-foot) shrub. Extremely fragrant. Lush, dark, textured leaves. Gets large red hips in fall. Winter hardy and disease resistant. Does not need yearly pruning. Introduced in 1894.

'**Celsiana':** Damask. Pale pink, semi-double flowers with 12 to 15 crinkled petals. Nice fragrance. Grey-green foliage on a vigorous, upright plant that reaches about 1.2 to 1.5 metres (4 to 5 feet) high. Introduced prior to 1750.

'**Empress Josephine':** Gallica. Empress Josephine's gardener grew this rose in the Empress's palace gardens and named the flower after her. Luminous pink with deeper pink tones toward the centre, the ruffled blooms have a papery quality. 24 to 30 petals. Slight fragrance. Upright, compact bush is 0.9 to 1.2 metres (3 to 4 feet) tall with narrow, grey-green leaves. Winter hardy and disease resistant. One annual bloom. Known to be in existence as early as 1583.

'**Fantin-Latour':** Cabbage. Loads of petals (maybe 200) range from pale to deep pink. One profuse annual flowering. Intense fragrance. Upright, vigorous bush is 1.8 m (6 feet) tall with smooth, light green leaves. Disease resistant and reasonably winter hardy — protect in zones 5 and colder. Exact date of introduction unknown, but around 1850.

'**Felicia':** Hybrid musk. Large clusters of pink, double flowers grow repeatedly on long, arching canes. Very fragrant. Tolerates filtered light well. The plant is 1.5 metres (5 feet) tall with glossy green foliage. Hardy to –23° C (–10° F). Introduced in 1928.

'Grootendorst Pink': Rugosa. Small, rose-pink, continuously blooming flowers with lightly toothed or serrated petals that resemble carnations. 25 petals. Slight fragrance. Mounded shrubs grow 1.2 to 1.5 metres (4 to 5 feet) tall and wide. The foliage is bright green and crinkled. Disease resistant and winter hardy. Introduced in 1923.

'Ispahan': Damask. Also known as 'Pompon des Princes'. Bright pink, double flowers with an intense fragrance. Blooms over a long period. Small green leaves. Grows about 1.2 metres (4 feet) high and equally as wide. Can be trained as a climber. Introduced prior to 1830.

'Jacques Cartier': Portland. Also known as 'Marquise Bocella'. Blooms continuously — clear pink flowers with hundreds of petals resemble powder puffs. Richly fragrant. Compact, upright plant with closely spaced, light green leaves. Reaches 1.2 metres (4 feet) tall. Introduced in 1842.

'Königin von Dänemark': Alba. Clear pink flowers with up to 200 petals have a deeper pink centre that resembles a button. One annual flowering. This extremely weather-tolerant rose has an intense perfume. Upright bush forms a mounded shrub that is 1.2 to 1.5 metres (4 to 5 feet) tall with blue-green foliage. Large scarlet hips. Very disease resistant and hardy. Introduced in 1826.

'Louise Odier': Bourbon. Deep pink, cupped flowers are very full and fragrant. 35 to 45 petals. The bush is slender and 1.2 to 1.8 metres (4 to 6 feet) tall with light green foliage. Keeps well as a cut flower. Blooms from spring to fall. Disease resistant and one of hardiest Bourbon roses. Introduced in 1851.

'Madame Ernest Calvat': Bourbon. Light pink petals twirl and swirl, creating a petticoat effect. The flowers are large, cupped, and intensely fragrant. Blooms lavishly in late spring and again in autumn. Upright, bushy plant grows 1.5 to 2 metres (5 to 7 feet) tall and has dark, glossy leaves. Susceptible to black spot. Will be damaged by temperatures below –23° C (–10° F). Needs protection. Introduced in 1888.

'Madame Isaac Pereire': Bourbon. The parent of 'Madame Ernest Calvat'. The flowers are large, cupped, and intensely fragrant. Blooms lavishly in late spring and again in autumn. Upright, bushy plant grows 1.5 to 2 metres (5 to 7 feet) tall and has dark, glossy leaves. Susceptible to black spot. Similar hardiness to 'Mme Ernest Calvat'. Introduced in 1880.

'Maréchal Davoust': Moss. Deep pink flowers with a lighter pink reverse have 100 petals and are wonderfully fragrant. The plant blooms once in early summer. The upright, vigorous bush is 1.5 metres (5 feet) tall and bears some sparse moss. Disease resistant and one of best winter-hardy Moss roses. Introduced in 1853.

'Marie Louise': Damask. A lovely mauve-pink rose that Josephine grew at Malmaison. The flowers are large with many petals and an intense fragrance. Blooms only once a year, in spring. The plant is full foliaged, reaching about 1.2 metres (4 feet) high. Introduced prior to 1813.

'Paul Neyron': Hybrid perpetual. Tightly packed with petals in various shades of pink, blossoms bloom lavishly in late spring and then again in autumn. 65 to 75 petals. Fragrant. The bush has glossy green leaves and grows to 1.5 to 1.8 metres (5 to 6 feet) tall. Disease resistant and winter hardy. Introduced in 1869.

***Rosa eglanteria*:** Species. Light pink blooms with five petals show off bright yellow stamens in one annual blooming. The flowers and leaves are scented — the flowers having a true rose fragrance, the leaves a fresh apple scent. Clusters of bright red hips appear in fall. Upright, vigorous bush reaches 2.5 to 3 metres (8 to 10 feet). Copious, glossy green foliage. Disease resistant and winter hardy. In cultivation before 1551 and known in Europe as the Sweet Briar Rose. Introduced prior to 1551.

'Sarah Van Fleet': Hybrid rugosa. Extremely fragrant pink blossoms with showy yellow stamens bloom repeatedly all summer. 18 to 24 petals. The 1.8- to 2.5-metre (6- to 8-foot) bush is upright and vigorous with dark green, leathery, patterned leaves. Makes an excellent hedge. Disease resistant and winter hardy. Introduced in 1926.

'Souvenir de la Malmaison': Bourbon. Immense, wonderfully fragrant blooms start out cupped and then open flat. The flowers are the palest of pinks — a cream blush — with rose shading at the centre. 65 to 75 petals. Repeats blooming steadily throughout the season. The bush is compact, 75 centimetres (2.5 feet) tall and wide, with large, leathery leaves. The climbing form reaches 2.5 to 3.6 metres (8 to 12 feet) tall. Does not like wet weather. Hardy to –23° C (–10° F). Moderately disease resistant. Extremely popular rose but difficult to establish in a garden. Introduced in 1843.

'Stanwell Perpetual': Scotch. Light pink, fading to white, blossoms bloom singly on very short stems. 45 to 55 petals. Fragrant. Blooms repeatedly after the plant is well established in the garden. The bush is attractive, vigorous, and spreading, 0.9 to 1.5 metres (3 to 5 feet) tall. Leaves are small and blue-green. Disease resistant and winter hardy. Introduced in 1838.

'Thérèse Bugnet': Hybrid rugosa. Produces abundant large, rose-red, double blossoms that are outstandingly fragrant. Repeat bloomer. 35 to 40 petals. The bush is round and shrubby and covered with quilted grey-blue-green leaves. Exceedingly disease resistant and winter hardy. Recommended for all climates. Does not like chemical sprays. Introduced in 1950.

'Tour de Malakoff': Cabbage. Double flowers with about 55 petals are intensely fragrant. They begin as pink but age to mauve. Bloom occurs only once in a season. The plant is vigorous, sprawling, and 1.8 to 2 metres (6 to 7 feet) tall. Disease resistant and winter hardy. Introduced in 1856.

'Zéphirine Drouhin': Bourbon. You can safely plant this rose along walkways because it is almost thornless. It is also very fragrant and produces peppermint-pink, loosely cupped blossoms all season. 20 to 24 petals. The plant is a climber, 2.4 to 3.6 metres (8 to 12 feet) high in warm climates. Medium green, glossy leaves. Shade-tolerant. Disease resistant but not as hardy as other Bourbons. Will likely need protection if used as a climber in zones 6 and colder. Introduced in 1868.

Yellow roses

The following are the class of the yellow old garden and species roses:

Rosa harisonii: Species. Also known as 'Harison's Yellow Rose'. A tough, hardy, disease resistant, and drought-tolerant shrub. Deep yellow, semi-double flowers are fragrant and bloom in spring. Rich green, fernlike foliage covers the spreading plant, which can grow to 3 metres (10 feet) tall. Can grow in poor conditions, including shade. In cultivation since 1830 and extremely hardy.

Rosa hugonis: Species. Also know as 'Father Hugo Rose'. Produces sprays of pale yellow, single flowers in spring. Five petals. Little or no fragrance. Blooms are borne on arching stems reaching 1.8 to 2.5 metres (6 to 8 feet) high and covered with fernlike, deep-green leaves. Disease resistant and extremely hardy. Introduced in 1899.

'Spring Gold': Scotch. A mid-yellow, semi-double blossom with heavy fragrance makes this a delight in almost any garden. One of the hardier Scotch roses, the 1.8-metre (6-foot) tall canes can be trained as climbers. Unfortunately, it is a non-repeat bloomer but has good disease resistance. Introduced from Germany in 1937.

'Topaz Jewel': Hybrid rugosa. The first re-blooming yellow rugosa rose. The frilly, light yellow blossoms emerge all season in scented clusters on the arching, dense bush. Old flowers drop off cleanly. 25 petals. The 1.5-metre (5-foot) tall and 2-metre (7-foot) wide bush has crinkled leaves. Disease resistant and winter hardy. Introduced in 1987.

Orange you going to tell me about orange roses?

We've only got one orange species rose to mention: *Rosa foetida* 'bicolour'. This rose's orange-red, simple blossoms with five petals bloom early in the season, giving off a heavy fragrance. In cultivation since 1590, the upright plant is irregularly shaped and has rather sparse, dull green leaves. Prone to black spot and not reliably winter hardy. If you have to grow it, protect it in zones 6 or colder.

White roses

Here are some of our favourite white old garden and species roses:

- **'Blanc Double de Courbert':** Hybrid rugosa. Ruffled, snow-white, intensely fragrant blossoms appear early in the season and repeat their performance later. 18 to 24 petals. Spent blooms tend to hang on, looking a little like dirty white socks. The bush is upright and vigorous. 1.2 to 1.8 metres (4 to 6 feet) tall with light green, leathery leaves. Disease resistant and very winter hardy. Introduced in 1892.

- **'Boule de Neige':** Bourbon. The name means "snowball" in French, and that's what these flowers look like when they're in full bloom. Made up of about 100 petals, the outer petals curl inward, giving the flower a big ball effect. Fragrant. Repeat bloomer. The bush is 1.2 to 1.5 metres (4 to 5 feet) tall, upright, and slender with dark, leathery leaves. Disease resistant and winter hardy. Introduced in 1867.

- **'Madame Hardy':** Damask. 'Madame Hardy' is a study in style. Elegant, tight buds open to lush, snow-white flowers with an eye-catching green point in the centre. The blooms occur in clusters, with the centre blossoms opening first. The flowers have probably 200 petals. Richly fragrant. The plant is sturdy and vigorous, covered with grey-green leaves; 1.5 metres (5 feet) tall. Disease resistant and winter hardy. Introduced in 1832.

- **'Madame Plantier':** Alba. Not for a small garden, 'Madame Plantier' is a large, dense, arching bush that you can train as a climber. It sends out clusters of extremely fragrant, pompon-like blooms once, early in the summer. Over 200 petals. The plant grows 1.8 to 2.5 metres (6 to 8 feet) tall with smooth, long, medium green leaves. Disease resistant and winter hardy. Introduced in 1835.

- **'Sir Thomas Lipton':** Rugosa. Double, cupped, white blooms grow abundantly and repeatedly throughout the season on a vigorous, bushy plant. Leathery, dark green foliage. 1.8 to 2.5 metres (6 to 8 feet) tall. Introduced in 1900.

Lavender roses

Of these two lavender antiques, 'Hansa' is the most versatile in the landscape:

- **'Charles de Mills':** Gallica. 'Charles de Mills' has been known to flower in many variations of purple and red: maroon, crimson, grape, wine, and violet. The fully opened, fragrant blossoms have about 200 swirling petals and a flat-topped appearance because the petals are so evenly spaced. Only one bloom occurs, midseason, on the upright, vigorous bush. 1.2 to 1.5 metres (4 to 5 feet) tall and 1.5 metres (5 feet) wide. Rough green leaves. Disease resistant and winter hardy. Origin date is unknown, probably 19th century.

⚜ **'Hansa':** Hybrid rugosa. This tall, arching shrub produces plentiful, intensely fragrant, purple-red blooms in late spring, with good repeat blooms. The flowers have 35 to 45 petals in a loose, cupped form. Large red hips appear in late summer, adding to the interest that this plant can provide in a garden. The shrub grows 1.8 to 2 metres (6 to 7 feet) tall and wide and is covered with green, wrinkled leaves that turn bronze in the fall. Disease resistant and winter hardy. Introduced in 1905.

Multicoloured roses

Here's a kaleidoscope of multicoloured antique roses:

 ⚜ **'Camaieux':** Gallica. Rose-pink-and-white-striped blossoms with 65 petals decorate this compact, rounded bush in the spring. Wonderfully fragrant, the flowers are cupped and camellia-like. The bush grows 90 centimetres (3 feet) tall and wide and is easy to grow. Prone to mildew in warm, humid regions. Winter hardy. Introduced in 1830.

 ⚜ **'Félicité Parmentier':** Alba. Ivory buds, tinged green, open into fluffy, flesh-pink and cream flowers of exceptional fragrance. The flowers arrive in abundance in the spring on a compact, 1.2-metre (4-foot) tall and wide bush with grey-green leaves. Disease resistant but occasionally susceptible to mildew. Grows well in a variety of climates. Winter hardy. Introduced in 1834.

'**Honorine de Brabant**': Bourbon. Pale lilac blossoms striped in crimson and violet grow abundantly in spring and autumn on a large, bushy plant. The flowers are richly fragrant, full, and double. The bush grows to 1.8 metres (6 feet) tall and is covered with medium green foliage. Disease resistant. Will require winter protection in zone 6 or colder. Date of origin not known, probably mid-19th century.

'**Léda**': Damask. Soft, fragrant flowers with 200 petals, white edged in red, bloom once in the summer. The bush is low, 60 to 90 centimetres (2 to 3 feet) tall, and grows in a spreading, trailing fashion. The bush can be trained upright as a climber (see Chapter 5 for more information). Disease resistant and winter hardy. Introduced before 1827.

'**Nymphenburg**': Hybrid musk. A most beautiful and fragrant rose. Flowers of salmon-shaded yellow at the base are borne in clusters all summer. 18 to 24 petals. The bush has large, glossy leaves and grows 1.2 to 2 metres (4 to 7 feet) tall and 1.8 metres (6 feet) wide. Vigorous and disease resistant. Introduced in 1954.

'**Vick's Caprice**': Hybrid perpetual. Reliable, repeat-blooming rose with large, pink- and white-striped flowers. Cupped, fragrant blooms. Bush grows 1.2 metres (4 feet) tall and less wide. Not reliably disease resistant. Introduced in 1891.

'**York and Lancaster**': Damask. For history buffs, this rose is an interesting one — named after rival families in 15th-century England. The emblem of York was the white rose (White Rose of York), the emblem of Lancaster the red rose. The battles between these two for the English throne came to be known as the Wars of the Roses. The wars seem to be still going on in this rosebush — the white and pink petals battle for dominance. Some flowers may be half pink and half white, and others are almost all one colour or the other. The fragrant blossoms have 24 to 30 petals formed in a loose cup shape. They bloom once in the summer on a 0.9- to 1.2-metre (3- to 4-foot) tall bush with rough grey-green leaves. Not vigorous — a slow grower. Disease resistant and winter hardy. Originated in 1551.

Chapter 15

Explorer and Parkland Roses

*I*f you have trouble growing roses, Explorers and Parklands are the plants for you. Grown and bred in Canada for the rigours of our Canadian winters, they're naturally a little tougher than your average rose — we're not living in the tropics, you know.

Breeders working for Agriculture Canada developed the Parkland and Explorer series of roses, and they continue working on the development of the perfect all-Canadian rose. Many wonderful plants in the series have been released to the public and we describe them all here.

What's So Wonderful about Them?

In our recommendations throughout this chapter, we indicate for each rose whether it is an Explorer or a Parkland. We think you should just grow the rose that appeals to you whether it's an Explorer or Parkland — they're all great roses, and here's why:

- **They are extremely hardy:** Most thrive to zone 3 and even zone 2 with a bit of winter protection.

- **All new shoots flower:** Even if old rose canes are killed to the ground by winter cold, the new canes can flower in the first year of their growth.

- **They are disease resistant:** While not immune to problems such as black spot, they are less likely to be killed by infestations.

- **They are heavy bloomers:** Some, such as 'Champlain', bloom all summer while others, such as 'John Cabot', bloom heavily in July with sporadic blooms the rest of the summer.

✔ **They are very versatile:** Explorer roses are available in three types — climbers, bush, and semi-miniatures. They make great hardy climbers, hedges that need little care, or beautiful container roses. A wealth of possibilities arises.

✔ **They grow easily on their own roots:** No rootstock for us hardy Canadians — we'll do it on our own roots. (See Chapter 16 for the advantages of own-root roses.)

If an Explorer is propagated on its own roots, there is no need to plant it deeply. If it is on a rootstock, plant the rootstock so the bud union is 5 to 10 centimetres (2 to 4 inches) deep to protect the graft from winter damage.

Getting Your Hands on Them

Funny thing is, even though they are wonderful roses for the North, most garden centres only stock one or two of the Explorers and Parkland roses each spring. To obtain the newer varieties like 'Marie-Victorin' or those that haven't been adopted by major propagators (who supply the garden centres), you'll have to use specialty catalogues. See the lists in Appendix B.

You'll also find more success obtaining *own-root* roses through the specialty catalogues, such as Corn Hill Nursery, which grow their own roses. (In Chapter 16 we explain why own-root roses are a good thing.) Major propagators find it faster and more economical to bud all their roses on rootstocks. You may have to search a bit if you want to collect all these roses, but sources such as Corn Hill, Pickering Nurseries, and Hortico are good places to start. (Appendix B tells you how to find these sources.)

Really Canadian, eh?

We should tell you that the Parkland roses are mostly named "Morden" something or other, after the Research Station in Morden, Manitoba. While there are a few exceptions to this (don't ask us how or why the government plant breeders choose names), this is the general rule.

The main difference between a Parkland and an Explorer rose is that the Parkland roses used the native species *Rosa arkansana* as the main breeding parent, while the first Explorer roses were based on Rugosa type roses as their parent stock. Climbing Explorer roses have a healthy dose of *Rosa kordesii* in their genetic makeup to give long canes. Through breeding, both *Rosa laxa* and *Rosa spinosissima altaica* pass along their disease resistance to both classes. Repeat-blooming characteristics were found in ever-blooming hybrid shrub and tea roses.

Looking for something specific?

You may have a particular gardening project in mind that requires a good hardy Explorer or Parkland rose. Keep these suggestions in mind:

✔ **For a container** try 'Royal Edward' or 'Morden Cardinette'.

✔ **For a hedge** try 'Jens Munk', or 'Prairie Joy'.

✔ **For fragrance** try 'Louis Jolliet', or 'Cuthbert Grant'.

✔ **For ground cover** try 'Charles Albanel', or 'William Booth'.

Some garden centres are quite good about ordering rose plants for their customers. If you have a favourite nursery, phone them early in the year (the earlier the better — like January or February) and ask them to find the rose you're looking for and bring it in for you. You might pay a premium for this service, but at least you'll get your rose.

A Canadian Mosaic: Explorer and Parkland Roses by Colour

Because they share the same kind of hardiness and Canadian origins, we group the Parkland family with the Explorer series in the following lists of recommendations by colour:

Red roses

Lots of great scarlet numbers to try here — grow any of these for a guaranteed bright spot in your garden:

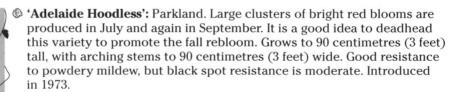

🌼 **'Adelaide Hoodless':** Parkland. Large clusters of bright red blooms are produced in July and again in September. It is a good idea to deadhead this variety to promote the fall rebloom. Grows to 90 centimetres (3 feet) tall, with arching stems to 90 centimetres (3 feet) wide. Good resistance to powdery mildew, but black spot resistance is moderate. Introduced in 1973.

🌼 **'Alexander MacKenzie':** Explorer. A tall, upright, and vigorous shrub reaching 1.5 to 1.8 metres (5 to 6 feet) with a spread of 1.2 to 1.8 metres (4 to 6 feet). Deep red, cup-shaped flowers produced in clusters with a single large flush followed by sporadic reblooming. Will die back in zone 3b without protection and some cane damage in zone 4 is not uncommon. Highly disease resistant. Introduced in 1985.

'Captain Samuel Holland': Explorer. Tall, pillar type of rose that grows up to 1.8 metres (6 feet) tall and 1.2 to 1.8 metres (4 to 6 feet) wide. When grown in full sun, it blooms regularly all summer. Medium red blooms with 23 petals are not fully double, produced in clusters of 1 to 10. Quite hardy in zone 3. Use this rose as a climber. Good resistance to black spot and mildew. Introduced in 1990.

'Champlain': Explorer. Exceptional shrub-type rose that freely blooms all summer long with velvety dark red, slightly fragrant blooms. Grows 0.9 to 1.2 metres (3 to 4 feet) tall and wide. Hardy to zone 3, it will require some deadwood pruning in the spring as the canes do suffer winter injury. Good resistance to mildew and moderate resistance to black spot. Introduced in 1982

'Charles Albanel': Explorer. This is our ground cover rose as it only rarely reaches more than 30 centimetres (1 foot) in height but spreads out to 90 centimetres (3 feet) in width. Repeat and free blooming all summer long with fragrant, medium red blooms. 20 petals to each blossom. Good hip development for fall display. Fully hardy into zone 2, this is one tough rose. Highly disease resistant. Introduced in1982.

'Cuthbert Grant': Parkland. An upright growing shrub with dark red, velvety flowers. Chosen as Manitoba's Centennial Rose in 1970. Strongly fragrant, the semi-double crimson blooms develop in June and again in September. Excellent disease resistance. No difficulty surviving in zone 3. Introduced in 1967.

'David Thompson': Explorer. This shrub flowers freely all summer with fragrant, 25-petalled medium red flowers. A medium-sized shrub 1.5 metres (5 feet) tall and 1.2 metres (4 feet) wide. Highly disease resistant. Quite hardy, with only minimal damage into zone 2. Introduced in 1979.

'George Vancouver': Explorer. Continuous bloom from July through September with medium red blooms that fade to pink. Flowers average 5 centimetres (2 inches) across in clusters of 1 to 6. An upright form, 90 centimetres (3 feet) tall and wide. It resembles 'Champlain' but is hardier and more resistant to mildew. Hardy right into zone 3 with minimal damage. Introduced in 1994.

'Henry Kelsey': Explorer. Flowers are medium red with a spicy fragrance. Petal count is 25 and flowers appear in clusters of 9 to 18 flowers. Upright, excellent climbing rose with 1.8- to 2.5-metre (6- to 8-foot) tall canes. Medium resistance to powdery mildew and slightly less to black spot. Hardy into zone 3. Introduced in 1984.

'Hope for Humanity': Parkland. This ever-blooming rose has a good, double blood-red blossom. Blooms appear from July through to September with two to five blooms per cluster. 60 to 90 centimetres (2 to 3 feet) in height. Disease resistance is good for powdery mildew and fair for black spot. Hardy into zone 3a. Named in honour of the 100th anniversary of the Canadian Red Cross. Introduced in 1995.

🌼 **'John Cabot':** Explorer. Heavy bloomer in July with fragrant, medium red, 40-petalled blossoms. Sporadic bloomer for the rest of summer. Strong, arching canes can easily reach 2.5 to 3 metres (8 to 10 feet) in full sun and fertile soil. Good disease resistance. Hardy into zone 3, it requires the removal of deadwood in most years in zone 4 and colder. Introduced in 1978.

🌼 **'John Franklin':** Explorer. Flowers freely all summer with medium red, slightly fragrant blooms. 25 petals to a blossom and these can grow together to upwards of 30 blossoms per spectacular cluster. Vigorous shrub that reaches up to 1.5 metres (5 feet) tall. Moderate disease resistance. Hardy into zone 3, it will require winter damage cleanup in zone 5. Introduced in 1980.

🌼 **'Morden Amorette':** Parkland. The carmine red (fading to rose) blossoms with 25 to 30 petals are unique in that the inside petals roll inward, covering the flower centre. If you deadhead the blossoms they tend to set more blooms. Ignore them and the flower production slows down. A compact rose shrub growing to only 60 centimetres (2 feet) tall and wide. Moderate disease resistance. Good hardiness into zone 3. Introduced in 1977.

🌼 **'Morden Cardinette':** Parkland. Blooms all summer with cardinal red, double blossoms. 25 petals per flower in clusters of 2 to 8 per stem. A compact, dwarf-type grower of only 45 to 60 centimetres (1.5 to 2 feet) tall. Excellent for container growing. Moderate disease resistance. Hardy right into zone 3b. Introduced in 1980.

🌼 **'Morden Fireglow':** Parkland. Scarlet red flowers are very dramatic. 28 petals in clusters of 1 to 5 with an explosion of late June blooms and then fewer ongoing blooms. Upright shrub to 90 centimetres (3 feet) tall and wide. Moderate disease resistance. Hardy to zone 2b. Introduced in 1989.

🌼 **'Morden Ruby':** Parkland. A repeat bloomer with double ruby red blooms. Excellent cut flower as the blossoms last for a long time. Upright shrub to 90 centimetres (3 feet) tall and wide. Moderate to good disease resistance. Hardy right into zone 2. Introduced in 1977.

🌼 **'Nicolas':** Explorer. A heavy bloomer, it produces medium red flowers all season long. Flowers have 18 to 20 petals in clusters of 1 to 3. A shrubby rose that grows to 60 centimetres (2 feet) tall, this is an excellent choice for large containers. Disease resistant. Hardy right into zone 3, but may show some winter injury in bad years. Introduced in 1996.

🌼 **'Quadra':** Explorer. Climber type deep red blooms are excellent with a main flush in June and sporadic blooming afterwards. Blossoms have 66 petals each in clusters of 1 to 4. Canes reach 1.8 to 2.5 metres (6 to 8 feet) in height and spread 90 centimetres (3 feet). Highly disease resistant. Hardy into zone 3 with only slight tip dieback over winter. Introduced in 1994.

◉ **'William Baffin':** Explorer. Climbing type. Flowers repeatedly with a medium red blossom. 20 petals in clusters of up to 30 flowers. Canes reach to 2.8 metres (9 feet). Highly disease resistant. Very hardy — right into zone 2a — with little winter injury. Introduced in 1983.

◉ **'William Booth':** Explorer. Flowers consistently all summer with a deep red unopened bud, medium red opened flower and light red fading bloom. Single flowers have 5 petals and cluster in groups of 8 to 10. Shrub rose with a trailing habit — it reaches 1.2 metres (4 feet) tall and 2.5 to 2.8 metres (8 to 9 feet) wide. Excellent disease resistance. Requires little pruning and is hardy into zone 3. Introduced in 1999.

◉ **'Winnipeg Parks':** Parkland. Slight fragrance to the medium red flowers that are produced all summer. 22 petals in clusters of 1 to 4. Dense shrubby growth to 90 centimetres (3 feet) tall and 60 centimetres (2 feet) wide. Fall foliage is red tinged. Moderate disease resistance. Hardy into zone 2b. Introduced in 1990.

Pink roses

Pure pink delights fill this list:

◉ **'De Montarville':** Explorer. Shrub-type rose is a repeat bloomer with a dark red bud opening to a medium pink when the blossom is fully open. Each blossom has 26 petals and averages about 8 centimetres (3 inches) across in bunches of 1 to 4 on a stem. A shrub-type rose, only 90 centimetres (3 feet) tall and wide. Resistant to powdery mildew but less so to black spot. Little pruning is required. Fully hardy into zone 3. Introduced in 1997.

◉ **'Frontenac':** Explorer. Heavy bloomer with deep pink blooms in June and sporadically thereafter, right through to another flush of flowers in September. Flowers average about 8 centimetres (3 inches) across with 20 petals. Upright growth habit to 0.9 to 1.5 metres (3 to 5 feet) and heavy blooming makes this shrub a desired garden performer. Resistant to powdery mildew and blackspot. Quite hardy right into zone 3. Introduced in 1992.

◉ **'Jens Munk':** Explorer. Fragrant, medium pink blossoms with 25 petals. Heavy flush of bloom in July, sporadic afterwards. Upright shrub 1.5 to 1.8 metres (5 to 6 feet) in height. Canes are heavily thorned. Good red hips in most years. Disease resistant, hardy right down into zone 2. Introduced in1974.

◉ **'John Davis':** Explorer. Flowers freely with medium pink blooms of 40 petals. Up to 17 blooms in each cluster on this showy plant. Upright arching canes grow to 2.5 metres (8 feet) long. Good disease resistance. Hardy into zone 3, with little or no winter damage in zone 4. Introduced in 1986.

If you need a hardy climber...

If you find climbing roses hard to keep alive, you might try one of these Explorer or Parkland roses that make tremendous climbers with a little training:

✔ 'Captain Samuel Holland'

✔ 'Henry Kelsey'

✔ 'John Cabot'

✔ 'John Davis'

✔ 'Louis Jolliet'

✔ 'Marie Victorin'

✔ 'Quadra'

✔ 'William Baffin'

✔ 'William Booth'

See Chapter 12 for more on climbing roses.

'Lambert Closse': Explorer. Flowers most of the summer with medium pink blooms. Buds start out deep pink, flower is mid-pink, and fully opened it fades to soft pink. Over 50 petals in this fully double bloom in clusters of 1 to 3. Shrub form reaching to 90 centimetres (3 feet) tall and wide. Disease resistant. Hardy into zone 3. Introduced in 1995.

'Louis Jolliet': Explorer. Blooms almost continuously from June to September with medium pink blossoms in clusters of 3 to 10. Spicily fragrant, it is well worth growing. Canes reach to 1.5 metres (5 feet) tall. Its rangy growth habit makes it suited for climbing. Disease resistant. Hardy to zone 3 with little winter injury. Introduced in 1990.

'Marie-Victorin': Explorer. Another 1.5-metre (5-foot) climber but with a major flush of bloom in July and sporadic blossoms afterwards. Colour is unusual deep peachy pink with 38 petals in clusters of 1 to 7 blooms. Highly disease resistant. Hardy to zone 3 but will need some spring pruning in some years to control damage. Introduced in 1998.

'Martin Frobisher': Explorer. Flowers are soft pink and fragrant, with 40 petals.1.5- to 1.8-metre (5- to 6-foot) tall canes mark this, the first Explorer introduction, as a tall, well-proportioned shrub spreading to 1.2 metres (4 feet). It flowers with an early summer flush and then produces sporadic blooms for the rest of the summer. Highly resistant to powdery mildew but may sometimes get black spot. Hardy to zone 2, it may experience some winter damage there. Introduced in 1968.

'Morden Blush': Parkland. The flower colour varies depending on temperature: when it is hot, the blooms are blush pink to white and when it is cool, they revert to light pink. Blooms all season long. Very tight flower bud — excellent for cutting. Low-growing shrub to 90 centimetres (3 feet) tall. Moderate disease resistance. Hardy to zone 2b. Introduced in 1988.

- **'Morden Centennial':** Parkland. Blooms are lightly fragrant and medium pink. Heavy flush of blooms in July and then a repeat bloom in the fall. 40 petals and clusters of 1 to 4. Compact shrub grows to 90 centimetres (3 feet) tall. Good resistance to powdery mildew and moderate resistance to black spot. Hardy right into zone 2. In 1996, it won "The Outstanding Cultivar Award" from the Canadian Society for Horticultural Science. Introduced in 1980.

- **'Royal Edward':** Explorer. Flowers repeatedly all summer with a deep pink bud opening to a medium pink blossom that fades to a pale pink. 18-petalled flowers grow in clusters of 1 to 7. Semi-miniature reaches only 60 centimetres (2 feet) tall and wide. Can be used in containers or as a ground cover. Disease resistant. Hardy into zone 3 with only slight winter injury. Introduced in 1995.

- **'Simon Fraser':** Explorer. Blooms continually in full sun with medium pink flowers. First flush is single with 5 petals but secondary flushes are semi-double with 22 petals. A shrub-like bush grows to 60 centimetres (2 feet) tall and wide. Moderate disease resistance. Hardy to zone 3. Introduced in 1992.

A couple of lonely hearts…

These two roses are singular examples of the work of the Agriculture Canada folks — one in white, and one in yellow:

- **'Henry Hudson':** Explorer. Clear white blooms make this rugosa hybrid a winner in the garden. It flowers repeatedly. 90 centimetres (3 feet) tall and wide, with quite thorny canes. Highly disease resistant. Hardy into zone 2. Introduced in 1976.

- **'J.P. Connell':** This is the first yellow to be released by Agriculture Canada. Lemon yellow blossoms fade to a cream yellow upon opening and are either produced singly or in clusters of 3 to 8. Young plants bloom lightly for the first several years; blooms increase with plant maturity. A vigorous bush to 1.5 metres (5 feet) tall and 120 centimetres (4 feet) wide. Good resistance to powdery mildew but susceptible to black spot. Excellent hardiness to zone 3. This release is not part of either the Explorer or Parkland research. Introduced in 1987.

Part IV
Growing Healthy Roses

In this part . . .

We get down and dirty in this part, working with roots, soil, planting, pruning, watering, feeding, and bugs. There's no way you come out of these chapters with clean fingernails. But as messy as it may get, this stuff is important. You need to know what to do and what not to do when planting and caring for roses. Read this part slowly and carefully. You may get dirty, but you'll come out smelling like roses.

Chapter 16

Shopping for Roses

• •

In This Chapter

▶ Revealing where roses come from

▶ Buying bareroot roses

▶ Buying container-grown and packaged roses

▶ Revealing the truth about own-root roses

▶ Rose-buying tips

• •

So this rose deal is starting to sound pretty good to you. Maybe you want to get a couple of plants and give it a try. Good decision, but where are you going to get them? These days you can buy roses almost anywhere, from supermarkets to drugstores, not to mention the usual places like nurseries and garden centres. You can also shop in the convenience of your own home through mail-order catalogues and the Internet. (You can find a list in Appendix B.)

But before you rush out waving your credit card in hand, you need a little background information on how roses are grown and sold.

You can buy roses in three ways: bareroot, potted, or in packages. How you get them depends on where you buy them. Some nurseries and all mail-order sources offer bareroot roses early or late in the season. Many garden centres offer potted rosebushes, and discount stores often sell roses less expensively in special lightweight packaging. How your roses come to you dictates how you plant them, so knowing what you're getting into before you buy is important.

Whose Roots Are These, Anyway?

To really understand how a rose plant gets its start, you need to read Chapter 1, "Everything You Need to Know about Roses," and Chapter 23, "Making More Roses." Basically, most rose plants have two parts: the top part that produces the nice flowers, and the bottom of the plant that produces the roots, called the *rootstock* (see Figure 16-1). They are joined at the *bud union*. During winter, a small bud from the mother plant, say a 'Peace' rose, is slipped into the bark of a rootstock, another type of rose. In a few months, the two fuse together and become one plant.

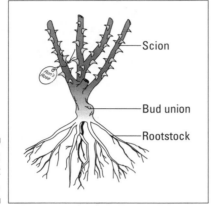

Scion

Bud union

Rootstock

Figure 16-1:
A bareroot
rose plant.

We know why growers want the top of the plant to be 'Peace' — it's a great rose. But why do they need the rootstock? A rootstock can provide a number of advantages that wouldn't exist if a 'Peace' were grown on its own roots, including the following:

- Greater vigour in growing and blooming
- Resistance to certain soil-borne insects and diseases
- Adaptation to certain soil types

Commercial rose growers choose which rootstock to use (they may have 10 or 15 to choose from), but they don't label them on the plant you buy. Roses grown in Canada will use hardier rootstocks than many imported roses but that's really all you need to know about rootstocks.

Some commercial rose growers propagate rose varieties, especially shrub and old garden roses, on their own roots and call them *own-root* roses. These roses are started as rooted cuttings and grown to maturity on their own roots.

The way an own-root rose sprouts *true to type* (meaning that it produces the type of flower you expect it to) is also an advantage when you grow shrub or landscape roses that need to be sheared. This type of pruning often causes the plants to sprout at the base, and if they're on their own roots — you guessed it — the sprouts are the type of rose you want.

Why your own-roots are good choices in Canada

Own-root roses can be an advantage in our Canadian winters. Here's why: Say the weather gets abnormally cold — so cold that the temperature kills the top of your rose plant. The roots are insulated by the soil, so they may live on to resprout next spring. If the rose was budded on a rootstock, the new sprouts might come from the rootstock, but you don't have any idea what variety that is. So instead of 'Peace' flowers, you get who knows what. If, on the other hand, the rose was grown on its own roots, the new sprouts are 'Peace', and you still have the rose you want.

Note that hybrid tea roses on their own roots are not much hardier than budded roses. Most of the advantages of own-root roses belong to the hardier roses, not the more tender types.

Own-root modern shrubs and floribundas are offered in the same venues as budded roses. Unless you inspect it very carefully, you don't know whether a plant is own-root or budded. It really doesn't matter, as long as the plant thrives for you.

Own-root roses have a possible downside, especially when you're dealing with a very vigorous shrub or old garden roses. On their own roots, these plants often spread by *root suckers* — sprouts that come from the roots, as shown in Figure 16-2 — and *spread* is the key word. These sprouts can literally take over a garden, sprouting everywhere you don't want them.

Figure 16-2:
Root suckers that can spread all over a garden are a downside of own-root roses.

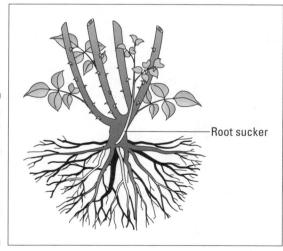

Root sucker

What Are Roots without Soil?

Come winter, when all the roses grown in nursery fields are dormant (resting) and leafless, they're pruned and dug out of the ground without any soil on their roots. These are called — surprise — *bareroot* roses. Removing all the soil from the roots doesn't hurt the plant. As long as the rose plant is dormant and the roots are kept moist, the plant is in great shape. And the plant weighs next to nothing — perfect for shipping.

Next, the bareroot roses are either bundled up, packed, usually in moist sawdust, and shipped off to retail nurseries or stored until the spring shipping season. Sometimes, they're packaged individually, with their roots packed in moist sawdust and enclosed in plastic.

Actually, not all the roses are shipped at the same time. Nurseries try to time their shipments to coincide with spring's arrival. Shipments to British Columbia will be earlier than those to Ontario and the Maritimes.

Back to those bundled roses that go to retail nurseries. Upon arrival, the bareroot roses are unpacked and displayed for sale, sometimes in large bins with their roots packed in — you got it — moist sawdust. Actually, the packing can be any lightweight organic matter that holds moisture, including peat moss or wood shavings. However, most retail nurseries immediately plant these bareroot roses in pots. (See Figure 16-3.) A potted rose is easier to take care of and if they do not sell during the spring rush, they can be more easily maintained for fall sales.

Bareroot roses from a nursery or catalogue company are fine as long as the weather is cold and the plants are dormant, but if it warms up and the plants start growing, you have to plant them — and fast.

Never, ever, allow the roots of roses to dry out. A dry root is a dead root. If you cannot plant your bareroot rose immediately on receipt, put it in a pail of water (for up to 24 hours) but never let it sit outside so the roots are exposed.

Some roses, particularly miniatures and old roses, aren't barerooted. Instead, they spend their entire lives in containers. The vast majority of miniature roses you buy are propagated and grown on their own roots in greenhouses and are offered for sale in leaf or even in bloom. They usually come in 6-centimetre or 10-centimetre (2½-inch or 4-inch) pots, ready for transplanting into a garden or into containers for outdoor or indoor culture. A huge selection of miniature roses is sold this way. Larger mail-order rose companies may send you field-grown bareroot miniatures that arrive looking more like big roses than minis. You should treat them the same way you do other bareroot roses.

Figure 16-3:
Roots of
container
roses grow
in potting
soil. Plant
them any
time of year.

For the most part, roses go from bareroot to you, or they are planted in pots for retail sale. A few wholesale growers even take bareroot roses, plant them in peat pots, and enclose them in plastic for shipping. A *peat pot* is a lightweight pot made of pressed peat or paper fibre. (Don't ask why we don't call them paper fibre pots.) You plant the rose, pot and all, and the peat/paper fibre pot breaks down quickly, allowing the roots to grow out into the surrounding soil.

Going Shopping

You now know — because we just told you — that you can purchase roses in three ways: bareroot, potted, or packaged. Bareroot roses are available during early spring and late fall. You can buy potted roses at retail nurseries or garden centres, or, for greater variety, you can purchase bareroot plants from one of the sources listed in Appendix B.

Buying bareroot has one main advantage. In general, these roses are less expensive than those sold in containers. Obviously, the pot and the soil add to the cost of a container plant. So if you're going to plant a lot of roses, you're better off buying during the dormant season and having the nursery ship these plants to you at the proper time for planting.

Buying roses in containers also has its advantages — the main advantage being that you can get roses in containers almost anytime. But you can also buy growing, even blooming plants. These babies are ready to go in the ground now and give you instant beauty. Wahoo! Instant colour! If you plant in the middle of summer, make sure you don't allow the rose to dry out. (See Chapter 17 for planting and watering directions.)

Getting only the best

Most mail-order nurseries send you top-quality bareroot plants, and the plants arrive in good condition. If they don't, you're entitled to a replacement. But if you're shopping in a nursery or garden centre, you get to examine plants closely before you buy. You want to be able to tell what's really a bargain and what isn't. You need to be able to recognize a plant that's been hanging around too long or has been neglected.

Bareroot roses are graded according to standards set by the Canadian Nursery Trades Association. The grades — #1, #1½, and #2 — are based on the size and number of canes (main branches) on the plant. A #1 is the highest-grade rose and represents a more vigorous, sturdy plant that should grow faster and make more blooms the first year after planting. #1½ and #2 are usually the roses you find on sale and, in many cases, they may be a good deal. However, if you want to get off to the best start, we think that you should pay a little extra for a #1. Most roses have the grade listed on the package.

Other things to look for when buying bareroot roses include the following:

- ✔ Make sure that the packaging and the roots haven't dried out — a sure sign that trouble is ahead.

- ✔ If you can examine the roots, choose a plant that has a moist, well-developed root system. Avoid those with dry, broken, or mushy roots.

- ✔ Look for plants with thick, dark green canes — the more the better. Avoid plants that look dry, brownish, or shrivelled.

Going home a happy rose shopper

So you think you know all about buying roses, with bare roots or with roots in soil, budded or on their own roots? Well, here are a few tips to ensure you make great rose purchases that flourish in your garden.

When buying potted roses, keep these points in mind:

- ✓ The optimal time to buy potted roses is as early in the season as possible when new growth is minimal, or late in the season just after the rose has gone dormant.

- ✓ If you do buy potted roses later in the season before dormancy has set in, choose plants with healthy, deep green foliage that is free of insects and disease. Vigorous new growth — deep red in many varieties — is a good sign.

- ✓ Don't hesitate to purchase roses late in the fall if they are in good shape — disease free and with strong canes. Fall is an excellent time to plant roses. If you plant a potted rose in the fall, water regularly to ensure it does not dry out before the ground freezes.

- ✓ Check the soil in the top of the pot. A pot full of twisting, circling roots may be a sign the plant has been in the pot too long. Skip this plant unless it is a really good deal — it will be slower to establish itself.

- ✓ Flower buds are a good sign. They mean that the plant has been well kept. Choose them over plants that have just finished blooming.

When buying packaged bareroot roses, do the following:

- ✓ Buy early in the season when packaged roses have no foliage. Avoid packaged roses that have foliage — they resent transplanting. Never buy a packaged rose after early spring.

- ✓ Try to buy plants with complete root systems rather than those with pruned, short roots.

- ✓ Never buy any package that has dry soil.

Chapter 17

Planting Roses

Vou're probably ready to get those roses in the ground so that they start growing and, better yet, start blooming! But wait just a minute. First, we need to discuss some timing issues. Also, planting means dealing with dirt — actually, soil in gardeners' parlance. Because that soil will be your rose's home for its entire life, you need to know some things about it before you go rushing outside with your shovel.

The way you plant your roses is the most important step in growing them. Because they may be living in the place you plant them for many years, you really have only one chance to start them off right. You should pay special attention to soil chemistry, the rose hole, and drainage. If you just skim any chapter in this book, don't let it be this one!

If Roses Aren't Sick, Why Do They Need Heeling?

Chapter 16 explains the different ways you can buy roses. So *when* do you buy 'em? After you get started with roses, you'll probably find yourself waiting with anticipation for new rose catalogues to arrive in late fall and winter. You can order mail-order roses just about anytime — in fact, the earlier the better to ensure that suppliers are not sold out of the varieties you want. Mail-order nurseries send the plants when it's time for planting in your area, or they ask you when you want to receive them. Planting these bareroot roses when the forsythias bloom is a good time. Basically, if your springtime garden soil can be walked on without clumping up and sticking to your boots — you can plant roses. The same rules hold true for pre-packaged roses.

Buy potted roses all season long — plant them when the roots are well established in the pot. Having the option of buying a blooming rosebush in a pot in midsummer to fill in an unplanned space or to replace a winter-damaged plant has certainly saved a few gardeners' reputations.

Storing bareroot roses

So you plant your roses as soon as you get them, right? That may seem like good advice, but it's not always practical. What if your bareroot roses arrive in the dead of winter and the ground is frozen solid? Or what if it rains for 40 days and nights? Then what are you going to do?

When you purchase or get your bareroot rose order in the mail, inspect the plants. Make sure plenty of moist packing surrounds the roots and that the top canes are green and firm. If the temperatures outside are still too cold to plant, the rose can be stored in one of two ways. For a week or two, the crisper of the refrigerator makes a good temporary home. Kept cool without freezing, the rose canes don't grow and the plant stays fully dormant. Alternatively, if the buds start to grow and swell and you can't plant the rose for more than two weeks, it can be potted. Just buy yourself a peat pot from a local nursery and grow your rose plant in a cool, sunny spot. If only rain is stopping you from planting, wait until it stops and plant, or just do it in the rain. The showers won't hurt the plant one tiny bit!

Heeling in is a way to store bareroot roses by packing their roots in moist (not soggy) soil until planting time. Where and how you heel in your roses depends on how many roses you have and on the soil conditions outdoors.

> ✔ If you have just a few roses, place them in a bucket or box and pack the roots and top third of the plant with moist sawdust, compost, peat moss, or soil. Store the whole thing in a cool (1° to 4° C or 35° to 40° F) place and check the packing often to make sure that it's moist. Unpack the roses at planting time, being very careful not to do too much harm to the tiny root hairs that may have grown along the main roots.

✔ If you have to store a lot of roses (say until the weekend when you can spend time doing the planting job properly) and can work the ground outdoors, dig a shallow trench about 30 centimetres (1 foot) deep, as shown in Figure 17-1, slightly slanted on one side, in a shady area of the garden (like the north side of the house). Lay the roses on a 45-degree angle and pack the roots and the bottom third of the plant with moist soil or compost. Check the packing often to make sure that it's moist. Add water if necessary. Gently remove the roses from the trench at planting time.

Don't keep roses heeled in much past the earliest planting time in your area, because the plants start to develop fragile new roots and fragile new top growth, both of which can be damaged when you start handling the plants.

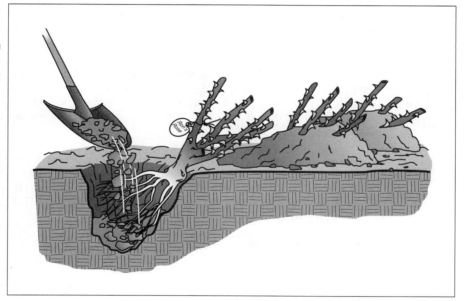

Figure 17-1:
If you can't plant bare-root roses immediately upon arrival, heel them in by laying them in a shallow trench and covering their roots with moist organic matter.

Storing potted roses

Potted roses are easier to store temporarily until planting time. Just make sure to keep the soil moist so that the plants don't dry out. If you store growing roses for more than a week or two, you may want to fertilize them with a liquid fertilizer, following the label instructions. Regular houseplant food works well.

Of course, you may want to grow your roses in pots or other containers. In this case, you can rest assured that you'll need a bigger pot than the one in which you bought your rose. See Chapter 7 for more information about growing roses in containers.

Getting in Touch with Your Inner Soil

We think that any gardener worth his or her salt should have an intimate relationship with soil. You need to grab it, squeeze it, smell it — you need to love it so much that you know everything about it: the good, the bad, and the ugly. Why? Because healthy soil means healthy roots, healthy roots mean healthy plants, and healthy plants mean fabulous flowers.

Provided that drainage is good, roses grow well in most soils. But if you wait until after you plant to find out that your soil has problems, you'll find those problems difficult or impossible to correct.

Basically, *soil* is a combination of mineral particles and *organic matter* (the remnants of living things such as leaves, animal waste, and so on). The size of the particles and the amount of organic matter determine soil texture. And your soil's texture determines not only how you plant but also how often you have to water and fertilize.

The ideal soil, and you probably don't have it, is well aerated; space for air in a soil is absolutely necessary for healthy root growth. It also retains some moisture and nutrients and drains well (water passes through it freely). Poorly drained soil often becomes waterlogged, suffocating roots and killing the plants that try to grow in it.

Although many in-betweens exist, you can conveniently break soils into three types:

- **Sandy soils** are made mostly of large mineral particles. Water moves through these soils quickly and, as it does, takes nutrients with it. Sandy soils are well aerated, quick to dry out, and often lacking in nutrients that plants need.

- **Clay soils** are made mostly of small mineral particles that cling tightly together. They hang on to water, are slow to dry out, and are poorly aerated.

- **Loamy soils** are a happy mixture of large and small mineral particles, and they usually contain an abundance of organic matter. They are well aerated and drain properly, while still being able to hold water and nutrients.

You can get a pretty good idea of what kind of soil you have by grabbing a moist handful and squeezing. When you let go, sandy soil falls apart and doesn't hold together in a ball. Clay soil oozes out between your fingers as you squeeze and stays in a slippery wad when you let go. A loamy soil usually holds together after squeezing, but it falls apart easily if you poke it with your finger.

You can also get some idea about your soil by watching what happens when it rains:

✔ Water passes through clay soils slowly, so rainfall quickly puddles up and drains away slowly. As clay soils dry, they often crack and become hard-crusted.

✔ Water passes quickly through sandy soils, leaving the soil barely moist.

✔ Loamy soils maintain just the right amount of moisture — not so little that your plant dries out quickly, and not so much that the roots are swimming.

Plumbing for poorly drained soils?

The quality and texture of the soil just a few inches down may be completely different from the topsoil. So even though you may have good loam on the surface, something completely different may be 6 to 12 inches (or farther) below. If a big rock or a compacted or impenetrable layer of soil (called *hardpan*) lurks beneath the surface, it may prevent water from properly draining away from the root area. And that's trouble.

Check your soil drainage by digging a 30- to 45-centimetre (12- to 18-inch) hole where you want to plant. Fill the hole with water, let it drain, and then fill it again. If the hole takes longer than two hours to drain after the second filling, you have a problem. You may be able to break through a thin hardpan that's near the bottom of the hole, but you'll probably get a sore back from doing so. If you've won the lottery lately, call a landscape contractor. He or she may be able to install drainage pipes to carry excess water away. But when we encounter bad drainage, we either plant somewhere else or plant in containers or raised beds (see Chapter 7).

Adding the big O

The *big O* is organic matter — leaf mould, shredded bark, compost, peat moss, manure, and the like. Organic matter helps to loosen and aerate clay soils. It also improves the water- and nutrient-holding capacity of sandy soils. If you don't have some organic matter lying around, your local nursery or garden centre should have several different kinds for sale.

If you're planting a large area with a lot of roses, you can incorporate organic matter into the whole area with a shovel or rototiller. Just lay down 5 to 8 centimetres (2 to 3 inches) of the stuff and turn it in to a depth of at least 15 to 20 centimetres (6 to 8 inches).

If you're planting just a few roses, mix in the organic matter with the backfill soil when you plant. *Backfill soil* is the soil you take out of the hole while you're digging it. If you mix this soil with about 25 percent volume (or more) organic matter, your roses should get off to a better start.

If you have good loamy soil and no problems with excess clay or sand, you don't *have to* add any organic stuff, but we always add as much as we can, no matter what the soil looks like. It can never hurt, and it always helps.

Is having acerbic soil an insult?

The chemistry of your soil is the single most important element in successful rose culture. Before you even think about immersing those rose roots in your garden, you have to check the soil's *pH*.

Soil pH is a measurement of the soil's acidity or alkalinity. A pH of 7 is neutral. Soils with a pH below 7 are acidic and become more acidic the lower the number goes. Soils with a pH above 7 are alkaline and become more alkaline as the number goes up.

Roses prefer a slightly acidic soil pH. Ideal soil pH for most roses is between 5.8 and 6.2. If soils are overly acidic or too alkaline, adjusting the pH with one of several soil amendments is vital. A soil pH that is too high or too low interferes with or prevents the chemical reactions that make nutrients available to plants.

Your local nursery or provincial soil-testing laboratory (contact the provincial agricultural ministry for the address) can give you a general idea of what your soil pH is or perform a soil test using a sample of your garden soil. Your favourite garden centre may even be able to sell you a small test kit so you can do the job yourself. While not as accurate as the professional tests, they will give you adequate results. You can adjust acidic soils by adding *dolomitic limestone*. Correct alkaline soils by adding *sulphur*. Again, a local professional is the best source of how much and what to add. Be aware that modifying the soil pH in a small spot such as a single rose-growing area will not work for very long. You have to modify a large area if you want the effects to last.

You can also test your soil's pH with inexpensive testing tapes or more expensive testing monitors that you can get via mail order or from nurseries and garden centres. See Appendix B for soil testing centres in your area.

Returning Roots to Their Rightful Home

The basic procedure for planting bareroot roses is shown in Figures 17-2 through 17-4. The key idea to remember: Don't plant a $10 (or more!) rosebush in a 50¢ hole. Whether you're planting several roses in a new bed, or just one in the middle of nowhere, dig a proper hole.

Dig a hole at least 60 centimetres (2 feet) deep and 60 centimetres (2 feet) wide. Put the backfill into a wheelbarrow or in one pile where you can mix it with fertilizers or amendments. This is, after all, the best time to add nutrients that are in short supply. For instance, a friend in Kingston adds one cup each of ground limestone, blood meal, and triple superphosphate fertilizer to the backfill soil. We simply mix several shovels of compost to each pile of soil.

Planting at the proper depth is very important. In mild-winter climates of Southern Ontario and coastal British Columbia, position the plants so that the bud union is just below to 5 centimetres (2 inches) below the level of the surface soil. In the rest of the country, plant so that the bud union is 10 centimetres (4 inches) below the soil surface. Plant own-root roses so that the point where the roots join the branches is just below the soil surface. In areas that face severe freezing, plant the bud union up to 15 centimetres (6 inches) below the surface. If you live in a cold area and only plant the bud union 5 centimetres (2 inches) deep, you will have to add extra insulation during the winter to avoid killing the rose.

Here are some tips for planting bareroot roses:

✔ Before planting bareroot roses, we prefer to soak the roots in a bucket of muddy water overnight. The water moistens the roots and the mud lightly coats them to slow drying out during planting. Soaking the roots is optional if you turn the planting hole into a muddy bath.

✔ Prune all the canes to about half their length. Most bareroot roses have 25- to 40-centimetre (10- to 16-inch) canes to start with, so shorten them to between 12 and 20 centimetres (5 and 8 inches). This technique forces the new canes to start lower on the plant — giving a bushier look.

✔ Before putting the plant in the ground, cut off any broken or mushy roots. *Don't* prune just to shorten them or stimulate their growth.

✔ Set the roots into the hole and cover with a few inches of soil. Pour water around the roots to wash the soil into the spaces between the roots. Add more soil and then turn this into mud by adding more water. Continue adding soil and watering it until the hole is filled with soil.

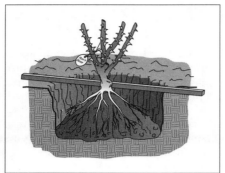

Figure 17-2:
Placing the
rosebush in
the hole.

Figure 17-3:
Watering
around the
roots.

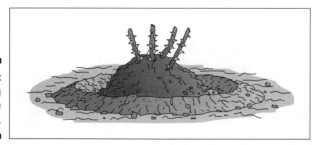

Figure 17-4:
Mounding
soil over the
bud union.

🖝 If, after planting, the rose settles too deep, grab the main stem (you might want to wear gloves for this) near the bud union and gently pull upward. When you let go, the plant should settle slightly higher. If the plant has settled too high, it's best to pull it out and start over again.

🖝 After planting, add lots and lots of water to the filled hole. Doing so settles the soil and eliminates air pockets. After that water drains away, the soil and rose may settle lower than you want. If so, add more backfill, and water again.

✔ After you water the rose in, mound the soil over the top of the plant so all but the last few inches of the cane tops are covered. Doing so helps to keep the plant from drying out. Once you see new growth, carefully remove the soil from around the canes.

Here are some tips for planting roses that come in containers:

✔ Water plants thoroughly before planting. Ensure that water is pouring out the bottom of the container before stopping. This means that the entire root ball is well soaked.

✔ Dig a large hole and add soil amendments just as for a bareroot rose, but leave the bottom of the hole flat to support the shape of the rootball.

✔ Place your new rose into the hole, pot and all, so that you can estimate proper planting depth. Remember to plant the bud union at the proper depth for your winter area.

✔ It is best to disturb growing roots as little as possible during planting. If your container rose is in a wood-fibre pot, use a heavy knife to cut the bottom off the pot before placing the plant in the hole. When you've got it in just the right position, slit the pot from top to bottom and remove it.

✔ If your rose is in a metal or heavy plastic container, remove the rootball from the pot. If the roots form a solid, circling mass, gently loosen or cut them, or the rose will be slow to adapt to the new soil. If the roots are really tight, make three or four vertical cuts along the sides of the rootball with an old knife. The roots will eventually branch at the cuts and grow out into the surrounding soil.

See Figures 17-5 and 17-6 for the procedure for planting container-grown roses.

Figure 17-5: Setting a container-grown rose into a planting hole.

Figure 17-6:
After correcting the soil level and adding the backfill, water thoroughly.

✔ If you're planting in hot weather, don't let the new plant dry out. Until the roots grow into the surrounding soil, you have to treat the plant like it is still in a pot. That means you may have to water every few days, if not more.

✔ Water all newly planted roses every few days, or more often if the weather is hot.

Planting Miniature Roses

Miniature roses are usually sold in 6- to 10-centimetre (2½-inch or 4-inch) pots, whether you buy them at a local retail nursery or by mail order. They should have fully developed root systems. In fact, they may be rootbound and more than ready to be transplanted.

Remember that these little plants were grown in a comfy greenhouse, so they may need time to adjust to natural, outdoor conditions. This process is called *hardening off*. Help potted plants adjust to your weather conditions by gradually moving them to more extreme temperatures and sunlight. From the porch to outside in partial sun and finally to full sun over a week's time should do the trick. If you don't have a porch, put them outside for the day in a shady spot protected from the wind and bring them back indoors for the night. Gradually give them more and more sunshine over a week-long period during their daytime outdoor periods. Do not leave them outside if freezing temperatures are forecast.

Miniatures can be planted at the same times as their larger cousins.

Digging the hole

Digging a hole for a potted mini is somewhat easier than digging a hole for a big rose. You can do it with a trowel, although removing a couple of spadefuls of soil ensures that the roots have a generous area in which they can spread.

In any case, prepare the hole much as you would for a big rose. Because your plant is smaller, the hole should be smaller — about 30 centimetres (1 foot) wide and 30 centimetres (1 foot) deep. Add smaller amounts of the same soil amendments you use for big roses.

Putting the plant in the ground

As with big bareroot roses, minis do a lot better when you cut half the length off the canes. This may mean cutting off some flowers and buds, but bite the bullet. Doing so pays off big-time later on.

Your mini rose should come out of its pot quite easily. Notice how all those roots have grown round and round inside the pot? To encourage the roots to spread out and grow into the new soil in your rose bed (or container), you can do one of two gardening tricks. The first is to insert both your thumbs into the bottom of the rootball and tear it apart for about two-thirds of its depth. The second is for more timid gardeners and that is to gently tease the roots away from the soil ball as you did with the larger pot-bound roses. Backfill and water exactly as described for full-sized roses earlier in this chapter.

Remember that miniature roses always have shallower root systems than big roses and need more frequent watering.

Chapter 18

Watering and Mulching Roses

• •

• •

*H*ow often should you water your roses? How much water should you apply? How should you apply the water? Should you use a hose? A sprinkler? Or do you just let Mother Nature take care of it all with summer rainfall?

Questions like these are often hard to answer even for the most experienced rosarian. The reason is that, like any other plant, a rose's water needs depend on a number of factors, many of which are determined by conditions that may be unique to your own garden. And what does that mean? It means that the only person who really can know the answers to tough watering questions is you.

Watering is really a matter of common sense and careful observation. You may even find watering to be one of the more enjoyable gardening chores. This chapter gives you tips that make setting up a watering schedule and applying the right amount of water painless and easy.

The Basic Watering Rules

First, you need to accept the fact that your roses need water to be healthy and bloom beautifully. Then tattoo these rules on your arm:

✔ Roses need more water more often in hot weather than in cool weather.

✔ Even if it rains often, that rain may not be enough water to keep your roses healthy.

✔ Roses growing in sandy soil need more frequent watering than roses growing in clay soils. (See Chapter 17 for more information about the different types of soils.)

✔ When you water, water deeply so that you wet the entire root zone. Don't just sprinkle lightly! It does little good.

✔ If you really want to know whether your roses need water, get down and dig in the dirt. It's the only way to know for sure. If the top 5 centimetres (2 inches) of soil is dry, you probably need to water.

✔ To reduce disease problems, water the soil, not the leaves. Roses can, however, benefit from overhead watering once in a while. Just make sure that you do so in the morning on sunny days so that the foliage can dry before nightfall.

✔ *Mulch! Mulch! Mulch!* Doing so conserves water. See "The Wonderful World of Mulches" later in this chapter.

Now we're getting somewhere. In the following sections, we get down to the nitty-gritty and answer the tough questions.

How often should I water?

Naturally, if you live where summers are dry (like the prairies most years) you need to water more frequently than you do if you live in rainy Vancouver.

"Yeah, sure," you say. "And if the soil is sandy, I have to water more frequently than if the soil is mucky clay. My tattoo tells me that. But exactly *how often* should I water?"

A good basic guideline is that a mature, full-sized rosebush needs about 3 centimetres (an inch or so) of water a week. Therefore, if you received at least 3 centimetres (1 inch) of rain last week, no problem. If you didn't, you need to water. But watering is usually not that simple. Soil type and weather are major influences.

Clay soil holds more water, so you need to add water less often. Sandy soil holds little water, so you need to water more often. If the weather is blistering hot and dry, common sense suggests more water is necessary. Likewise, if weather has been cool, perhaps the roses can go well beyond a week between drinks.

Keep in mind that, theoretically, you can't overwater a rose. Of course, with no sun and ten days of steady rain, your roses won't be thrilled. But if drainage is good, the extra water won't hurt them, either.

Start with a watering schedule, watering once every five or six days, for example. Watch the plant carefully, especially when you get to the fifth or sixth day. If the new growth starts to look dull or wilts a bit, dig down near the base of the plant and see whether the soil is moist. If it's bone dry about 5 centimetres (2 inches) from the surface, you're ready to water. If it's still moist, wait a few days and check again.

Over time, you'll get to know your soil and how quickly it dries out, whether it's warm or cool, rainy or dry.

How much water should I apply?

Water deeply so that the entire root zone is wet — for roses, that means to a depth of at least 45 centimetres (18 inches). How far a given amount of water can penetrate into the soil depends on the soil type. For example, if you applied about 3 centimetres (1 inch) of water evenly over sandy soil, it would go down about 30 centimetres (12 inches). In a clay soil, it would reach only about 10 to 12 centimetres (4 to 5 inches). In a loam soil, 3 centimetres (1 inch) of water would go down about 15 to 25 centimetres (6 to 10 inches).

Chapter 17 gives you some general guidelines on determining what type of soil you have. But what you really want to know is *how long* you have to water to wet your particular soil to the proper depth. To find that out, you need to play in the mud a bit.

We consider different types of irrigation systems and how fast they apply water later in this chapter. But for now, assume that your watering system, even if it's just a hose, is in place. Fill up your *water basin* — the 8- to 15-centimetre (3- to 6-inch) high circle of soil you make around your rose when you plant it — once. Let the water soak in and then probe the soil with a stiff rod or stick.

The rod or stick should move smoothly through wet soil, and then be hard to push when it reaches dry soil. Digging with a spade, you can see exactly how deep the water has gone. From there, calculating how long to water is easy. For example, if the soil is wet to a depth of 15 centimetres (6 inches) after 10 minutes of watering, you need to water for a total of 30 minutes to get the water down 45 centimetres (18 inches).

You may want to water a little longer than it takes to get the water down 45 centimetres (18 inches), just to make sure that you're doing a good job and watering your roses thoroughly.

Tools of the Watering Trade

Two tools can help you fine-tune your watering schedule. The first is a *soil probe*, a hollow metal tube that removes a small core of soil from the ground. By examining the soil core, you can tell how deeply you're watering or how dry the soil is.

The second useful tool is a *rain gauge*. It can tell you exactly how much rain has fallen, and you can adjust your watering schedule accordingly.

You can purchase soil probes and rain gauges through the irrigation supply stores listed in the Yellow Pages, the Internet, or from your favourite garden centre. Or, if you're handy, you can make your own after seeing what they look like in a catalogue. We use an old margarine tub as a rain gauge, which has worked fine (with regular replacement) for twenty years or more.

Ways to Water

There are many ways to water roses. The key is to apply the water only over the soil where the roots are — and not so fast that it runs down the gutter toward the next town. Slower is better.

Building a basin

One simple way to water is to build an 8- to 15-centimetre (3- to 6-inch) high basin of soil around the plant and fill it using a hand-held hose. Just make sure that the basin is wide enough. It should be at least 45 centimetres (18 inches) wide for new plants, and at least 90 centimetres (36 inches) wide for really big roses. And don't forget, you may have to fill the basin twice to get the water deep enough.

Using sprinklers

There are many types of sprinklers — ones that attach to the end of a hose (see Figure 18-1) and ones that are connected to underground pipes (see Figure 18-2). You can hook both types to timers or controllers to prevent overwatering. They can even water while you're on vacation.

Figure 18-1:
If you have just a few roses and a long hose, a hose-end sprinkler is a convenient way to water roses.

Figure 18-2:
An underground irrigation system delivers water either overhead or right at the roots.

Set up a rain gauge and run the sprinklers to find out how long it takes to apply about 3 centimetres (one inch) of water. This is the time you set the sprinkler to run once per week on an automatic system, or you could set it to run half of that time twice per week. Just don't water any more than twice a week or you'll encourage *shallow rooting*. Shallow rooting makes a rose more susceptible to winter damage as well as to dry soils if you ever forget to turn on the sprinkler.

Sprinklers are very democratic waterers. They give equal amounts to all plants and they don't stop because it's hot or the ball game has started. Consistent watering is the key to good rose flower production, and sprinklers — even the kind you turn on and off yourself — are better than hand watering.

Using drip irrigation

Drip irrigation (see Figure 18-3) is a particularly useful watering system for areas that are dry in summer, in areas where water shortages are common, or for busy gardeners who don't have time to water as often as they'd like. Most drip irrigation systems are built around 1- to 2½-centimetre (⅜- to 1-inch) black tubing and specifically designed emitters. The emitters drip or spray water slowly, no faster than the soil can absorb it. And only the root area gets wet.

Figure 18-3: Watering roses with a drip system is convenient if you have many roses, and it is efficient if you live where water is a precious resource.

A good way to test out the timing for drip irrigation systems is to put an emitter into a 20-litre (5-gallon) bucket of water and measure how long it takes to fill the bucket halfway. This is the time the drip system should run every week if you have average to good soil. After a watering, do a moisture test by digging down 12 to18 inches with a spade or probe to see whether you should lengthen the time (needs more water) or shorten the application time to get the water to that depth.

Most garden centres carry a variety of sprinklers and watering devices. In most cases, garden centre staff can help you with design and installation. See Appendix B for other resources.

Black spot, and rust, and mites, oh my!

You have to think about one last thing before you decide how you're going to water. Many rose diseases, including black spot, rust, and downy mildew, thrive on wet foliage. If you live in areas where such diseases are problems (see Chapter 4 for more information about where these diseases are most troublesome), you may want to water in a way that keeps the leaves dry. Drip systems or bubbler-type sprinkler heads apply water at the base of the plant and do a good job of keeping the leaves from getting wet.

To complicate matters, some diseases, such as powdery mildew, spread more rapidly on dry foliage. And insect pests like mites thrive on dirty, dusty leaves. In both cases, drenching the entire plant cleans the foliage of disease spores and dust, reducing pest problems. But if you're going to water with overhead sprinklers, be sure to do it early in the morning on a sunny day so that the leaves have a chance to dry before nightfall. And whether or not you water overhead, keeping dead leaves and pruning debris out of the garden really pays off.

The Wonderful World of Mulches

Mulch is any material, organic or not, that you place over the surface of the soil. But mulches *really* are a waterer's best friend. By reducing soil temperatures and evaporation, and by smothering greedy weeds (the seeds won't germinate if they're covered by several centimetres of mulch) that compete with roses for moisture, mulches not only conserve water but also even out rapid changes in soil moisture that can spell disaster in hot weather.

The best time to apply mulch is in early spring, about the same time you remove winter protection (see Chapter 21 for more information).

Organic mulches

Organic mulches include grass clippings, compost, wood chips, leaf mould, pine needles, shredded bark, straw, hay, grain and fruit by-products, composted manure, mushroom compost, sawdust, and even newspapers. Some are easier to find in specific parts of the country. We recommend organic mulches for roses because, as the mulch breaks down, it adds organic matter to the soil, improving soil texture and adding nutrients. Mulch also makes your garden look better by giving the ground a cleaner, more orderly appearance.

Many organic mulches break down fairly rapidly, so they need to be replenished regularly. Apply a good, thick layer in spring before the weeds start to grow. Then check the plants in the fall to top it up if necessary. Figure 18-4 shows a properly mulched rosebush.

Figure 18-4:
A layer
of organic
mulch,
shown on
the left side
of the plant,
improves
root growth.

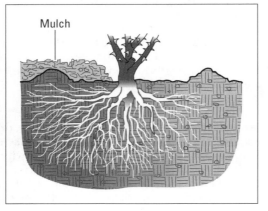

To be effective, a mulch should be at least 8 to 10 centimetres (3 to 4 inches) thick. Spread it evenly under the roses, over an area that is slightly wider than the diameter of the plant. Mulching is that easy!

Composted manures make particularly good mulches, looking neat while adding nutrients to the soil as they break down. Just make sure that the manure is fully composted and that you don't add too much. Fresh manures contain salts that will damage the plant and make its leaves look as if they've been burned by a blowtorch. Basically, uncomposted manure is too much of a good thing. (Too much of any fertilizer, manure included, supplies excess nitrogen.) So compost fresh manure for at least six months before using it. Think of having too much salt in your soup. A little is good . . . too much and it's inedible.

You can buy bags of composted manure in most nurseries and garden centres. Some farmers will sell composted manure, and horse-riding stables can be a good source of fresh manure for those in nearby areas, but remember to let the fresh manure age six months before using it.

Mulches are the topic of much advice and even myths in the gardening world. Here are some of the most common stories you'll encounter.

- **Bark mulches, such as pine, are quite acidic.** Luckily, they decompose very slowly, so they will not influence the pH of the soil at all. Use these large chunks freely, contrary to advice that says to avoid them. The same goes for evergreen needles as mulch.

- **Grass clippings make terrible mulches.** Actually, fresh grass clippings make a wonderful mulch if you don't pile it higher than 3 inches. (Higher than 3 inches and it might start to compost and heat up.) Grass clippings are usually pretty abundant, although if the grass goes to seed before you cut it, you could end up with grass growing in your rose beds. Also, make sure that no herbicides (weed killers) have been used on your lawn, the residue of which can damage or kill your roses.

- **Some organic mulches — such as fresh sawdust — rob nitrogen from your soil as they break down.** As long as you don't dig the mulch into your soil, you won't have a problem with nitrogen robbing. You may have a problem with softwood sawdust as it contains oils that may reduce growth rates on some plants. It's usually best to avoid softwood sawdust. If you do use sawdust, throw on an extra shovelful of compost to be on the safe side. Sawdust from pressure-treated wood should not be added to your garden.

- **Peat moss makes a good mulch.** Water will not penetrate dry peat moss, so the water runs off instead of soaking through to the roots. Best to avoid peat as a mulch.

- **Tree leaves should never be used as mulch around roses.** The best thing to do with leaves is to compost them first to make a more dense mulch material. Chopping them up with a lawnmower and then applying them around your roses is a good idea. The only leaves we don't apply whole and unchopped around our roses are maple leaves because they do mat down.

- **Mushroom compost is a good mulch.** The truth is that this compost is largely devoid of nutrients and often has a very high salt residue. If you use this as a mulch, do not expect it to feed your plants, and thoroughly soak it to dissolve and wash away any excess salts. The easiest way to do this is to spread it and then turn the sprinklers on for three to four times longer than you normally would.

You can purchase organic mulches like shredded bark, compost, and leaf mould in bags, or sometimes in bulk, from nurseries and garden centres. Grass clippings, compost, and wood chips come free from the garden. Municipalities now regularly make compost available to residents.

Inorganic mulches

Inorganic mulches include plastic, gravel, stone, and sand. As we said, we usually prefer organic mulches because they improve the soil and look better. Some gardeners like the look of gravel under their roses. We find that garden chores are more difficult with these mulches. Weed seeds germinate well in them so you'll constantly see small dandelions trying to establish themselves in the gravel. Any digging is difficult with a rock mulch and cleaning it of plant debris is harder than cleaning up an organic mulch. Once the gravel works its way into the soil, you have a gravel rose soil — a delight we're sure to avoid in our gardens.

Chapter 19

Fertilizing Roses

. . . .

In This Chapter

▶ Applying the nutrients roses need most

▶ Testing your soil

▶ Knowing when and how often to fertilize roses

▶ Using specific fertilizer programs

. . . .

Most roses need frequent applications of fertilizer to keep them growing vigorously and blooming repeatedly. If that's all you want to know about the mind-boggling world of fertilizers, that's fine. Go to your local nursery, buy a bag or box of fertilizer labelled "Plant Food," and follow the directions on the package. You'll get perfectly fine roses. If, however, you want to go for perfectly spectacular roses, we can tell you about that, too. So in this chapter we spell out the theory of fertilizing, and then we give you a few options.

The Whats, Whens, and Whys of Fertilizing

For some people, plant nutrition is a complicated science that they spend their whole lives studying. But it doesn't have to be that complicated. We're just talking about how and what to give roses so that they grow their best. The following sections give you the nitty-gritty of feeding roses.

But before we launch into all the whys and wherefores, keep in mind that no fertilizer on earth will help your roses if the pH of your soil is too high or too low. When the pH is off, important nutrients already in the soil are unavailable to plants. As we explain in Chapter 17, roses prefer a slightly acidic soil with a pH between 5.8 and 6.2. When the pH is right, your roses' roots can interact with the bacteria and enzymes in the soil and get full benefit of natural nutrients and those you add.

Keep in mind, too, that fertilizers come in three basic forms:

- **Granular:** Designed to be scratched into the soil at the base of the plant
- **Liquid:** Either a liquid or powder designed to be dissolved in water for liquid feeding to the soil or foliage
- **Timed-release:** To be mixed with the soil for constant release over a long period of time

Note: Roses growing in containers need special care — see Chapter 7.

Nitrogen is the element needed most

Plants actually require 16 different elements for healthy growth, but most of these elements are already in your soil (or in the air!) and don't need to be added regularly. Nitrogen, however, is what fuels the growth of a rosebush. This chemical stimulates dark green, healthy foliage growth, and because a plant's energy to make flowers is manufactured in its leaves, healthy leaves mean more flowers.

Nitrogen comes in several forms; some are fast acting, and others are slower. But when you buy packaged fertilizer, the amount of nitrogen it contains (the first number in the formula on the bag — see Figure 19-1) is what's important.

Alkaline soils need iron

In areas where the soil is on the alkaline side, a rose plant may need applications of fertilizers containing iron. You know when your roses need iron because their leaves are yellow with green veins.

Working your fingers to the bone meal

Along with nitrogen, phosphorus and potassium are called *macronutrients* because they are needed in larger supplies than other nutrients. However, some soils contain enough phosphorus and potassium for healthy rose growth; adding more to them does little good. Besides, phosphorus doesn't move easily through the soil like nitrogen and potassium — it gets "tied up" and has to stay put. If your soil is short on phosphorus,

you should add it directly to the planting hole when you put in your roses so that it gets where it needs to go. That is why gardeners have been adding bone meal (a good source of phosphorus) to planting holes for centuries.

Only testing can tell whether your soil needs either phosphorus or potassium.

Figure 19-1:
The numbers on a package of fertilizer show the percentages of major nutrients: nitrogen (N), phosphorus (P), and potassium (K). Fertilizers made especially for roses also include directions on the label.

Iron is called a *micronutrient*, meaning that the plant needs it only in small quantities. Zinc and manganese are other micronutrients that problem soils may need. The fastest way to correct these deficiencies is to apply a liquid fertilizer containing *chelated* micronutrients (forget about all the terminology — it just means that they work better) to both the foliage and the soil. That's right, just spray the fertilizer over the whole plant. But look for cautions on the fertilizer label. Most manufacturers recommend *not* spraying if the plants need water or if temperatures are over 29° C (85° F).

Salty secrets for roses

Many experienced rose growers swear by magnesium applications. And who are we to argue? Magnesium sulphate — simply the Epsom salts you find in drugstores — is the form that's usually applied. This chemical can intensify flower colour and increase production of new flowering canes. Apply about ½ cup per plant per month and water in.

If you have doubts, have the soil tested

Nutrient deficiencies aren't always this cut and dried. If you're having problems keeping your roses green and growing, have your soil tested or show a sample of the foliage to a local nursery worker. If the nursery can't help, the employees should be able to recommend a private lab that can. A soil test tells you exactly what's wrong with your soil, and then your nursery can help you correct the problem. Costs vary from area to area and depend on how detailed the test is. Your provincial agricultural ministry and its Web site will also have soil lab contact information. See Appendix B.

Feed often, but don't overdo it

To keep roses blooming again and again, fertilize them about every six weeks, although the type of fertilizer you use may alter this rule a bit. (Refer to the basic fertilizer programs later in this chapter.) However, if you go overboard and apply too much or too often, you can *burn* a plant — the edges or the entire leaf turn brown and scorched looking. And if that doesn't happen, the overly lush growth is a favourite of many insect pests. Always follow label instructions when determining how much fertilizer to use.

Roses that bloom only once in spring, like many of the old garden roses, don't need to be fertilized as often. Fertilizing once in early spring is enough.

If you do overfeed your plants and get fertilizer burn, simply turn the hose onto the plant and overwater it drastically. This excess water dissolves the fertilizer salts and washes them away from the root zone. It won't help the damaged leaves but it will stop the plant from absorbing any more.

Start in early spring, stop in late summer or fall

Make your first application about four to six weeks before growth begins in spring or when you take off your winter protection. Continue through summer until about six weeks before the average date of your first frost. (Employees at your nursery can tell you exactly when that date is.) Later fertilization may encourage growth that will be damaged by frosts and can result in roses that are not fully "cold resistant." (For more information about rose hardiness, see Chapter 4.) If in doubt, make your last feeding for the season during the last week of July.

Water before and after fertilizing

A plant stressed from lack of water is more likely to be burned by nitrogen fertilizers, so make sure that the soil is wet before fertilizing. Watering afterwards helps to move nutrients into the root zone.

A Fertilizing Program Just for You

Fertilizing is kind of a personal thing. Of course you want to keep your plants healthy, but how you do so really depends on the type of gardener you are. So in this section we describe a few successful fertilizer programs we've seen. Take your pick.

Lazy and cheap formula

Fertilizers that contain all three major nutrients — nitrogen, phosphorus, and potassium — are called *complete fertilizers*. They are the types usually packaged as "Rose Foods." Although phosphorus and potassium are needed for healthy growth, they are often already present in the soil in sufficient amounts and don't need to be replaced on a regular basis. Some fertilizers, such as ammonium sulphate, contain only nitrogen. They are dramatically cheaper than complete fertilizers and are often all that's needed. However, they are easier to make a mistake with and burn your rose. Don't exceed the label directions.

Figure 19-2:
Spreading fertilizer at the base of a rose plant.

Ammonium sulphate has the added advantage of being an *acidifying fertilizer* (it gradually lowers soil pH), which is ideal for alkaline soils. One rose grower we know saves money and time by running through the garden giving each rose one handful of ammonium sulphate (he wears gloves) every six weeks. He spreads the fertilizer evenly under each plant, shown being done with a can in Figure 19-2, and then waters thoroughly to dissolve the granules and wash the nutrients into the soil. Simple, cheap, and his roses look great.

Just plain lazy formula

You can apply several types of timed-release fertilizers once or twice a year, and they provide enough nutrients for an entire season. Follow the label instructions carefully and watch your roses closely. If they slow down and stop blooming, the fertilizer may have run out early. Most rose growers who use timed-released fertilizers supplement their use with one or two applications of a regular fertilizer just to make sure that the plants have enough nitrogen.

Tree-hugger's formula

Many gardeners prefer to use organic fertilizers — ones that occur naturally — over chemical-based fertilizers. And their reasons are good ones. Organic fertilizers, such as fish emulsion, composted manures (fresh manures can burn plant foliage), and *blood meal* (dried animal blood, which is high in nitrogen), contribute organic matter to the earth and are better for all those weird micro-organisms that populate the soil and are responsible for plant health.

One successful formula we've seen mixes even amounts of alfalfa meal and cottonseed meal. Ten cups of the formula are spread at the base of each plant every ten weeks and then covered with a thick mulch of compost. Try it; your worms will love it.

You can grow superior roses (particularly container roses) if you feed them weekly with a liquid fish emulsion mixed at recommended rates. Compost tea — a shovel of compost in a 20-litre (5-gallon) pail of water — is also a wonderful pick-me-up for summer rose feeding.

Water and spray, water and spray, oh how I love to water and spray

You can't argue with the fact that half the fun of gardening is actually spending time in the garden. One friend of ours combines work with pleasure. She applies liquid or water-soluble fertilizers through a hose-end sprayer, as shown in Figure 19-3. She applies the fertilizer to the leaves and soil, so she gets the immediate effects of *foliar feeding* and the long-term benefits of soil application. (Believe us, applying fertilizers to the leaves works if the label says that doing so is okay — try it! Roots are not the only part of the plant that can absorb nutrients; leaves can do so, too.) She follows this routine at least every two weeks, but sometimes she mixes the fertilizer at half strength and applies it weekly.

If only we had the time. . . .

Figure 19-3: A hose-end sprayer allows you to fertilize both the leaves and the soil.

Gung-ho fertilizer for gung-ho rose growers

Rose society members, especially those who show their roses at local and national rose shows, are pretty finicky about how they care for their plants. But you can't argue with their results, which are large, perfect flowers and wonderful foliage. One trophy winner we know has a particularly high-powered fertilizer program:

1. About a week after his plants leaf out in spring, he applies a water-soluble 20-20-20 fertilizer (refer to Figure 19-1 for more information about what this means), diluting 2 tablespoons of fertilizer in 8 litres (2 gallons) of water and giving each plant the whole 8 litres (2 gallons).

2. A week later, he puts a ½ cup of Epsom salts (magnesium sulphate) around each bush.

3. The third week, he applies fish emulsion at the same rate as the 20-20-20 fertilizer applied two weeks earlier.

4. During week four, he applies a liquid fertilizer (16-4-2), which includes chelated micronutrients, at 1 tablespoon per 4 litres (1 gallon), 8 litres (2 gallons) per bush. In week five, he starts all over again.

Whew, a lot of work — but, he says, twice the bloom and bigger flowers.

Chapter 20

Pruning Roses

*I*f you think that pruning is a complicated thing, think again. Although pruning trees and other types of plants may be met with lots of head scratching, pruning roses is so simple and straightforward that you're not going to believe it. And you won't believe the big-time results you'll get from performing a little lopping at the right time.

Feel better? Good. Because if you want to grow roses, you're going to have to prune them. Roses are tough plants, and even if you make every mistake in the book, your roses will be better off than if you hadn't pruned them at all.

When you prune, you cut the canes of a rosebush. You may cut them near the top of the plant, you may cut them at the base of the plant, or you may cut them somewhere in the middle. You cut 'em in all kinds of different places, depending on the result you're trying to achieve.

What pruning *isn't* is something you do for the sake of doing it. Whenever you take a pruner to a rose cane, ask yourself why.

Why You Need to Prune

What is pruning, anyway? Obviously, it means cutting something or other. But what? When? And most of all, why? Roses need to be pruned for several reasons. Most of them have to do with keeping the plant healthy, and a couple of them have to do with keeping the plant pretty. And some of them have to do with keeping the plant from getting out of bounds.

Here's the skinny on why you really *do* want to prune your roses:

- **To improve flowering:** Proper pruning results in more and bigger blooms. Especially with hybrid teas grown for cut flowers, good pruning practices give you those huge flowers atop long, strong stems.

- **To keep plants healthy:** Pruning removes diseased or damaged parts of the plant. It also keeps the plant more open in the centre, increasing air circulation and reducing pest problems. (For more on controlling pests, see Chapter 22.)

- **To keep plants in bounds:** Without pruning, many rose plants get huge. Some of these monsters can take over an entire yard! Pruning keeps them where they're supposed to be. Pruning also keeps the flowers at eye level, where you can enjoy them up close.

- **To direct growth:** More than just keeping them in bounds, pruning can direct growth (and flowers) to a spot you pick. The best example is pruning a climbing rose to grow on a trellis or an arbour.

Tools of the Pruning Trade

Before you can start pruning your roses, you need the proper equipment:

- **Heavy gloves:** We shouldn't have to tell you this. You do know that roses have thorns, right? Choose gloves that are flexible but not easily punctured. Your nursery can recommend some types designed especially for roses.

- **Hand pruners:** This tool does most of the work. We prefer bypass pruners — the type with a curved blade and cutting arm, as shown in Figure 20-1. This tool provides the cleanest cut and is less likely to crush the cane below the cut, which often happens with anvil-type shears. Buy professional quality hand pruners rather than cheap ones — your hands will thank you.

- **Loppers:** These are similar to hand pruners but have long handles to give you better leverage when cutting thicker canes. (See Figure 20-2.)

- **Pruning saw:** This saw is necessary for cutting really old, woody canes or dead wood. We like the folding type with a slightly curved blade, shown in Figure 20-3. This type fits neatly, if slightly uncomfortably, in your back pocket.

Figure 20-1:
Bypass hand
pruners with
a curved
blade and
cutting arm
make the
cleanest
cuts.

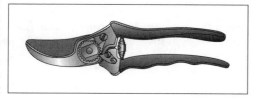

Figure 20-2:
Loppers
have long
handles,
providing
leverage
that makes
cutting
thick canes
easier.

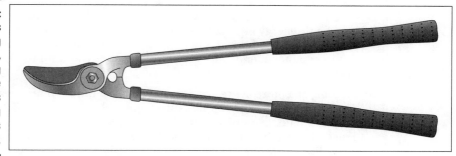

Figure 20-3:
A folding
pruning saw
fits in your
pocket. This
tool is best
for cutting
dead wood.

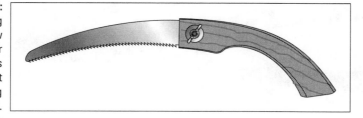

One thing you don't need is any kind of pruning paint or black goop to seal your pruning cuts. The rose does quite well on its own, healing itself. Using goop of any kind seals in and protects problems rather than excluding them.

Deep cuts and the same old response

Even though each type of rose prefers to be pruned a little bit differently, we like to simplify rose pruning into three types of pruning cuts. Each one generates a very predictable response from the plant. You'll probably want to use a combination of all three types of cuts:

- ✔ *Thinning* removes a branch at its origin — that is, it cuts a branch back to another branch or to the base of the plant. Usually, thinning does not result in vigorous growth below the cut. The result of thinning is that the plant is more open and less densely branched.

- ✔ *Cutting back* to a dormant bud stimulates that bud to grow. If you're pruning during the dormant season — when the rose is resting and leafless in winter — the bud won't grow until spring, but this type of cut focuses the plant's energy into that one bud and maybe one or two buds below it. Pruning back to a bud, at any time, is the best way to direct plant growth and to channel energy into specific canes that you want to bloom. Always prune to an outward facing bud.

- ✔ *Shearing* is a more aggressive type of pruning but is sometimes effective. You simply use hedge clippers (see Figure 20-4) to whack off a portion of the plant. The result of shearing is vigorous growth below the cuts and a denser, fuller plant. This cut is particularly effective with landscape roses, like shrubs and floribundas, especially if you plant them as hedges.

Figure 20-4: Hedge clippers are effective for aggressive pruning.

On a cool, crisp, early spring day . . .

Whenever we're asked when people should prune their roses, we always answer, "Whenever the weather's right and you have the time." And that's the truth. There's no exact day, or even exact week, for pruning roses.

Just before growth begins in early spring — exact timing depends upon your climate — is the best season for big pruning. And if you do a good job in the spring, you shouldn't have much to do throughout the rest of the season beyond deadheading and cutting great roses.

You do want to wait until after the coldest weather has passed and any winter damage to the plant has already occurred. That's usually about six weeks before the average date of the last spring frost. Your local nursery can give you exact frost dates for your area.

Avoid pruning in early fall. Any pruning after the first frost but before really cold weather usually signals the plant to grow. These new canes or shoots are very tender and will be killed by cold weather. Late fall pruning of species and hardy roses — after the leaves have fallen — is acceptable, but it is preferable to wait and see what the winter brings (and damages) before doing any major renovation pruning. Hybrid tea rose canes will be damaged by winter cold so it is preferable to cut them back as per our instructions later in this chapter.

For bigger flowers, get after those hybrid teas and grandifloras

Because hybrid teas and grandiflora roses are usually grown for large, long-stemmed flowers, you prune them more severely than other types of roses. This harder pruning channels the plant's energy into fewer canes, which produce bigger and better flowers.

Here are the basic steps for pruning hybrid tea and grandiflora roses. Figure 20-5 shows the "before" picture.

1. **In the early spring, remove dead or damaged canes.**

   When you remove the winter insulation, you'll likely see winter damage on the canes. This is dark brown, dead looking wood. Canes that are alive have a green tinge. You can tell for sure whether a cane is alive by cutting off a piece. A dead cane is brown inside; a healthy one is whitish. Scratching the bark will also show you the cane's status: a dead cane is brown when the bark is removed; a living cane is green right below the bark.

   Anyway, remove the dead canes, cutting back at least far enough so that the insides of the canes are white again. After a really cold winter, you may have to prune all the way to the ground. If the plant looks dead, don't despair; wait a few weeks and it may still put out new shoots. If it doesn't, you may have to practise another type of pruning — shovel pruning — to remove the dead rose plant and its roots.

   Gardeners who plant their bud unions quite deep to aid in winter survival may find that the rose canes die right to the ground every winter. The below-ground canes will throw out new shoots approximately three weeks after the more traditionally shallow-planted roses. Have patience.

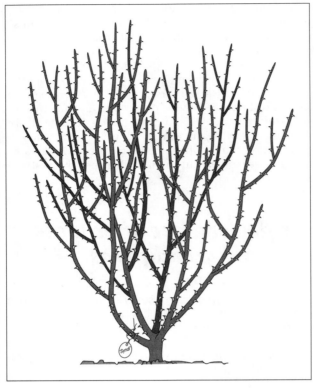

Figure 20-5:
A typical
hybrid tea
bush before
winter. The
darker canes
are the best
ones to cut
during the
growing
season. In
the fall,
shorten the
rest of the
canes as in
Figure 20-7.

2. Remove suckers.

If you're pruning budded plants, and you probably are, remove any *suckers* — vigorous canes that arise from the rootstock below the bud union. But be careful: Don't mistake desirable new canes for suckers. If you suspect that a new cane is a sucker, let it grow awhile. If its leaves are distinctly different from other leaves on the plant, go ahead and cut it away. (If you're growing own-root roses, or roses that have not been grafted but have their original roots, don't worry about suckers.) For more about rootstocks, bud unions, own-root roses, and the like, see Chapter 16.

Suckers should be removed as close to the rootstock as possible. Some gardeners use a claw hammer to pull them off the root, just like pulling a nail out of a board. The lower down you prune them, the less likely they are to regrow.

Suckers come all summer and they don't bloom. So if you have a large, vigorous cane without blooms, you likely have a sucker. Not only that, but sometimes, in the spring, the desirable top of the rose dies and the rootstock throws suckers to try to stay alive. These will grow like crazy, producing huge long arching canes and you'll think you're growing a great rose. Unfortunately, you're growing a non-blooming rose that should be compost. To positively identify a sucker, excavate around the base of the rose to expose the bud union. If the cane comes from below the bud union, it is a sucker.

3. **After you have pruned out the damaged canes and removed the suckers, select the flowering canes.**

The healthiest canes are thicker and usually bright green; older canes are brown or grey and sometimes shrivelled looking. Remove any spindly, twiggy branches. You want the flowering canes to be as evenly spaced around the plant as possible, and you should try to leave the centre of the plant open, without any canes. After you finish, the plant should be sort of cup-shaped with flowering canes around the outside.

The number of flowering canes you select depends on the vigour and age of the plant. With recently planted roses, leave about three to five flowering canes. Older plants can support more.

4. **Cut back the flowering canes you select by a third to a half.**

Cut back to an outward-facing bud, as shown in Figure 20-6. If you've left 30 to 45 centimetres (12 to 18 inches) of cane above ground for the winter, plan on pruning these back to 15 to 25 centimetres (6 to 9 inches) in the spring. In really tough winters, you may find yourself cutting further back than that to find live wood. This is another reason to put that bud union just a bit deeper if you're in a colder climate.

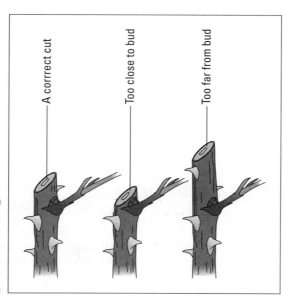

Figure 20-6: Prune about ¼ inch from an outward-facing bud.

A corrrect cut

Too close to bud

Too far from bud

5. **After the blooming season, in the late fall, cut back the entire plant.**

   After a wonderful growing season and fall frosts knock the leaves from the rose, it is time to start pruning for winter. With our tender roses, we prune for several reasons. The first is to stop the winter wind from whipping the canes around; this whipping can damage the bud union if the base of the cane is close to this joint. The second is to eliminate excess canes that might allow blackspot spores to overwinter. And the third is that the canes are going to die anyway and will not be used in next year's growth so we might just as well cut them back in the fall as wait for spring. We want to use fresh strong new canes next year to support next year's flowering so this year's canes can be pruned in the fall.

   Most rose growers cut the canes back to 45 to 60 centimetres (18 to 24 inches) in the fall and hill up to the top of the canes to protect the rose. In the colder parts of the country, some growers prune the canes down to 30 centimetres (12 inches) as the canes will be killed off that far anyway. See Figure 20-7 for details.

   And don't forget to insulate for winter after the leaves have fallen. See Chapter 21 for wintering tips. The following spring, return to step number one (above) and start all over.

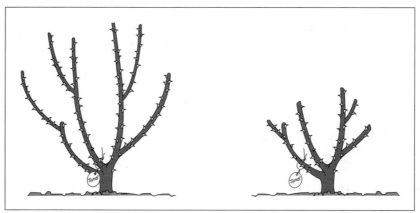

Figure 20-7: Cut back less if you live where winters are mild (left) and more if you live where winters are cold (right).

The shear pleasure of pruning floribundas and polyanthas

In the spring after you've removed the winter's protective cover, remove all canes that were damaged by winter. Again, just like hybrid teas, cut about one-third to one-half of the growth. Instead of picking three strong branches, shape the plant into as nice a rounded dome as possible, as shown in Figure 20-8.

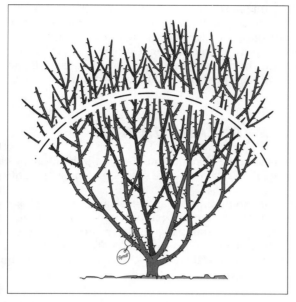

Then do a quick pass with a hand pruner, removing dead or very crowded branches and opening the centre of the plant a bit. Again, take the stronger and remove the weaker. The result will be a denser plant covered with blooms.

During the summer, you can prune floribunda and polyantha roses much like hybrid tea roses, but because they have a more twiggy growth habit (more, but smaller, stems and canes), you need to leave more flowering canes. However, because floribundas and polyanthas produce clusters of small flowers instead of those long-stemmed single beauties of the hybrid teas, and because they are more often used en masse as landscape plants, you can prune in a much easier way — simply lop 'em back with hedge clippers.

Pruning a mixed bag of shrubs

Shrub roses represent a real mishmash of different kinds of plants, from low-growing, spreading ground covers to neat, compact shrubs, to vigorous, upright monsters. Consequently, there are no hard-and-fast rules about how to prune them. Still, the basic techniques we've gone over in this chapter work — remove dead and diseased branches, remove any rubbing or crossing branches, try to open the centres a bit, and whack back whatever gets out of bounds.

The problem with giving hard and fast directions is that winter ruins these rules. What and how much you'll prune back varies from year to year. A tough, long winter with lots of Arctic highs (with their corresponding low temperatures) can sometimes burn even the toughest of species roses to the ground. At the risk of repeating ourselves, remove the dead, diseased, and rubbing branches and both you and the rose will be better for the exercise.

Tiny pruners for tiny plants?

You can shear miniature roses like floribundas and polyanthas, which is especially timesaving if you have several plants on landscape duty.

Because miniatures are so diminutive and often admired up close, many gardeners prefer to handle them more gently. If you are one of those gardeners, treat minis like hybrid teas, opening the centre, removing dead or twiggy branches, and selecting healthy flowering canes. To keep the plants compact, shorten the flowering canes a little more — by as much as three-quarters of their original height.

Pruning antiquity

Old garden roses, like shrubs, are a greatly varied group of plants. We believe in a less-is-more approach to pruning. Take out the damaged and dead branches, shear back a bit — but not by over a third, or you may reduce bloom — and remove anything that's out of bounds.

Old roses that bloom only once in spring should be pruned after flowering. Otherwise, pruning during the dormant season reduces the bloom. But the rules still apply — go lightly.

Taking pruning to new heights

Pruning climbing roses is a bit different from pruning other roses.

The first thing you need to know is that climbing roses don't climb like true vines. They don't twist around or attach to whatever they come in contact with like ivy or grapes. Instead, they put out long, longer, and longer yet, vigorous, arching canes. If you just leave them alone, they form a huge, sprawling shrub. Consequently, to get them to climb, you have to tie them (we like to use the green plastic tape sold in any nursery) to some kind of a support, such as a fence, arbour, or trellis. Different types of supports for climbing roses are discussed in Chapter 5, "Landscaping with Roses."

The most common types of climbers are the climbing sports of hybrid teas and large-flowered climbers, which bloom repeatedly throughout the growing season. Hardy Explorer roses that can be used as climbers are described in Chapter 15. (Climbing roses are further described in Chapter 12.) After planting, you should pretty much leave these climbers alone for two years so that they can develop long, sturdy canes. Just keep them within bounds and remove any dead or damaged growth. Tie them to the support if you need to keep them out of the way.

The fun begins after the second or third year of waiting. Think of your climbing rose as having two parts: the flowering shoots and the main structural canes on which they grow. Your goal in pruning is to select the sturdiest canes and tie them to the support in some evenly spaced manner, ideally in an angled or nearly horizontal fashion. The pattern doesn't have to be fancy. The number of canes you choose depends on the size of your support and the age of the plant — three to five is common. As the rose gets older, you can select more canes to fill up, say, a large fence. These main canes form the basic structure of the plant. Other canes should be removed.

After you bend these structural canes and tie them to the support, new growth sprouts along their length. These are the flowering shoots that — surprise! — flower. During dormancy, you should cut back these shoots to about two to three buds above the structural canes. After pruning, your climbing rose should look something like Figure 20-9.

Figure 20-9: A pruned climbing rose. The inset shows how to shorten flowering canes of climbing sports of hybrid teas and large-flowered climbers.

Occasionally, one of your structural canes may become too old and woody and not bloom as well as it used to. So get rid of it. New canes that you can train as replacements arise every year from the base of the plant.

The rules change a bit with climbing roses that bloom only once in spring. Wait until after they bloom to prune; then remove more of the older structural canes and replace them with new ones. The new canes produce most of the next season's bloom.

Post-pruning cleanup

After pruning, cleaning up and discarding or destroying the plant debris is important. Many insects and diseases live on dormant leaves and branches. And even though you remove dormant leaves and branches from the plant, pests can find their way back to the bush if you leave the prunings hanging around.

Start by removing any leaves left on the rose plant during dormancy. Then rake everything up and either discard or burn it. You can run the stuff through a shredder and add the debris to a compost pile, but you still risk harbouring some pest organisms. To avoid future problems, keep the compost pile far away from your roses.

Deadheading: No Free Rides on This Rose

You do most of the pruning described up to this point during the dormant season, when plants are leafless. But you also need to prune a bit during the growing season. Most important, you have to deadhead. *Deadheading* is removing spent flowers — those that have withered and died — so that the plant can channel its energy into producing more flowers instead of seeds.

As with other types of pruning, you can deadhead the hard way or the easy way:

- ✔ You should prune most hybrid teas the hard way — cutting back each spent flower shoot down to at least the first leaf with five leaflets, as shown in Figure 20-10. Done this way, the plants maintain a neater appearance, rebloom sooner, and produce sturdier stems that are less likely to result in droopy flowers. Remember, buds arising from thicker parts of a cane grow into sturdier canes themselves. Therefore, in order to get the largest possible new cane to grow from a bud eye, you have to cut down to where the main cane is fairly substantial. However, never remove more than a third of the plant at one time during the growing season. Doing so may weaken the plant unnecessarily.

✔ With more floriferous landscape roses like floribundas, shrubs, and miniatures, deadheading in the preceding manner can take forever. So if you don't have time, get out your trusty old hedge clippers and whack off the faded flower clusters. The disadvantage of the whack method is that the plants take a little longer to rebloom. But the plants are much better off than if you hadn't whacked at all.

Other than deadheading, prune during the summer as you see fit. If a branch gets in the way or is out of bounds, give it the axe.

Right after spring pruning is the ideal time to apply a dormant spray to your plants, as long as the plants are still dormant and leafless and have not started to grow. See Chapter 22 for instructions.

Figure 20-10:
Deadhead hybrid teas by cutting back spent flowers to just below the first leaf with five leaflets.

Chapter 21

Protecting Roses Where Winters Are Cold

*L*ove those hybrid teas but fear our Canadian winters will be too much for them? No worries. With a little extra effort (which is entirely worth it), you can keep those babies alive no matter how wild the winter gets. That's what this chapter is about: protecting roses — any kind of roses — where winters are cold. Mounding soil over the base of your plants is one secret, but you can make your mounding more effective in some easy and inexpensive ways. Planting the bud unions deeper is another secret, but hey, we're going to describe all our best secrets in this chapter.

How Hardy Are They?

Most plants are judged by the minimum low temperatures they can withstand in winter without being killed or damaged. This is called the plant's *hardiness*. Unfortunately, rose hardiness is not a cut-and-dried matter because conditions other than cold temperatures can devastate a rose plant. And these conditions vary from winter to winter.

Even within rose classifications, different varieties can be hardier than others. For example, the new, fragile-looking, striped floribunda called 'Scentimental' is surprisingly so hardy that if you live in zone 6 or warmer, it doesn't need much winter protection. But the lovely white floribunda 'French Lace' is so tender that it often has to be replanted every year no matter where you plant it. Unfortunately, there's no sure-fire way to tell which varieties will be hardy in your yard, other than having experience in your yard.

But generally, if you live anywhere in Canada where winter temperatures predictably reach –12° C (10° F), and most of us do, many of the most popular roses — such as hybrid teas, floribundas, grandifloras, miniatures, and climbers — need some kind of protection to survive the winter. You can find more information about rose hardiness, as well as a list of the hardiest varieties, in the descriptive chapters on rose types. Also see Chapter 15 on hardy Explorer and Parkland roses.

Without protection in areas where winters get colder than a variety's hardiness can tolerate, parts or all of the top of the plant will be killed or damaged. If a tender variety is budded onto a hardy rootstock, the rootstock may survive, but the flowering top of the plant can be killed or damaged. Who knows what will grow from the rootstock next spring? What we know is that it won't flower much, if at all. That's the main advantage of own-root roses — they sprout true from the base. (For more information about roses and rootstocks, see Chapter 16.)

Luckily, protecting roses is not a difficult task.

Preparing for a Cold Winter

Even though different types of roses are given general hardiness ratings, how you care for specific plants prior to the onset of cold weather can affect their hardiness. A good analogy is the difference between a car with a radiator full of fresh antifreeze and one that has only water.

A rose that is properly prepared for cold weather is said to be *hardened off*.

Most roses harden off by themselves during the gradual onset of fall and winter. During this time, the plant's cell walls thicken as they prepare for dormancy. In many rose varieties, this process manifests itself by the canes taking on a purplish cast. Unfortunately, purple canes indicate the onset of dormancy only and don't give much of an indication as to whether the variety is hardier than varieties that harden off without turning purple.

The better care your roses receive throughout the growing season, the better chance they stand to get through the winter unscathed, or at least without too much damage. If the plant suffers from lack of water or nutrients or was devastated by disease during the summer and fall, it will be in a weakened state when winter arrives.

The key to hardening off a rose is to make sure that the plant stops growing and becomes fully dormant before the onset of the coldest weather. You can encourage full dormancy in two ways:

> ✔ **Stop fertilizing six to eight weeks before the first frost.** Late applications of nitrogen fertilizers can keep a rose growing longer into fall or winter than is safe. If you don't know the average date of your first frost, ask an employee at your local nursery.
>
> ✔ **Let hips develop.** Instead of cutting off (*deadheading*) the spent flowers from the last fall blooms, let the spent flowers go to seed. That is, let the hips — or the seedpods — develop fully. Doing so slows growth and encourages dormancy.

Keeping Roses Cold

Why would you want to keep your roses cold? You're supposed to be trying to protect them from cold, not keeping them cold, aren't you?

Well, the two are kind of the same thing. You see, whether or not a rose plant is damaged by cold is not purely a matter of how low the temperatures get. Strong winter winds can burn or dry out the canes. And fluctuating temperatures, which can cause plants to freeze and thaw, refreeze and thaw again (that hurts just to think about it!), can kill a cane in a snap.

So what you really want to do when you winter-protect a rose is to insulate the plant not only from the coldest temperatures but also from unusually warm weather that may cause the plant to thaw prematurely. And you also want to protect the rose from drying winds.

Here's the easiest way to winter-protect roses:

1. **Make sure that your plants are well watered.**

   Fall rains usually do the job, but if the weather has been dry, water deeply after the first frost but before the ground freezes.

2. **In mid to late fall, after most of the leaves have fallen from the rose and when the nights are getting regularly frosty, mound spadefuls of soil over the base of the plant, extending the soil up at least 30 to 45 centimetres (1 to 1½ feet) above the soil line.**

   Take this soil from another part of the garden, not from around the roots. You don't want to dig around the roots and you don't want to expose them to more freezing than they need.

3. **When the ground is thoroughly frozen, cover the soil mound with a thick layer — at least 30 centimetres (1 foot) — of mulch, such as straw, leaves, or compost.**

   Doing so ensures that the ground stays frozen. If any leaves are left on the plant, pull them off. Besides harbouring disease, leaves can increase drying. Cut off the canes above the soil line.

4. Start pulling back the mulch as soon as it thaws in the spring and put it aside to be reapplied as a summer mulch once the soil mound is removed.

When the ground begins to thaw, slowly remove the pyramid of soil from around the rose canes and spread it in another section of the garden. But don't get started too early; a sudden cold snap can be brutal. Watch for the yellow blooms of the forsythia or buds swelling on trees. Once these are in bloom or swelling, it's okay to remove the mound of soil. Remove the soil carefully, because you may find that growth is beginning — you can tell if buds are swollen and are beginning to stretch. Those new buds are very easy to break off, which is why working carefully around the plant is important. Applying a gentle stream of water is often better than using your hands.

Late frosts hurt only the buds that have opened up and are tender (having been protected by the mulch and mounded soil). So, if you have new, tender shoots and a forecasted frost is on its way — protect those shoots by carefully covering the plant with mulch or damp cloth coverings (see Figure 21-1) and watering heavily (hopefully before the temperature drops). Some rose growers from southerly climates suggest that a good snow cover takes the place of soil mounding and mulch insulation. Snow is a good insulator on top of mounded soil and 30 centimetres (1 foot) of mulch, but it doesn't help much by itself when it comes to protecting tender roses in Canadian winters.

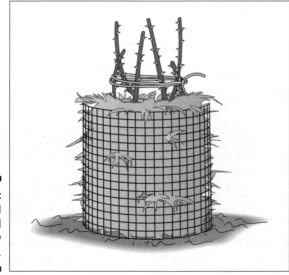

Figure 21-1:
A mulched and wrapped rose ready for winter.

Rose growers are an ingenious lot when it comes to protecting their roses. Some gardeners wrap the mounded soil with wire fencing and then fill the fencing with insulating material, as shown in Figure 21-1. Some cover their roses with polyfoam pyramids. Others, led by the Royal Botanical Gardens in Hamilton, Ontario, use a nursery overwintering foam cloth to cover their rose beds. We would prefer to move our roses (with the gardener) to a more southerly clime for the winter. Instead, we deep plant.

Planting Deep

As we've mentioned before, deep planting is another Canadian trick to protect tender roses from the predations of Old Man Winter. When you plant, put that bud union between 10 to 15 centimetres (4 to 6 inches) deep. It is like having a permanent insulating mound installed on the rose. The key to success with deep planting is adequate summer feeding to get the food down to the deeper-than-normal root system.

If you're having trouble overwintering your tender roses, you can also dig and replant the rose when it is dormant. Simply dig up the rose, trying to keep as many of the roots intact as possible, and excavate a deep enough hole to install it at the lower depth. See Chapter 17 for planting instructions.

If you're not having trouble overwintering your tender roses, don't bother experimenting with deep planting. On the other hand, it really doesn't matter where in Canada you live — if you're killing your tender roses, try deep planting to see how it works for you.

Protecting Climbers and Tree Roses

Because climbing roses and tree roses are more upright and more exposed to cold and wind, they need special protection. If you live in zone 5 and colder, take tender climbers off their supports. Tie the canes together and wrap them with burlap or insulating material. Dig a trench 30 to 45 centimetres (12 to 18 inches) deep and bury the rose in the trench. It helps to do this as late in the fall as possible and include some mouse bait along with the rose. Put the bait in an old boot right next to the rose so it stays dry and available all winter long. Tree roses can be stored the same way. Alternately, dig up tree roses and store them for winter in a cool garage or basement where they can be kept moist but not frozen solid.

Some gardeners use what is called a tip-over method of overwintering roses, as shown in Figure 21-2. To do this, dig up half the roots and lean the rose over on its side. Use stakes to hold the rose down and in place. Then cover the rose with soil and 30 centimetres (1 foot) of mulch to protect it for the winter. It's sort of like having an aboveground trench. This works well in areas where the roses being grown are almost but not quite hardy enough to grow on their own.

Figure 21-2:
You can protect a tender rose through the winter in marginal areas of winter cold by uprooting one side of the plant so that you can lean it over and bury it.

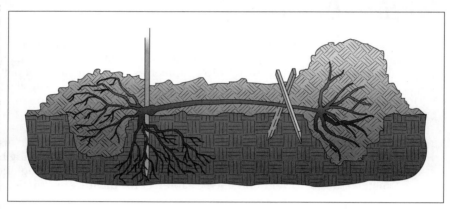

Chapter 22

Outsmarting Rose Pests and Diseases

Certain insects and plant diseases probably like your roses as much as you do — but not more so than they like many other kinds of plants. Yeah, right. Then how come every time you walk into a nursery, garden centre, or even a grocery store, all you see are rose care products — sprays, dusts, combination fungicides and insecticides, and preventative three-way cure-alls piled up to the roof?

Big surprise. Roses are, after all, among the most popular garden plants, and gardening is big business. Millions of dollars are made each year from products that catch the eye of rose growers, whether growers actually need those products or not.

The truth is that more than one approach to controlling rose pests exists. Some gardeners are determined to have their plants produce perfect flowers; these growers are looking for the perfect flower to display at a rose show and spray their plants every seven to ten days to prevent every insect and disease from touching their roses. On the other hand, many gardeners never spray with strong chemicals and still have beautiful rose gardens.

We recommend a flexible, common-sense approach to controlling rose pests. Take a little and give a little. We can live with a few bugs — they make for a more diverse garden. But if they try to wipe out our plants, we do something to stop them. But even then, we use only products that have the least impact on the environment. This common-sense approach to pest control is what this chapter is all about.

Preventing Problems

You can do several things to prevent insects and diseases from becoming problems on your roses:

- **Grow healthy plants.** A good, strong rose plant is less likely to be seriously bothered by pests or diseases than one that is weakened by under- or overwatering or that is planted where it doesn't get enough sunlight. Proper pruning to keep the plant open and free to good air circulation helps prevent disease. Even too much of a normally good thing — like nitrogen fertilizer — can result in excessive, lush growth that attracts insects like aphids. The tender leaves are just too luscious to pass up. So read Chapters 17 through 20 on caring for roses; they're the first step in preventing insects and disease.

- **Use compost as a primary food source.** Compost promotes the growth of beneficial soil organisms that eat fungus spores and other bad guys. As a midsummer food source, use a compost tea, fish emulsion drench, or foliar spray. (See Chapter 19 for details.) Fish emulsion has tons of minor nutrients that your rose will thrive on. A strong-growing rose is a healthy rose.

- **Plant problem-free varieties.** Many rose varieties, especially the newer ones, have natural resistance bred into them. On the other hand, some of the loveliest roses are also the most disease prone. It's like anything else — for the best you have to pay a price, in this case more pests. Roses of all types vary in their susceptibility to pests, and where you live plays a part, too; some problems that are common in one region are rare in others. Regional disease problems are discussed in Chapter 4.

  If a rose has good pest resistance, we say so in the variety descriptions beginning with Chapter 8. Rose mail-order catalogues (see Appendix B) are also a good source of information about pest and disease resistance.

- **Encourage and use beneficial insects.** Beneficial insects are the good bugs in a garden — the insects that feed on the bugs that bother your roses. You probably have a bunch of different kinds in your garden already, but you can also purchase them and release them into your garden. The more beneficials, the fewer the pests. File that in your memory for now; we give you specifics later in this chapter.

✔ **Keep your garden clean.** Many insects and diseases spend the winter or go through various stages of their life cycle in garden debris, like fallen leaves or prunings left on the ground. If you remove these hiding places, you also likely reduce the number of future pests. So occasionally rake around the base of your plants to clean up fallen leaves, and always discard or burn your prunings. And apply a mulch to prevent water from splashing disease spores onto the foliage.

✔ **Know the enemy.** The more you know about specific pests and diseases common to your area — when they occur and how they spread — the more easily you can avoid them. For example, the fungal disease black spot runs rampant on wet foliage. By simply adjusting your watering so that you don't wet the leaves of your plants, or by watering early in the day so that plants dry out quickly, you can reduce black spot's occurrence.

✔ **Apply a dormant spray.** This application is the most important preventative spray you can make, and the only one we recommend that you apply every single year. Usually a combination of fairly benign horticultural oil and a fungicide like lime sulphur or fixed copper, a dormant spray smothers insect eggs and kills disease organisms before they become a problem. Apply the spray right before you put the rose to bed and again in the spring after you uncover. The following summer your roses will be much more disease free.

Identifying Rose Pests

Before you wrestle with any insect or disease problem, make sure that you properly identify the problem. For a start, consult our list of common insects and diseases that follows, and also take a look at the information we give about the best products and materials to use. If you need further help, contact a local nursery that has a variety of reference books to consult and is familiar with local problems.

If you like to look things up for yourself, ask at your local nursery or library for the *Ortho Problem Solver*. It's a 1,000-page encyclopedia of garden pest problems, each one with a colour picture.

Insects that prey on roses

Here are the most common insect pests that you are likely to find infesting your roses and the best ways to control them. Later in this chapter we go into full details on the insecticides, pesticides and other treatments recommended in the following list.

✔ **Aphids** are tiny, pear-shaped pests that come in many colours, including black, green, and red. (See Figure 22-1.) They congregate on new growth and flower buds, sucking plant sap with their needlelike noses. They leave behind a sticky sap that may turn black if infected with sooty mould.

Aphids are easy to control. You can knock them off a plant with a strong jet of water from a hose or use insecticidal soap. The soap helps to wash off the sooty mould, too. Sometimes, if you just wait a week or two, the aphid population boom is followed by a build-up in beneficial insects, especially lady beetles (commonly known as ladybugs), and they take matters into their own hands before serious damage occurs. We knock the first flush off our roses with a water spray and then depend on the developing beneficials to provide protection for the rest of the summer.

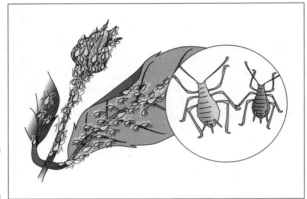

Figure 22-1:
Aphids.

✔ **Cucumber beetles** are easy to recognize — they're about ½ centimetre (¼ inch) long and yellowish green, with black stripes or dots on their backs. Two different types exist. They feed mostly on cucumbers and vegetable plants, but they also love rose blossoms and take big bites out of them just as they open.

To control these pests, spray with *pyrethrin* (a botanical insecticide) or insecticidal soap. *Parasitic nematodes* (yes, worms) prey on the soil-borne larvae. Rotenone dust is another excellent insecticide for beetle problems. (See our description a little later in this chapter.)

✔ **Japanese beetles** are becoming more of a problem for Canadian gardeners. The 1-centimetre (½-inch) long beetles have coppery bodies and metallic green heads. (See Figure 22-2.) They feed on both flowers and foliage, often skeletonizing the leaves.

Figure 22-2:
A Japanese
beetle.

Control can be tough. Treating your lawn and garden soil with parasitic nematodes or milky spore may reduce the white, C-shaped larvae, but more adults will probably fly in from your neighbours' yards. Turning the soil to expose the grubs to birds may also help. Floral-scented traps that attract adult beetles are available, but the traps may bring in more beetles than you had before. If you try traps, keep them at least 30 metres (100 feet) away from your roses.

Insecticidal soap and pyrethrins are effective alternative sprays for controlling adult beetles. An excellent control is to enlist the help of predator nematodes, to attack and eat lawn grubs. (These nematodes also eat over 200 other pests; see the full details later in this chapter.) Your local garden centre or specialty nursery is the source for these tiny critters.

✔ **June beetles** are about 2.5 centimetres (1 inch) long and reddish brown to black. They usually feed at night and prefer the foliage of various trees, but they also feed on roses. Control is the same as for Japanese beetles, but milky spore is not effective against June beetle grubs.

✔ **Caterpillars** are the larvae of moths or butterflies. They occasionally feed on the foliage or flowers of roses. You can control them by releasing trichogramma wasps. Rotenone and diatomaceous earth work their magic on caterpillars.

✔ **Rose midges** are small, almost invisible pests that rasp new growth, especially flower buds, causing it to shrivel and turn black. If your rose plant looks healthy but you get shrivelled flowers, suspect rose midge. Insecticidal soaps sometimes work, as does rotenone, but the best environmental control is predator nematodes attacking the soil-borne larvae. Diazanon applied as a soil drench also works for this pest.

Figure 22-3:
A rose
chafer.

✔ **Rose chafers** are tan-coloured beetles with long legs, as shown in Figure 22-3. Again, control is the same as for Japanese beetles and June beetles, but milky spore is not effective against the grubs, which is why the predator nematodes are so useful.

✔ **Stem borers** (shown in Figure 22-4) are tiny, wormlike larvae that bore into canes and feed inside, causing the cane to wilt and, eventually, die. Borers are not hard to control. First, cut off the wilted stem well back into healthy tissue. You may be able to see a small hole where the borer entered the stem or two raised circular markings around the cane. Cut back below that and look to see whether tissue inside the cane is damaged. If so, cut lower still until the inside of the cane is healthy. Few sprays of any kind are effective, although you may get some of the larvae by using parasitic nematodes near the base of the plant. After feeding, the larvae drop to the ground to mature. Discard or burn the cuttings, do not leave them to compost. Some gardeners swear that putting a bit of white glue on the cut end helps stop subsequent borer problems.

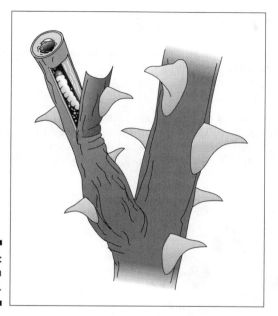

Figure 22-4:
A rose stem
borer.

✔ **Spider mites** are tiny, spiderlike arachnids that you can barely see without a magnifying glass. If the population gets big enough, you can see their fine webbing beneath the leaves. And as they suck plant juices, the leaves become yellowish with a silvery stippling or sheen. If things really get bad, the plant may start dropping leaves. Mites are most common in hot, dry summer climates and on dusty plants.

A daily bath with a strong spray from a hose should keep infestations down. You can control spider mites with insecticidal soaps, which also help to clean off a plant's leaves. Summer oil is also effective, as is releasing predatory mites. The key to controlling spider mites is consistent and regular action. You will not kill them all with one or even two sprays.

✔ **Thrips** are another almost-invisible troublemaker. They feed on flower petals, causing them to be discoloured and the buds to be deformed as they open. Often the first sign you see is an unopened bud that is bent over at a sharp angle. Thrips like all roses but are particularly fond of light-coloured varieties.

Many beneficial insects feed on thrips, especially lacewings. Insecticidal soaps are also effective, as are several stronger botanical insecticides, including rotenone.

Troublesome rose diseases

The following sections talk about five of the most common rose diseases and suggest some techniques for controlling them.

Black spot

Like its name says, this fungus causes small black spots on rose leaves and stems, as shown in Figure 22-5. The edges of the spots are fringed, and the tissue around the spots often turns yellow. In bad infections, the plant may drop all its leaves. This disease is most common during a warm, humid summer with frequent rain.

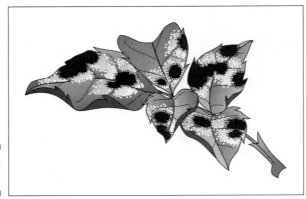

Figure 22-5:
Black spot.

The best advice to prevent black spot (besides planting disease-resistant varieties) is to clean up your winter prunings — the most common source of reinfection — and use a dormant spray that includes lime sulphur. Also, avoid overhead watering or water early in the morning so that the leaves can dry out quickly. Mixing baking soda and summer oil spray, as mentioned later in this chapter, provides some control, as does liquid sulphur.

Downy mildew

Often confused with powdery mildew and black spot, but much more serious, downy mildew has the capability to defoliate a plant in 24 hours. Greyish white fuzz forms on the bottoms of the leaves. Round, purple blotches with yellow edges form on the tops. Leaves often turn brittle and drop. Fortunately, downy mildew is less common than other rose diseases. It usually shows up after long periods of cool, wet weather and then clears itself up when the weather warms.

The disease needs moist conditions to spread, so avoid overhead watering and water early in the morning — that way, everything has time to dry out. Good cultural methods are the best control — prune to increase air circulation and clean up plant debris. In late fall or winter, use a dormant spray. An early spring spray with a copper-based fungicide is also effective if downy mildew has been a problem in your garden.

Powdery mildew

Greyish white, powdery fungus infects new leaves and flower buds, causing them to become distorted and crinkled-looking. (See Figure 22-6.) Unlike most other fungal diseases, powdery mildew spreads on dry foliage as well as wet.

Many rose growers prevent its spread by overhead watering or a sprinkling down each morning, thus washing the spores off the leaves before they can establish themselves. Other preventative measures include planting resistant varieties, planting in full sun, and pruning to encourage air circulation. Effective preventative sprays include antitranspirants and the baking soda and summer oil mixture, both mentioned later in this chapter.

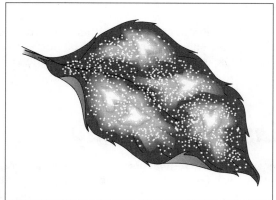

Figure 22-6:
Powdery
mildew.

Rust

On a plant that has rust, small, orange pustules form on the undersides of the leaves. Yellow spots appear on top. (See Figure 22-7.) If the rust is severe enough, the plant can lose all its leaves. This disease is most troublesome when days are warm but nights are cool; prolonged hot, dry weather usually stops its development.

Prevention is similar to black spot — winter cleanup and dormant spray. Make sure that you also strip off infected leaves. Spraying a lime-sulphur (or sulphur by itself) mix will provide some control, but there is not much that can kill rust.

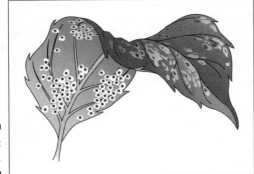

Figure 22-7:
Rust.

Rose mosaic viruses

Rose mosaic viruses cause yellow mottling on the leaves and deformed new growth. There's not much you can do about it. Most of the time, it shows up on a few leaves and doesn't do much harm to anything. It can't spread from plant to plant, but you should definitely avoid taking cuttings from or hybridizing with infected plants. The virus is passed on to offspring.

All reputable rose nurseries will replace a plant with a virus. Large commercial nurseries that grow roses now supply plants that are 95 percent virus free, but some older plants may be infected. Severely infected garden plants should be destroyed.

Encouraging Garden Good Guys

Okay, open your mental file on beneficial insects — the garden good guys — and fill it with some specifics. Following are some things you can do to encourage beneficial insects to populate your garden and reduce the number of rose pests:

- ✔ Avoid indiscriminate use of broad-spectrum pesticides, which kill everything, the good guys and the bad. If you do spray, use a spray that specifically targets the pest you want to eliminate.

- ✔ Have a diverse garden with many different kinds and sizes of plants. Doing so gives the beneficials places to hide and reproduce. Variety can also provide an alternative food source, because many beneficials like to eat pollen or flower nectar, too. Some plants that attract beneficials include Queen Anne's lace, parsley (especially if you let the flowers develop), dill, clover, fennel, goldenrod, milkweed, and yarrow. You'll find many of these plants described in *Gardening For Canadians For Dummies*.

If beneficial insects are not as numerous in your garden as you would like, you can buy them from garden suppliers (we list several in Appendix B). If you know that a particularly difficult pest is likely to appear, order in advance. That way, you can release the beneficials in time to prevent problems.

Following are some of the good insects that you can buy to help control rose pests:

- **Lady beetles:** These are your basic ladybugs, with black-spotted reddish shells. Both the adult and particularly the lizard-like larvae are especially good at feeding on small insects like aphids and thrips. Releasing adults is sometimes not very effective because Mother Nature has programmed them to migrate on down the road, so they leave your garden quickly. Try *preconditioned* lady beetles, which have been deprogrammed (you don't want to know how); they are more likely to stick around. And release them just before sundown. That way, they'll at least spend the night. Release a few thousand of them in your garden in spring as soon as you notice aphids.

- **Green lacewings:** Their voracious larvae feed on aphids, thrips, mites, and various insect eggs. These insects are one of the most effective beneficials for garden use. Release them in your garden in late spring after danger of frost has passed.

- **Parasitic nematodes:** These microscopic worms parasitize many types of soil-dwelling and burrowing insects, including the grubs of Japanese beetles, June beetles, and rose chafers. Because grubs usually inhabit lawns, you have to apply these worms there, too, as well as around the base of your rose plants. Apply parasitic nematodes to the soil around the base of your plants once a year in the spring.

- **Predatory mites:** This type of mite feeds on spider mites and thrips. Add them to your garden in spring as soon as frost danger has passed.

- **Trichogramma wasps:** Tiny wasps (harmless to people) that attack moth eggs and butterfly larvae (that is, caterpillars). Release these garden good guys when temperatures are above 22° C (72° F).

You'll find that by avoiding the use of sprays other than forceful water jets and by using your hands to control many pests, natural predators will make their appearance. If you use compost to control soil-borne problems and establish a natural order in the garden, your problems will usually be more easily controlled.

Aphid Hors d'Oeuvre

Good bugs are no dummies; they hang out in gardens that offer the most diverse and reliable menu. That's why eliminating every last insect pest from your garden makes no sense.

As we said earlier, our approach to pest control is to have maximum diversity in the garden. That's why having some "bad" bugs around all the time is important. Aphids are like hors d'oeuvre for so many helpful insects (not to mention hummingbirds), so you always hope to have a few in your garden. Otherwise, what will the good bugs eat? But accepting the bugs also means that you have to accept a little pest damage once in a while. So you're really just trying to manage the pests, not nuke them off the face of the earth. You want to keep them at acceptable levels, without letting them get out of control.

Spend time in your garden. Poke around, turn leaves upside down. Investigate. Knowing what's out there is important.

Controlling Pests and Disease

To manage insects and diseases successfully, you have to be a good observer, checking your roses frequently, if not daily, for developing problems. If an insect or disease does get out of hand, you want to treat it effectively without disrupting all the life in the garden. To do that, we start with what we consider our first line of defence against pest outbreaks: pesticides that can be very effective against a certain pest, are pretty safe to use, and have a mild impact on the rest of the garden's life forms.

In general, these products are short-lived after you use them in the garden — that's what makes them so good. However, in order to get effective control, you often have to use them more frequently than stronger chemicals.

Here are our favourites:

- **Biological controls:** This method involves pitting one living thing against another. Releasing beneficial insects is one example of biological control. Applying predator nematodes to control grubs is another.

- **Botanical insecticides**: These insecticides are derived from plants. The following two are especially useful against rose pests.

  - **Pyrethrins** are derived from the painted daisy, *Chrysanthemum cinerariifolium*. It is a broad-spectrum insecticide, which means that it kills a wide range of insects, both good (spray late in the evening to avoid killing bees) and bad. That's the downside. The upside is that this insecticide kills pests like thrips and beetles quickly, breaks down rapidly in sunlight, and has low toxicity to mammals, which means that it's essentially harmless to people, pets, and the environment.

The terminology can be confusing, however. *Pyrethrum* is the ground-up flower of the daisy. *Pyrethrins* are the insecticide components of the flower. *Pyrethroids,* such as permethrin and resmethrin, are synthetic compounds that resemble pyrethrins but are more toxic and persistent. Consequently, we prefer to avoid pyrethroids for home garden use.

- **Rotenone** is derived from roots of some tropical trees. It is an extremely potent dust for killing a wide range of pests. Its advantage is that it breaks down very quickly in sunlight — disappearing within a day or two. Do not confuse short-lived with ineffective. Also, do not treat it lightly just because it is a botanically derived insecticide. Always wear a mask and long sleeves when using it. Pregnant women should not apply this product.

✔ **Horticultural oils:** When sprayed on a plant, these highly refined oils smother pest insects and their eggs. The words *highly refined* mean that sulphur and other components of the oil that damage plants are removed. They are relatively non-toxic and short-lived. Two types exist:

- **Dormant oils** are sprayed on roses when they are leafless in winter. They are often combined with a fungicide like lime sulphur or fixed copper to help kill overwintering disease spores.

- **Summer oils** usually are more highly refined (or further diluted) than dormant oils — they're thinner. They can be used on roses during the growing season, as long as the plants have been well watered and temperatures are not above 29° C (85° F).

Avoid using oil sprays when temperatures are likely to reach above 29° C (85° F). When it's that hot, the oil can damage plant leaves.

✔ **Insecticidal soaps:** Derived from the salts of fatty acids, insecticidal soaps kill mostly soft-bodied pests like aphids, spider mites, and whiteflies. They can also be effective against Japanese beetles. They work fast, break down quickly, and are non-toxic to humans. Insecticidal soaps are most effective when mixed with soft water. Soaps sometimes burn tender foliage.

✔ **Baking soda (sodium bicarbonate):** Regular old Arm & Hammer has been a popular powdery mildew remedy (partially effective against black spot) in the rose underground for the past few years. If you want to try it, do it like this: Mix 1 rounded tablespoon of baking soda with 1 tablespoon of summer oil in a gallon of water. Apply weekly to well-watered plants, and don't spray if temperatures are above 29° C (85° F). The combination of the spray with the heat damages leaves. Ongoing research has revealed that potassium bicarbonate might work a little better and be less prone to damage leaves. We expect to see products containing potassium bicarbonate and summer oil soon. An alternative recipe is to use 2 tablespoons of baking soda with a gallon of water and a squirt of household detergent or soap to help with the mixing. Whichever recipe you experiment with, be sure to keep the solution well mixed even while spraying.

Baking soda can burn leaves. Apply it in the early morning and not at all during very hot weather.

- ✔ **Sulphur** is a good fungicide and can be used as preventative for black spot or a slow-down agent to reduce the spread of rusts. Obtain it at your garden centre and follow the directions for mixing. It stains concrete or wood yellow, so be careful mixing it. If you experiment with powdered sulphur as a dust for pest control, remember to wear goggles. When sulphur combines with water (as it will if you get a bit of the dust in your eyes) it forms sulphuric acid. Your eyes will sting and itch for some time.

- ✔ **Antitranspirants:** When sprayed on plant foliage, these form a thin, waxy layer that can prevent fungal disease like powdery mildew from invading the leaves. Antitranspirants don't kill disease, but they may prevent a disease from getting worse.

Pesticide Double-Speak

People call pesticides such as carbaryl, diazinon, and malathion the "traditional" pesticides. Such a label would make George Orwell proud. These pesticides are not traditional at all, unless you figure that only what happened after World War II is "traditional." Most of the petroleum-derived pesticides that line the shelves in garden centres weren't available to home gardeners until the 1950s.

Many chemical pesticides are labelled for controlling rose pests. They are generally effective but usually kill beneficial insects as well as pests. And in some cases, pests have developed resistance to a particular spray, so the spray no longer provides adequate control.

A Rosarian's Approach to Pest Prevention

One of the things we do in our gardens, even with environmentally sound methods such as rotenone or sulphur, is to use at least two products in rotation. For example, in a season when black spot is a problem, we'll spray with a baking soda mix in week one, and we'll switch to liquid sulphur in week two. In week three we go back to baking soda, and we continue using the products in alternate weeks for the whole spray season. This reduces the ability of the problem to acclimatize itself and develop immunity to the control agent. We alternate sprays for insect pests as well as sprays for diseases.

Pesticide safety

No matter which pesticides you decide to use, you must use them *safely*. Even pesticides that have a relatively low impact on your garden environment can be dangerous to use and toxic to humans. This is true of several commonly used botanical insecticides.

Always follow instructions on the product label exactly. Doing otherwise is against the law. Both the pest you're trying to control and the plant you're spraying (sometimes plants are listed as groups, such as landscape shrubs or flowering vines) must be listed on the label.

Wear gloves when mixing and applying pesticides and fungicides. Dust masks are wonderful inventions. Long sleeves to protect your arms are good, as are rubber boots with pant legs tucked inside for cleaning with a water hose before you truck off into the house for a well-deserved cool drink. In other words, don't carry the spray residues with you on your clothing or shoes.

Spray when winds are calm. Store chemicals in properly labelled containers well out of the reach of children (a locked cabinet is best). Dispose of empty pesticide containers as described on the label, or contact your local waste disposal company for appropriate disposal sites.

We do not believe in using *combination products* (fertilizer, insecticide, and fungicide). They are a shotgun approach to pest control that often results in excess use of unneeded chemicals, which can harm the environment.

Chapter 23

Making More Roses

So you bought a couple of rosebushes, and now they're growing great. You love the flowers; you love the fragrance. You're hooked. It's time for more roses!

What's the best way to increase your collection? The easiest and most obvious is to go to a garden centre and buy more plants. Or if you spent hours poring over the newest rose catalogues, why not order from them? Make no mistake: Buying new, healthy, vigorous, young rose plants is the very best way to increase your collection.

But noooo. *You* have to be the ultimate rosarian and make your own plants. Okay, we can help. But know right now that there's nothing simple about it, no matter which method you use. The concept is simple enough, but a rose isn't a geranium or an impatiens. Roses are as easy to grow as other flowers, but they're not as easy to propagate. Roses certainly are fun to *propagate* (a heavy term for increasing their numbers), though, if you really enjoy the hobby.

You can propagate a rose plant in two ways:

  ✔ **Asexual propagation:** Like cloning, asexual propagation creates new plants that are identical to the original plant. You can use several methods to create new plants of the same variety: transplanting new shoots from own-root plants, rooting cuttings from the original plant, and budding the original variety onto rootstock. Also, if you have an expensive tissue culture lab, you can clone a new plant from just a single cell. But, as you can imagine, cloning a plant is complicated, so we won't get into it here.

One warning, however. As we mention in Chapter 1, new roses are patented (you see that weird little symbol on the rose label); therefore, asexually propagating patented roses is illegal. Although we doubt that the rose police will come to your yard to check for illegal propagation, out of respect for hybridizers who work so hard to bring new roses into the world, most rosarians gladly comply with the law. Don't worry; plenty of great rose varieties are off-patent and are prime candidates for propagating.

✔ **Sexual propagation (also known as _hybridizing_):** Pollen is taken from one rose to fertilize the eggs of another rose. Roses self-pollinate because they have both male and female parts. But the result is rarely as good as the original plant. So hybridizers take pollen from one plant, called the _pollen parent_, or dad, and brush it onto the female parts of another rose, called the _seed parent_, or mom. After seeds develop, they are planted to grow new varieties of roses. Sexually propagating patented roses, even the very newest varieties, is not illegal.

Raiding a Rose Garden

Own-root roses, usually of the old garden type and some modern shrubs, are not budded onto a rootstock (see Chapter 16 for more information about this rootstock business). Therefore, new canes grow from the crown (the base of the plant, right at ground level) of the plant. Often, the plant throws up a new shoot close to the main plant. You can dig up this cane, plant it elsewhere, and leave it to grow into a whole new plant.

Friends who grow roses, particularly the old garden roses that are more inclined to produce this type of growth, are often willing to share their bounty and give you new shoots to plant in your own garden. New shoots from own-root plants are always identical to the original plant.

To plant a new shoot, do the following:

1. **In early spring, dig up the new shoot with a spade, taking along a big clump of the soil in order to keep the roots relatively undamaged.**

2. **Plant the whole thing in a beautifully prepared hole, just like one you'd prepare for any other rosebush (see Chapter 17 for pointers).**

3. **Water thoroughly and mound the plant with soil, leaving the soil in place until new growth begins to appear, which indicates that the roots are working on their own to nourish the plant.**

In a month or two, you should have a healthy new rose plant.

Growing New Plants from Cuttings

Growing roses on their own roots has some advantages, such as increased winter hardiness. Although many rosarians and commercial growers believe that a plant must be budded to reach its full potential, that's not true for all varieties. Why not try rooting a few cuttings (pieces of rose stem) and compare for yourself?

Rooting new plants from softwood cuttings sounds easy, but unless you know what a cutting needs and faithfully provide those things, you will not have a successful experience. Here's how to do the job right:

1. **Take a cutting from a fairly young cane coming from a bud eye along a main cane.**

   Just after a new cane flowers is a good time to take your cutting. The diameter of the cane should be about the diameter of a drinking straw. You will have more success with cuttings taken from the tender growing ends of canes than with those taken further down the cane.

   An easy way to tell if the cutting is ripe to be taken is to press sideways on a thorn on the section of cutting you want to take. If the thorn bends over and does not snap off, it is too young to make good roots. If it fights back and punctures your thumb, it is too old to take a cutting. If, on the other hand, it snaps off with a small pop, it is exactly right to be taken and rooted.

2. **After you remove the small cane from the plant, cut off the bottom at a very sharp angle so that the cut is as close as possible to a bud eye.**

   Make this angled cut with a very sharp pruner.

3. **With a razor blade or X-acto knife, lightly score the bark vertically from the bottom, and up about 2 to 3 centimetres (1 inch), on the side of the stick opposite a bud eye.**

   Doing so encourages roots to form along the score.

4. **From the bottom of the cutting, measure up about 15 centimetres (6 inches), leaving two to three sets of five-leaf leaflets. Cut the top off the stick, about ½ a centimetre (¼ inch) above a bud eye.**

5. **Dip the bottom, angled end of the cutting into a liquid rooting hormone (such as Dip n' Grow), mixed according to package directions.**

   Dip the cutting to a depth of about 2 to 3 centimetres (1 inch) so that the score you made on the cane is immersed. If you use dry powder hormone instead of liquid, knock off all excess dust so only a sheen of dust is showing.

6. **Insert the coated cutting into a small peat pot filled with wet sterile potting soil.**

   With your fingers, squeeze down the soil so that the cutting stands up and is fairly stable in the pot.

7. **Place your cutting into a misting tent.**

   Making an effective misting tent is easy. Simply mist the cutting with water, place a clear or white plastic bag over the container, and secure the bag around the top of the pot with a piece of string, as shown in Figure 23-1. The tent keeps the cutting moist and prevents it from drying up and dying.

Figure 23-1:
A rooted
rose cutting
in a misting
tent.

8. **Place the misting-tent-enclosed cutting outdoors in a spot that gets indirect morning and afternoon sun but is in shade at midday, such as the north side of the house.**

   Avoid placing the misting tent in direct sun at all costs, or you will bake the contents of the bag rather than help root your cutting. You must mist the leaves several times each day, more often if it's sunny. Misting keeps moisture in the cutting, which it needs because it has no roots to get its own moisture. Don't forget to mist, or your cutting will die. If the leaves turn yellow and fall off before the first week ends, you may as well give up and start again.

If the leaves fall off after three weeks, it's not a great sign, but you still have hope. Mix 1 tablespoon of a high-nitrogen liquid fertilizer in 4 litres (1 gallon) of water and lightly mist your plant with the solution. Doing so may stimulate new leaf growth from the bud eye.

If all goes well, your cutting should root in less than a month. Strong white roots grow from the bottom of the cutting and fill the small pot. Now's the time to transplant into a larger pot.

If you are not able to mist regularly during the day, spray the cuttings (top and bottom of each leaf) with an antidesiccant. This is a waxy liquid that dries on the leaf and prevents it from losing water. We use it on all tricky cuttings to almost guarantee success.

9. **Plant the cutting, peat pot and all, into a 15-centimetre (6-inch) pot filled with regular potting mix, harden it off, and start dreaming while you grow it for a month or two in the sun.**

   To harden off a plant, move it from a shady, wind-protected spot out into full sun gradually, keeping it outdoors in the sun a little longer each day for a ten-day to two-week period. Never let the soil dry out.

10. **When the plant starts putting out strong, healthy growth, transplant it into the garden and treat it as you would any rose plant.**

   See Chapter 17 for planting instructions.

Sexual Propagation

You've heard about this kind of thing before, haven't you? Well, the process is pretty much the same for roses as it is for people, give or take a few steps. Here's how to go about it the rose way.

If you want to try your hand at creating a new variety of rose without a lot of effort, try growing the seeds in the hips that you find on your plants in the fall. They're already pollinated — by bees or by themselves. So the sex part is already over.

Follow these steps:

1. **After the hips (seed pods) change colour from green to orange or red, pick them off the plant.**

2. **Carefully cut open the hip with a knife, trying not to injure the seeds that are waiting inside. Gently remove the seeds.**

3. **Wrap the seeds in a damp paper towel and place them in a plastic bag.**

4. **Keep the bag in the crisper section of your refrigerator for 90 days.**

5. **Remove the seeds from their cool packaging and plant them ½ to 1 centimetre (¼ inch) deep in a shallow container or flat filled with sterile potting soil.**

6. **Place the container under lights or on a really sunny windowsill and wait for the seeds to sprout.**

   Not all the seeds will sprout, but that's normal.

7. **Leave the seedlings to grow in the container, keeping them moist but not soggy at all times.**

   They should bloom in about six weeks. The plant and the bloom will be small, and although you won't get a very accurate idea of what the flower will look like on a mature plant, you can tell whether it has potential.

8. **Destroy plants with really ugly flowers or those that become diseased when the others in the flat do not.**

9. **After the first flower blooms, carefully transplant the seedling into a larger pot.**

   To keep from damaging the fragile roots, take plenty of the surrounding soil along with the roots when you transplant.

10. **After the plant throws several new canes, harden it off (see Step 9 in "Growing New Plants from Cuttings" earlier in this chapter) and then plant it in the garden to mature.**

    Roses are heavy feeders, so give your new seedling plenty of nutrients to enable it to achieve maximum growth in its first season. (Chapter 19 explains fertilizing roses.) With proper care, many seedlings can reach a large size in the first season.

Hybridizing Roses

Hybridizing is best done in a greenhouse, rather than outdoors where bees can interfere with crossbreeding and your plants are subject to the whims of the weather. Of course, you *can* hybridize outside. Here goes:

1. **Choose two varieties of roses that you think have good characteristics that you would like to see passed on to a new variety.**

2. **Watch the plant that you have decided should be the seed, or female, parent. When you see a flower on which the first couple of rows of petals have opened but the centre is still tightly furled, gently remove all the petals from the flower.**

   Doing so leaves the yellow *stamens* exposed. (See our rose anatomy explanation in Chapter 2.) The *anthers*, or male parts that produce the pollen, are at the top of the stamens. The anthers must be removed to ensure that the rose does not self-pollinate, ruining your cross.

3. **Gently bending the rose stem, cut off or remove the anthers from the stamens with a pair of tweezers or manicure scissors.**

   Never allow the anthers to fall into the centre of the flower.

   Once you remove the anthers, your rose seed parent is *emasculated*.

4. **Cover the parent with a bag so that no new pollen drifts in.**

   Leave it alone for 24 hours so that the female parts can ready themselves to accept pollen.

5. **In the meantime, collect some pollen from the *pollen parent*, or male.**

   Pollen requires a couple of days to ripen after being harvested, so collect the anthers (removing them just like you did when you emasculated the seed parent) well in advance from a mature flower of the variety you choose as the pollen parent. Let the tiny anthers sit in an uncovered shallow container in a warm place until you can easily shake off the yellow pollen.

6. **When both the pollen and the seed parent hip are ready, use a small paintbrush to dab pollen onto the centre of the emasculated seed parent.**

   If you want to simplify this step, just cut the pollen source from the rosebush and dab the pollen on the seed parent when its centre looks slightly sticky. (See Figure 23-2.) The results are less reliable, but this method is much easier. Whichever method you use, place a bag back over the seed parent for a week.

Figure 23-2:
Dabbing pollen onto the seed parent.

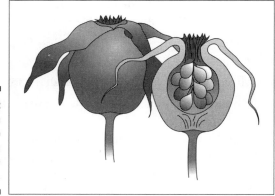

Figure 23-3:
A swollen
rose hip
showing
mature
seeds.

If the cross-pollination is successful, the hip begins to swell, as shown in Figure 23-3. The hip is ripe and the seeds are harvestable after six to eight weeks, when the hip turns red or orange. Like the self-pollinated seeds we discussed earlier in this chapter, the seeds must be chilled for 90 days before planting.

7. **Plant the seeds about ½ to 1 centimetre (¼ to ½ inch) deep in a pot or tray filled with sterile potting soil.**

   Put them in a warm, brightly lit area indoors (a heated greenhouse is ideal) and keep the soil moist. They should germinate in about six to eight weeks.

8. **When the seedlings have two true leaves, transplant them individually into small pots.**

   Keep them in a bright windowsill until the weather is nice enough to plant outdoors. But make sure to harden off the seedlings first, conditioning them to outdoor sun and temperatures gradually.

Keeping track of the cross you made is always a good idea. You can do so by attaching a label to the stem of the hip as you leave it to ripen. Write the seed parent's name first, then an x, meaning "crossed with," and then the pollen parent's name. For example:

'Pristine' x 'Folklore'

Some rose varieties make better seed parents, and some make better pollen parents. Hybridizers who have worked with roses for years have learned which is which, and you can share their experience by reading any of the books they've published or by subscribing to the *Rose Hybridizers' Association Newsletter*, published by the Rose Hybridizers' Association.

If you want to get rich hybridizing roses, try to come up with a large, red, fragrant hybrid tea with excellent form. It has to grow on long, sturdy stems and produce flowers generously. It must be disease resistant and do well in a greenhouse. If it does well outside, too, that's a great bonus. The colour must stay true for a long time, not bluing or blackening on the edges, and the flower should have a long vase life. Good luck!

For more information about hybridizing your own roses, contact the following organization:

Rose Hybridizers' Association
21 South Wheaton Road
Horseheads, NY 14845
607-562-8592

An annual Canadian membership fee of $10 (in U.S. funds) brings its quarterly bulletin to your door. An additional $5 will get you the RHA's *Handbook for Beginners* that outlines the basics of hybridizing.

One More Thing, Sport!

One other way to come up with a new variety of rose is to find a sport on an existing plant. A *sport* is an anomaly in a plant's cells that causes a cane and flower that look entirely different to grow from the bud eye of the original plant. Often these sports are really wonderful roses, sometimes even better than the original plant. For example, 'Chicago Peace', a sport of 'Peace', was discovered by a gardener in Chicago. And 'Gourmet Popcorn', a sport of the white miniature 'Popcorn', was discovered by a rosarian in Los Angeles. Many of the roses you can buy today are sports.

As with many types of plants, sporting is a fairly common occurrence, but finding a sport is always fun — especially if it's a good one.

If you observe a sport on one of your plants, make a cutting and grow the new variety. The plant may be wonderful beyond your wildest dreams. If so, invite one of the large commercial growers to take a look. If they like your rose, test it, and introduce it to the public, you're entitled to a royalty!

Chapter 24

Drying Roses and Making Potpourri

. . . .

In This Chapter

▶ Drying whole roses in silica gel

▶ Drying rose petals for potpourri

▶ Making potpourri

▶ Pressing roses

. . . .

*E*ver walk into one of those wonderful-smelling shops where they sell cookbooks, kitchen utensils, things to hang on the wall, and maybe soaps and towels — you know, just about anything frilly? They also sell perfect bouquets of dried roses and intensely fragrant potpourris filled with dried rose petals. Where does that stuff come from? A herd of hard-working grandmas must be out there somewhere growing and drying a heck of a lot of roses.

Actually, if a herd of grandmas is out there, they may not be working as hard as you think. Drying roses and making potpourri is not that difficult. In fact, it's pretty easy, as we show you in this chapter. And in the process, you not only find out how to preserve and spread the beauty of roses around your house 12 months a year, but you also can make great gifts to share with friends.

Drying Roses in Silicon Valley North

Computer nerds use silica gel to dry roses, of course. What did you expect? (Okay, so it's not funny and doesn't make sense. But every ...*For Dummies* book has to have a reference to computer nerds, and that was ours.) *Silica gel* is actually a sugar-like substance that sucks the moisture right out of a rose, leaving a perfectly dried flower. You can get the stuff from a florist or at a craft shop.

To get the best results when drying roses with silica gel, cut your roses in the morning after the dew dries. Pick the best roses, open just the way you want them and free of insects and disease. Leave very little, if any, stem on the flower.

Spread about 2 to 3 centimetres (1 inch) of silica gel in the bottom of a flat, wide container that has a snug-fitting top. A plastic microwave tray works well. Set the roses upright in the gel, making sure that they don't touch. Gently add more gel until the flowers are completely covered and then seal the container.

The roses take anywhere from a day or two to two weeks to dry, depending on their size and how humid the air is where you live. The roses are dry when they feel like crisp paper. Carefully remove the blossoms from the gel and blow on them gently to remove the excess gel. If some gel sticks, use an artist's brush to remove it. Don't leave the roses in the gel too long, or the colour will fade quickly after you take them out.

You can also dry rose leaves for making more realistic dried bouquets, but you should dry them in a separate container from the flowers. They become too brittle if left on the stem, and they may take longer to dry than the flowers do.

Which roses dry best?

Because they dry so quickly, miniature roses are favourites for preserving in silica gel. But with some practice, you can also dry larger roses successfully.

Which colours are best? Many of the deepest red roses dry black. However, some bright orange roses dry bright red. Deep pink roses usually dry nicely. White, light pink, and yellow roses tend to fade to dishwater white. Blended roses dry beautifully, but again they tend to fade after a while.

We asked some members of the American Rose Society who have been drying roses for years, which varieties they get the best results with. They made the following suggestions (some of these might be difficult to find, so consult the resources in Appendix B):

- **Reds:** Use hybrid teas 'Old Smoothie' and 'Olympiad', and miniatures 'Acey Deucy', 'Debut', 'Old Glory', and 'Starina'.

- **Pinks:** Try 'Century Two', 'Colour Magic', 'Dainty Bess', 'Electron', 'Miss All-American Beauty', 'Perfume Delight', 'Pink Peace', 'Prima Donna', 'Sheer Elegance', and 'Touch of Class' among the hybrid teas, and 'High Jinks' and 'Winsome' (actually a mauve rose) from the miniatures.

✓ **Oranges:** Good choices (which, oddly, dry to red) include 'Bing Crosby', 'Cary Grant', 'Command Performance', 'Dolly Parton', 'Fragrant Cloud', and 'Tropicana' of the hybrid teas, grandifloras 'Olé' and 'Prominent', and floribundas 'Impatient' and 'Marina'.

✓ **Multis:** Good choices include 'Milestone' and 'Mon Cheri' of the hybrid teas, and 'Child's Play', 'Holy Toledo', and 'Kristin' of the miniatures.

Preserving and arranging dry flowers

You can display dried roses in bowls or dishes with other dried flowers, or you can use them to make arrangements. However, to make arrangements like you do with fresh flowers, you need to attach the blooms to flower sticks, floral wire, or something stiff to support the dry flower. A craft shop is the best place to look for ideas and materials.

Making Potpourri

Who'd want to make "rotten pot"? Well, maybe the idea sounds better when you translate "rotten pot" into French, making it *potpourri*. Potpourri is an aromatic and colourful mixture of dried rose petals, herbs, spices, and aromatic oils. (You can make moist potpourri, but this chapter describes the dry kind, which is a lot easier to make, anyway.) The word *potpourri* is derived from a French process of aging rose petals in some type of container — the rotting pot.

Any rose, as long as it's fragrant, makes a good potpourri. Collect the petals in the morning after they have dried. Flowers that are about three-fourths to fully open are best. Anything older loses its fragrance.

To dry the petals, spread them out on an elevated screen placed in a well-ventilated, warm, dry area away from direct sun. The petals are dry enough when they break when bent — the process takes anywhere from a day or two to a week.

The basic procedure for mixing potpourri is as follows:

1. **Mix the dry petals with your favourite aromatic herbs and spices — cloves, allspice, mint, and cinnamon work well.**

   Use 30 millilitres (an ounce) of dry herbs for every litre (quart) of dried petals. You can also throw in dried citrus peel and other dried flowers.

2. **Add some aromatic oils, such as lavender, clove, or cinnamon, and a preservative.**

   Powdered or chopped orris root (available at craft shops) is a favourite preservative. You can either put a few drops of aromatic oil on the small pieces of orris root or drop the oil over the whole mixture into which you have added the powdered orris root.

3. **Mix everything gently and place the potpourri in a sealed container.**

   Store the potpourri in a cool, dark place. Gently shake or toss the mixture every so often. The mixture should be ready in a few weeks, although the scent is pretty strong at first.

   You can put your potpourri out in any attractive container, but a glass bowl looks especially nice. To prolong the aroma, keep the potpourri covered, and then open and gently stir it when you want to release the essence (like when guests come over). You may want to add more dried flowers occasionally to intensify the colour. When covered, a potpourri can last for years.

   You usually can find everything you need for making potpourri in craft shops. Aromatic oils can also be found in drugstores and health food stores.

Pressing Flowers

You can dry roses another way — by pressing them. The process is simple but works best with single roses or flowers with fewer than 10 or 12 petals. You can find flower presses in nurseries or craft stores, but you can just as effectively press flowers between the pages of a heavy book. Here's how:

1. **Place two pieces of blotter paper (even paper towels work) between the pages of a heavy book.**

2. **Pick some roses in the morning after they dry.**

3. **Place the roses between the pieces of blotter paper, arranging the petals just the way you want the flower to dry.**

4. **Close the book carefully and pile some other heavy books on top.**

5. **Check the flowers every few days.**

   If the blotter paper looks wet, replace at least one piece of it, carefully moving the flowers with tweezers, if necessary. The flowers dry in about two weeks.

Store the flowers in an airtight container, between pieces of paper, or even in the book itself. You can use pressed roses to make greeting cards, mount them in picture frames, or use them to decorate festive tables.

Friends of ours who do this kind of thing (we're too busy growing and smelling roses to be crafty too) tell us that the clay pressing boards you use in the microwave are wondrous technological advancements in flower drying. These are available through specialty garden stores and come highly recommended for those who want dried flowers in a hurry. As a bonus, our friends tell us the original colours are preserved better with microwave drying than with any other method they've used.

Part V
The Part of Tens

The 5th Wave   By Rich Tennant

"Oh sure, Hemlock, nightshade and foxglove I can grow. But try to grow a single lousy rose and all I get are thorns."

In this part . . .

This is a fun part of the book, filled mostly with ways to fine-tune your enjoyment of roses. Here, you can get answers to those burning questions about roses that you always wanted to ask (unless you're an expert and don't need to ask burning questions), pick up some *not*-to-do tips for growing roses, find out about the interesting history of roses, and see how to cut those beautiful roses you're growing so that they last for days in vases all over your house.

Chapter 25

The Ten Most Frequently Asked Questions about Roses

∙ ∙

In This Chapter

▶ All the things you wanted to know about roses but were afraid to ask

∙ ∙

From the Queen of Hearts School of Pruning

Q. How soon can I prune?

A. Never prune for the sake of pruning. Cut off dead parts of the canes in early spring after removing winter protection. Prune off dead or dying flowers (which is called *deadheading*). Prune out spindly growth from the bottom of the plant as soon as you see it. And cut as many flowers as make you happy. Never cut rose canes in late summer before frost. (See Chapter 20 for more information about pruning.)

From the Imelda Marcos School of Shopping

Q. Where can I shop for roses?

A. Seen a rose you simply must have but can't find it anywhere? Get on the Internet. Go to a meta search engine like www.dogpile.com and enter the name of the rose. If it exists, this will bring it up. Also check out Appendix B for specialty catalogues.

From the Absolutely Clueless School of Rose Culture

Q. What's wrong with my roses?

A. If your plants don't seem to have any of the pests or diseases that we describe in Chapter 22, get a soil test. You can find out more about soil tests in Chapter 17, or see Appendix B for soil-testing resources in your area.

From the Climbing the Wall Syndrome

Q. Why won't my climbing roses bloom?

A. Some older varieties of climbing roses bloom on old wood — that is, stems that are two years old or older. If you chop those climbers to the ground every spring, you'll never see a flower. In Canada, your best bet is to protect your climbers really well. See Chapter 21 for winter protection tips. If you haven't protected them, it is also possible that the tops are dead and the non-blooming growth is coming from the rootstock below the bud union. If so, dig it up and compost it.

From the Jaundiced Rose Garden

Q. Why do my rose leaves turn yellow and fall off?

A. First, check for spider mites by looking on the undersides of the leaves. You may need a magnifying glass. If you see little red spiders, they're sucking the very life from your rose plant. Try blasting them off with daily hose sprayings — the more powerful the better. If this doesn't work, try a spray with summer oil, which smothers the little suckers. If you don't see tiny spiders, check Chapter 22 about rose pests and diseases and see whether your plant has black spot or any other fungal disease. Our best guess is mites and/or black spot.

From an Insecure Rose Gardener

Q. What are the easiest roses to grow?

A. It really depends on the kind of gardener you are. But if you have absolutely no confidence in your ability to grow roses, give it a rest! You're as good a grower as anyone else. To start with, try roses in the Explorer series, such as 'John Cabot' or 'Champlain'. See Chapter 15 for more information on these hardy roses. If you can't grow Explorers — think silk.

From the "No Question Is Stupid" School of Higher Learning

Q. What's the difference between bareroot and potted roses?

A. One has its roots growing in a pot of soil, and the other has all the soil removed from the roots. We'll let you figure out which is which. For more information about how roses are sold, see Chapter 16.

From the "All That Glitters" School of Disease Control

Q. Why are my rose leaves silvery and shrivelled?

A. Your roses have powdery mildew. Kill it quick before it spreads to other plants in your garden. Try the summer oil and baking soda routine described in Chapter 22.

From the Runny Nose Department

Q. Why aren't my roses fragrant?

A. You may be growing varieties that have little or no fragrance. Or perhaps you're smelling them at the wrong time of day. Choose fragrant varieties if fragrance is important to you. See the list of fragrant roses in Chapter 3.

From the Freezer Section

Q. When should I prepare my roses for winter?

A. Wait until you think that your plants are pretty dormant. Hint: When the leaves start falling off in the fall, the plant is dormant. Some people wait until the ground is frozen, but chances are you'll have to do your winter preparing in the snow if you wait that long. You want the roses to have experienced a hard black frost or three to ensure they're well dormant and will stay that way. If you do get snow before you have a chance to protect your tender roses, pile the mulch on anyway, the deeper the better. (You did think ahead and leave the mulch where it was dry and not frozen, didn't you?)

Chapter 26

Ten Ways to Kill a Rose

If you decide that roses aren't for you and you want to kill them in your garden, here's how to go about getting rid of these pesky plants. Mind you, some of these tips are simply common mistakes made by beginning gardeners. Whether you're trying to kill the rose or simply making a common mistake is up to you.

Plant Them in the Shade

Roses need six hours of full sunshine each and every day. The more you reduce this amount, the fewer blossoms you'll get. Not only that, but the weaker your plant will become and one winter . . . well, after the winter, you'll have some extra material for the compost pile. Even those roses that are labelled as being shade tolerant will not tolerate much shade and still produce flowers. It will likely take three to four years for a shaded plant to die.

Plant Them with Lots of Grass around the Base to Compete for Nutrients

This is a favourite of some gardeners. They take a hybrid tea rose and plonk it down in the middle of the lawn. Having read that a rose is a shrub, they expect it to compete with grass for nutrients. *Nothing* competes with grass for nutrients, and a rose is certainly not going to win that contest. Get rid of the grass around your rose.

Plant Them Where They Get a Dose of Lawn Spray

The average rose does not appreciate the chemicals used to kill lawn weeds. Being woody plants with deeper roots, they are not immediately killed by lawn chemicals. However, several doses over the summer will set them back and they simply won't grow well or flower heavily. Remember that many lawn sprays are volatile. This means they form gases and float around on the breeze. If they float over to your rose — you get the picture, I'm sure.

Never Water Them during a Dry Spell

This is one of the truly creative ways to kill a rose. Roses are seldom killed outright by a lack of water unless it is a truly serious drought. Instead, they struggle along with reduced growth and blooms and enter the winter in a weakened condition. When they die over the winter, then winter damage becomes the cause, not your lack of gardening efforts.

Never Treat for Black Spot

Black spot will take a few years to weaken a rose (even a good healthy one) until it succumbs to winter death. This disease defoliates a plant over the course of the summer. Without leaves, the plant can't get enough energy to renew itself. Just like the above non-watering point, the gardener can hardly be blamed for winter losses.

Do Not Protect Tender Hybrid Teas during the Winter

This is a wimpy way to kill your roses. If you want to be creative, see the above two points. Everybody knows you have to protect tender roses — this is Canada, after all. However, you can always say you thought they were extra hardy Explorer roses. You still come out looking bad but at least you have somebody else to blame — like the nursery that sold you the wrong roses.

Don't Take Climbing Hybrid Teas off the Trellis for the Winter

Hey, these climbers are supposed to climb, right? What's with taking them off the trellis and burying them for the winter? You can confuse the issue for an extra season if the rootstock throws out suckers that will grow like crazy and not bloom. If in doubt, blame the nursery where you got the rose: "They said it would be easy to grow."

Prune Heavily and Do Not Feed At All

If you cut your rose to the ground every year, or it is knocked down over the winter, it takes a lot of food to grow strong canes and produce flowers. If you never feed your rose, slowly but surely it will weaken. It will produce pitifully thin canes and small flowers. If you combine this technique with growing in the shade and never watering, you can shorten the lifespan of most roses quite a bit.

Spray with Heavier Doses of Sprays Than Recommended

This is a good one. Ignore the warnings on the label that caution you to only use one tablespoon of something like baking soda. Heck, use four or five. If a little bit is good then a whole lot is better, right? So what if the leaves all turn brown and the flowers go purple after you spray. You've definitely knocked back the fungus problems!

Ask Your Neighbours to Water Your Plants for You

We don't know why, but every time we ask the neighbours to water the garden all heck breaks loose. You can substitute your mother-in-law, the minister, or anybody else you want to blame, but understand that when you leave for a holiday, the plants will resent it. They resent it so much they simply die for your return. This works particularly well on roses you are growing in pots or large containers.

Plant Roses in the Shade

We'll say it again as a bonus. See our first point in this chapter.

Chapter 27

Ten Tips for Cutting Roses

Anyone who grows roses and doesn't cut some to bring their beauty and fragrance indoors is missing the boat. No matter what your home looks like, from campy to castle, bringing some roses inside can make it look regal. And having roses around the house makes you feel great, too. Try it if you don't believe us.

Really, almost any rose makes a great cut flower. It's true that some varieties last longer than others, and we tell you about those varieties in this chapter. But if you like a rose — any rose — then cut it, bring it inside, and put it in a vase. Who cares whether it lasts two days or ten; this isn't a contest! If the thing wilts, you can always cut another one.

Anyway, that's our approach to cutting roses. But we may be in the minority. To many people, cutting roses is an art. And artists can be a little nutty. You know the type:

"My cut roses last longer than anyone's. The secret is to cut them while standing on your head and singing John Denver songs. Then chew off all the thorns while gargling with beer and put them in water measuring exactly 47 degrees Celsius."

Yeah, right.

To be honest, cutting roses is a little bit craziness and a little bit science. And that's what this chapter is about. If you want your cut roses to last as long as possible, follow as many of our ten suggestions as possible. If you don't care whether they last five days or six, do whatever you want.

Following a Flipped-Out Florist

Here are ten ways to get the longest-lasting cut roses:

- ✔ Cut flowers late in the afternoon, when stem and flower are loaded with food reserves. The second best time is very, very early in the morning before the rose starts growing for the day.

- ✔ Make sure that the plant you're cutting from is not dry, especially in hot weather. If it is, water it several hours prior to cutting flowers.

- ✔ Choose flowers at the right stage — roses that are one-third to one-half open, or still closed in the bud but whose sepals are separated and turned downward. The bud shouldn't be rock hard. Instead, it should be slightly soft when you squeeze it.

- ✔ Carry a bucket of water with you. Cut the stem at a 45-degree angle and place it immediately in the water. You can cut as far down the stem as you want, but try to leave at least two or three leaves on the stem below the cut. Those leaves feed the remaining stem.

- ✔ When you get inside, cut the ends of the stems again, but this time cut them under water. That's right, under water. Doing so keeps the stem's vessels open so that it can take up water. Just use a pruner or a pair of scissors that you don't mind getting wet and cut the stems at an angle right in your bucket. If you take only one suggestion — this is the one to take!

- ✔ Let the flowers stand in a bucket of room-temperature water, in a cool, dark place for at least a few hours before arranging them. This conditions the roses so that they'll have a longer vase life.

- ✔ Doctor the water in the vase. Roses last longer in clean water that is a little on the acidic side. You can buy little packs of flower preservative that add all the right stuff at florist shops, or you can make your own. The florist's one works best but homegrown ones are better than nothing. Our favourite mix adds one part lemon-based soda pop, like Sprite or 7-Up, to three parts water. Or just add two good squeezes from a fresh lemon, a tablespoon of sugar, and a few drops of household bleach to a quart of water.

- ✔ Before putting the flowers in a vase, remove the lower leaves and thorns (they snap right off when you push them sideways) that will be beneath the water. If left on the stem, they'll rot quickly and mess up the water. Also, use a clean vase.

✔ Change the vase water often. The cleaner you keep the water, the longer the flowers will last. This is the second most important suggestion we'll make. And, when you change the water, recut the stems (under water!) half a centimetre (one-quarter inch) shorter to extend their blooming life a bit more.

✔ Last but not least, say something nice to the roses. It can't hurt. Besides, if you do all the other stuff, you probably talk to your flowers already.

If, even after all this, your roses still wilt (or maybe the phone rang and you forgot all about the flowers in the yard), recut the ends, submerge the entire bunch in cold water, and let them sit for an hour. That may revive them.

The Best Roses for Cutting

In general, the more petals a rose has, the longer it lasts as a cut flower, simply because it takes longer to open. So, fully double modern roses, especially hybrid teas, are ideal as cut flowers because they usually have those great long, sturdy stems. Old rose flowers tend to have a shorter life than modern varieties, but the great character and fragrance of most old roses really make them wonderful in bouquets.

How you handle the rose is more important than the *variety* you grow. Follow as many of the above suggestions with any rose you like to grow in your garden. If you like it in your garden, you're going to love it in your kitchen.

Chapter 28

Ten Roses and Rose Gardens That Made History

In This Chapter

▶ Facts and fancy on roses throughout history

Roses have a royal history that few other plants can match. You can trace them back over 5,000 years, when they were grown by many an ancient civilization, including the Egyptians, Chinese, Greeks, and Romans. Even Confucius wrote about roses around 500 B.C. Since then, roses have been cherished by kings and queens, described by poets and philosophers, and just plain loved by us commoners.

Even if you're not a history buff, you can't ignore the historical significance of roses and some rose gardens. This chapter talks about roses and gardens that made history, giving you just enough to whet your appetite for what might be the start of a new career: Rosarian Historian. Or is it Historian Rosarian?

The Rose the Romans Loved

Rosa damascena sempervirens, known as the autumn damask rose, caused quite a stir in ancient Rome around 50 B.C. Until then, the Romans knew only roses that bloomed once a year. When they saw this new rose from North Africa that bloomed *twice* a year, they went bonkers. Imagine what would have happened if someone had walked into Rome with the floribunda 'Iceberg', which never stops blooming. A Caesar might *still* rule the world!

Cleopatra's Secret Weapon

The cabbage rose, *Rosa centifolia* (at least we think the plant was a cabbage rose — we weren't actually there), was another rose that those decadent Romans loved. They learned how to grow these roses in heated greenhouses so that they flowered almost year-round. Picture this: Emperor Nero, sipping wine while lounging on cushions filled with rose petals. Fountains flowing with rose-scented water, with guests strolling through halls strewn with rose petals. And — how come we didn't see this in the movie? — Cleopatra supposedly had rose petals piled knee-deep in the room where she first entertained Mark Antony.

Fighting over Roses in England . . .

Roses were even involved in the fight over who would be king of England. The five-petalled White Rose of York, *Rosa alba,* is infamously linked to the House of York, who used it as its emblem in the 15th-century Wars of the Roses. Their enemies, the House of Lancaster, chose the red apothecary's rose, *Rosa gallica officinalis,* as its symbol. One fable says that the two parties stopped fighting when they found a rosebush bearing both red and white individual flowers, and flowers that were both red and white, in the English countryside. The pink and white damask rose 'York and Lancaster' is often credited with being that rose, but it actually wasn't introduced to England until much later.

. . . and the Rose to Commemorate the War's End

The 'Peace' hybrid tea has long been one of the world's favourite roses. In 1965, Antonia Ridge published the story of 'Peace' and the Meilland family that bred her. If you're interested, the book was called *For Love of a Rose.* We've borrowed liberally from her story.

'Peace' can be traced back to Lyon, France, where, in 1935, the 23-year-old hybridizer Francis Meilland made the cross that would first be known as #3-35-40. The rose caught everyone's eye. Meilland himself described it, saying that it "produced flowers quite marvelous in shape and size with a greenish tinge, warming to yellow, and progressively impregnated with carmine around the edges of the petals."

Buds from #3-35-40 were passed to several nurseries around the world. In the confusion surrounding the start of World War II, the rose was given three different names: 'Gloria Dei' by a German company, 'Gioia' by an Italian nursery, and 'Mme A. Meilland' in memory of the hybridizer's mother.

Even during the war, #3-35-40 gained notoriety. The Duke of Windsor himself said, "I have never seen another rose like it. It is most certainly the most beautiful rose in the world."

Meanwhile, the Conard Pyle Company introduced #3-35-40 as 'Peace' to commemorate the end of suffering of World War II. Under the auspices of the American Rose Society, 'Peace' was formally introduced on April 29, 1945, a date that also marked the fall of Berlin. Shortly after this event, at a meeting of 49 delegations of the United Nations in San Francisco, the head of each delegation received in his or her hotel room a small vase with a single 'Peace' rose accompanied by a card carrying the following message:

"This is the 'Peace' rose, which was christened by the Pacific Rose Society exhibition in Pasadena on the day Berlin fell. We hope the 'Peace' rose will influence men's thoughts for everlasting world Peace."

Besides being inseparably linked to world peace, the 'Peace' rose is also one of the most widely used roses for creating new varieties. No fewer than 285 progeny of 'Peace' exist, including 236 hybrid teas, 32 floribundas, 11 grandifloras, and 6 shrubs.

What a rose!

The World's Biggest Rose Plant

The 'Tombstone' rose, a single Lady Banks' rose growing in Tombstone, Arizona, was originally planted in 1885. It now covers over 720 square metres (8,000 square feet) and has a trunk that is approximately 2.4 metres (95 inches) in diameter. It is listed in the *Guinness Book of World Records* as the world's largest rose plant.

Build It and They Will Come

Empress Josephine, wife of France's Napoleon I, put together probably the world's most famous, if not most important, rose garden at her imperial chateau, Malmaison. In 1798, she started collecting every species and natural hybrid of rose she could find. Plants came from all over the world until she had a collection of about 250 rosebushes.

Visitors who saw the great garden were stunned. At once, the great diversity in the rose family was plainly visible, and people saw the possibilities of new varieties and types. Soon there were new hybrids galore, heralding the era of modern roses to come.

The Hangover Rose?

Roses have a long history as medicinal and perfume plants. Rose oils were used to treat everything from eye problems to wrinkled skin to hangovers. As far back as the 13th century, the apothecary's rose, *Rosa gallica officinalis,* was widely used to make perfume and medicine in the French town, Provins. Eventually, the apothecary's rose became a symbol for modern pharmacology.

Roses on the Gridiron

Pasadena, California's annual Rose Parade and Rose Bowl football game is an all-American tradition on New Year's Day. It got its start in 1890 as a celebration of California's mild winter climate, where roses can still bloom in January. The founders of the Tournament of Roses, as the day's events are called, created a floral festival patterned after the Battle of the Flowers held in Nice, France. Initially, the Tournament was a modest procession of flower-covered carriages. The afternoon "games" included foot races, tug-of-war contests, and sack races.

Today, the Rose Parade features animated floral floats, high-stepping equestrian units, and precision marching bands and is viewed by an estimated 425 million people worldwide. In the afternoon, the championship collegiate football teams of the Pac-10 and the Big Ten conferences meet for a gridiron showdown in the Granddaddy of Them All (a trademarked name, no less), the Rose Bowl.

'Tournament of Roses', the pink grandiflora rose, was named to celebrate the 100th anniversary of the Tournament of Roses.

The Canadian Heritage Rose Garden

Rideau Hall, the home of Canada's Governor General, is the site of a unique rose garden commemorating Canada's heritage. Open to the public, this garden has 260 specific rose species and varieties in 11 different garden areas. These roses were chosen to represent all of Canada's immigrant populations as well as the aboriginal peoples. The granite columns flanking the garden are inscribed with the histories of each of the native and immigrant communities that built this country. Constructed with private funds, this heritage rose garden is the only one of its kind in the world.

Provincial Roses

Only one province in Canada uses the rose as its provincial emblem. And the winner is . . . Alberta.

You have to understand that we aren't saying that Albertans are either "wild" or "prickly" but that's what their rose is.

The wild rose or prickly rose (*Rosa acicularis*) was adopted as the provincial emblem in 1930. It is a hardy rose found throughout much of northern Canada but particularly in Alberta. A spiny shrub rose with a delicate scent, it presents a single flush of pink flowers (variable from light to dark pink) in July. You can make a wonderful jam from the rose hips too.

Hmmm, nice fragrance, great sweet jam, but prickly and wild. Who does that remind you of?

Part VI

Appendixes

The 5th Wave   By Rich Tennant

Walt's Rose Nursery

♪ I beg your pardon ♪
I never promised you a...

HEY!! WHAT DID I TELL
YOU ABOUT SINGING THAT SONG?!

In this part . . .

Because you're having so much fun growing roses, you're going to need more of them. So in this part, we show you how to increase your supply without having to visit a nursery — by buying roses through the mail or even via the Internet! Now that's fun. Of course, we also supply you with a list of Canadian rose growers so that you can visit their nurseries in person, if you're happier seeing roses up close and personal rather than on a catalogue page. And you can find contact information on provincial agriculture offices, soil-testing facilities, and "bug stations" to help you identify and conquer your rose gardening challenges. Here's also where you can discover how to access online rose articles and newsgroup discussions, and how to join rose societies across the country.

Appendix A

Rose Societies and Newsletters

*W*ith such widespread love for the rose as a flower and a plant, it's no surprise that people get together to share their experiences. Joining a rose society is a great way to meet people with similar interests and a fantastic way to get information about growing roses, particularly on a local level.

Canadian Rose Society

If you are falling in love with this wonderful plant, there is no better way to learn and meet fellow enthusiasts than to join the Canadian Rose Society. This will open the door to meeting rose enthusiasts in your province as well.

The Canadian Rose Society produces several publications, including the following:

- ✔ *The Rose Annual* contains full colour pictures of new and interesting roses as well as informative articles on the techniques of growing and showing roses in Canada.
- ✔ *The Rosarian* magazine is published three times a year, giving current developments in the world of roses and practical tips on rose growing. It also serves as a way for members to communicate with each other.

Benefits of membership include the opportunity to consult rose experts who can answer your questions, and a book-lending library that operates by mail to give you access to all the books on rose growing that you'll ever want or need to read. A large slide collection on roses is available to members for an evening's entertainment or to show during lectures or seminars. A special added bonus of membership is getting access to other member's gardens. These private rose gardens (some quite spectacular) are only open to other members and not the public.

To join the Canadian Rose Society write to them at 10 Fairfax Crescent, Scarborough, Ontario M1L 1Z8 or call 416-757-8809 or fax 416-757-4796 or visit their Web site at www.mirror.org/groups/crs/index.html (membership is only $25.00 /year).

Local Rose Societies across Canada

For something a little closer to home, you should try contacting these local rose societies, which are happy to receive new members:

Vancouver Rose Society. This is the oldest and largest rose society in Canada. Contact: Wendy Caywood, 4623 55th St., Delta, BC V4K 3P6; phone and fax: 250-946-0822; www.hedgerows.com/Canada/club brochures/VancRoseSoc.htm

Fraser Pacific Rose Society. Contact: Peter Howard, 625 Cottonwood Ave., Coquitlam, BC V3J 2S5; phone: 250-931-5120; www.hedgerows.com/ Canada/clubbrochures/FrasPac RoseSoc.htm

Calgary Rose Society. Contact: Evelyn Salamanowicz, 324 Cantrell Dr. SW, Calgary, AB P2W 2C6; phone: 403-281-3786; fax: 403-281-6621

Saskatchewan Rose Society. Contact: Doug Bradford, 60 Mathieu Cres., Regina, SK S4R 3J2; phone: 306-543-8189; www.dlcwest.com/ ~rhs/rose.html

Golden Triangle Rose and Garden Society. Contact Ed Mansz, 83 Belmont Ave. W., Kitchener, ON N2M 1L5; phone: 905-827-2628

Hamilton and Burlington Rose Society. Contact: Elaine Sparrow for membership, 905-827-2628; President Ron Bishop, 905-387-4936. The society meets at the Royal Botanical Gardens, 680 Plains Road West, Burlington, ON L7T 4H4 on the first Wednesday of every month.

Huronia Rose Society. Contact: Edna Caldwell, RR1, Shanty Bay, ON L0L 2L0; phone: 705-721-0484

William Saunders Rose Society. Contact: 26 Guildford Court, London, ON N6J 3Y1; e-mail: wsrose@ netcom.ca

Société de Roses du Québec. Contact: 31 Lorne Ave, Saint-Lambert, QC J4P 2G7

Prince Edward Island Rose Society. Contact: Leo McIsaac, RR5, Charlottetown, PEI C1A 7J8; fax: 902-569-1476

Don't Forget Our Friends in the U.S.A.

We would be remiss if we didn't mention the American Rose Society (ARS). Founded in 1899, the ARS is a huge resource that should not be ignored by Canadian rose fanciers. They produce a yearly *American Rose Annual* as well as a monthly magazine, *The American Rose*. Like the Canadian society, they have many resources for members, including consulting rosarians to solve problems, annual garden visits, get-togethers, and trial gardens. A Canadian membership costs $42 (payable in U.S. funds only).

For information on the American Rose Society, write to them at Box 30,000, Shreveport, LA, 71130-0030, or call them at 318-938-5402.

Take a look at their Web site at www.ars.org/ for more details.

Newsletters

Harry McGee writes a newsletter every second month about rose growing in Canada. Called *The Rosebank Letter,* after his own garden's name, this is an excellent resource for Canadian gardeners.

The newsletter varies in size (he guarantees 10 pages but it's usually larger than that) and is Harry's way of helping out the Canadian rose-growing community rather than a money-making venture. For only $15 a year, you can learn all about the newest roses, the oldest roses, and what roses are doing well in various parts of the country. This is practical information written by a practical gardener and other gardening authors.

You can subscribe by sending a cheque for $15 (payable to Rosecom). Mail it along with your complete address to Rosecom, 41 Outer Drive, London, ON N6P 1E1.

Visit Harry's Web site at www.mirror.org/people/harry.mcgee/rosebank. html if you'd like to see the collection of articles written over the history of the newsletter. You can reach him by e-mail at rosecom@lonet.ca.

Where to Find Roses, Information, and More in Canada

So many catalogues, so many roses — so little time. You can find more plants represented in these Canadian mail-order and online catalogues than any gardener needs to grow. Ah, but wants to grow — that's another matter.

You'll be able to find most of the good beginner roses, such as the Dream and Explorer series, at your local garden centre. But when you branch out and start growing harder-to-find varieties, you'll need some of these sources. A few of the nurseries in this list do not provide retail services but will refer you to other garden supply merchants where you can purchase their roses. If you want to place a special order with your local garden centre, it helps to know the source of the rose you want. We collect many of the catalogues in this list just because they're fun to browse through on a winter's evening. They're cheap dreams.

Where to Find Roses

Brentwood Bay Nursery
1395 Benvenuto Road
Brentwood Bay, BC V8M 1J5
250-652-1507, fax 250-652-2761
home page www.coastnet.com/
~plants/index.html#toc
Old roses, David Austin English roses, modern shrub roses, and climbers. Mostly on old roots. See Web page for ordering information. Catalogue is $3, which is redeemable with your first order.

Canadian Rose Company
RR 2
Lowbanks, ON N0A 1K0
905-899-0776, fax 905-899-0778
David Austin, Explorer, old-fashioned, and modern roses. Free list.

Classic Miniature Roses
Box 2206
Sardis, BC V2R 1A6
604-823-4884, fax 604-823-4046
More than 150 hardy varieties of miniature roses, including micro-minis, mini-climbers, and mini-moss. Free list with business-size SASE; four pages.

Corn Hill Nursery
RR 5
Petitcodiac, NB E0A 2H0
506-756-3635, fax 506-756-1087
Mostly hardy roses, Explorer series.

Enderlein Nurseries Ltd.
RR 1
Lisle, ON L0M 1M0
705-466-2532, fax 705-466-2361
home page www.enderleingarden
roses.com
e-mail endernur@bconnex.net
Wholesale grower of many varieties
of roses, including hybrid teas,
grandifloras, floribundas, climbing,
shrub, rugosa, and David Austin
roses; most budded on vigourous
multiflora rootstock and some on
own roots. No mail-order catalogue
or retail services available. Web site
features good-quality colour photos
and information on each variety.
Will provide referrals to local garden
centres where you can buy their
roses.

The Fragrant Rose Co.
RR1, Site 19-C8
Fanny Bay, BC V0R 1W0
888-606-7673, fax 250-335-1135
Importers and distributors of
fragrant English-grown roses from
R. Harkness & Co. Ltd. of the U.K.
Bareroot roses shipped November
through March. Catalogue $2.

Greenbelt Farm
RR 5
Mitchell, ON N0K 1N0
519-347-2725, fax same
Ninety varieties of roses, woodlot
regeneration stock, perennials.
Catalogue $5; 88 pages, botanical
names, winter-care tips.

Hortico
RR 1, 723 Robson Road
Waterdown, ON L0R 2H1
905-689-9323, fax 905-689-6566
home page www.hortico.com/
e-mail office@hortico.com
A wide range of roses from the latest
hybrid teas to antique roses.
Catalogue $3. Full e-commerce
capacity.

J.C. Bakker and Sons Limited
1360 Third Street
St. Catharines, ON L2R 6P9
905-935-4533, fax 905-935-9921
home page www.jcbakker.com
e-mail nursery@jcbakker.com
Grows own-root roses and others
on multiflora rootstock. Wholesaler
only, no retail or mail-order services
available. Online catalogue of
products features lovely colour
photographs of all rose varieties. Call
or e-mail to arrange a nursery tour.

Lamrock's Little Roses
46 Marrakesh Drive
Agincourt, ON M1S 3W8
416-292-0321
e-mail clamrock@iionweb.com
Over 50 miniature rose varieties.
Information available upon request;
contact Cecil Lamrock via e-mail
address above. (Lamrock's Little
Roses has expansion and relocation
plans starting summer 2000.)

Martin & Kraus
Box 12
1191 Centre Road
Carlisle, ON L0R 1H0
905-689-0230, fax 905-689-1358
home page www.gardenrose.com
e-mail sales@gardenrose.com
Hardy roses grown on own roots or
on Rosa multiflora understock.
Hybrid tea, grandiflora, floribunda,
miniature, climbing, David Austin,
antique, shrub, Explorer, Parkland,
Meidiland, and Pavement roses;
garden accessories. Catalogue $1.

McConnell Nurseries Inc.
P.O. Box 248
Strathroy, ON N7G 3J2
English 800-363-0901, French
800-461-9445, fax 800-561-1914
home page www.mcconnell.ca
Approximately 35 rose varieties
available. Mail-order services only.
Free catalogue.

Mori Miniatures
Box 772
Virgil, ON L0S 1T0
905-468-0315, fax 905-468-7271
Specialists in miniature roses. Free
catalogue.

Old Rose Nursery
1020 Central Rd.
Hornby Island, BC V0R 1Z0
250-335-2603, fax 250-335-2602
home page www.oldrose
nursery.com
e-mail oldrose@mars.ark.com
Own-root, old-fashioned garden
roses; also English, ramblers,
climbers, rugosas, Explorers. Ships
to western Canada only. Catalogue
$4 plus SASE.

Carl Pallek & Son Nurseries
Box 137
Virgil, ON L0S 1T0
905-468-7262, fax 905-468-5246
Hybrid tea, floribunda, grandiflora,
climber, miniature, and old garden
roses. Free catalogue.

Pickering Nurseries Inc.
670 Kingston Road
Pickering, ON L1V 1A6
905-839-2111
home page www.pickering
nurseries.com
More than 900 varieties of antique,
rugosa, shrub, climbing, rambler,
David Austin, and modern hybrid
roses. Catalogue $3, 650 photos.

Russian Roses for the North
5680 Hughes Road
Grand Forks, BC V0H 1H4
250-442-1266, fax same
home page www.russianrose
forthenorth.com
e-mail jlhtech-rr@telus.net
Over 450 roses, including antiques,
Explorers, Morden, shrubs, David
Austin, Canadian heritage roses,
and miniatures; all on own roots
and hardy.

**Skinner's Nursery and Garden
Centre Ltd.**
Box 220
Roblin, MB R0L 1P0
204-564-2336, fax 204-564-2324
home page www.skinners
nursery.mb.ca
e-mail contact@skinners
nursery.mb.ca
Over 70 varieties of hardy roses,
including Canadian heritage roses,
Explorers, Parkland, and old garden.
Mail-order services available; shipping to all parts of Canada. You can
register to receive a free catalogue
via their Web site; a downloadable
format is also available.

Sylvan Roses
848 Stonybrook Road
Kelowna, BC V1W 4P3
250-764-4517, fax 250-764-0166
home page www3.telus.net/
Sylvan_Roses/
e-mail sylvanroses@bc.
sympatico.ca
English and Agriculture Canada
roses, all on own roots. (Their Web
site was under construction when
Roses For Canadians For Dummies
went to press.) Catalogue $3, 35
pages.

Valderose Gardens (Farm)
7470 Grande River Line
Chatham, ON N7M 5J7
519-354-6536
home page www.valderose.com/
homepage.html
e-mail valderose@ciaccess.com
Over 200 varieties: represents Fryer's
Roses in Canada, also grows David
Austin, Harkness, Explorer, and
Parkland roses, all on multiflora
rootstock. No retail purchases or
mail-order service available, but will
refer you to local garden centres
across southwestern Ontario where
their roses are available.

Where to Start Looking for Information

Need to know something about your local growing conditions? Try your province's agriculture Web site for a variety of gardening-related information.

Alberta Agriculture, Food, and Rural Development
home page www.agric.gov.ab.ca/navigation/crops/horticulture/specialties/col_index.html
A goldmine of online factsheets, including diseases, insects, weeds, turf grasses, trees, fruits, vegetables, and even houseplants.

British Columbia Ministry of Agriculture and Food
home page www.agf.gov.bc.ca/publicat/publications.htm
Most online information is for commercial growers, but some information of interest to home gardeners, such as late blight disease on tomatoes and potatoes, fruit tree diseases, and a few factsheets on insects and weeds.

Manitoba Agriculture
home page www.gov.mb.ca/agriculture/crops/index.html
Wide variety of online factsheets covering soil, weather, climate, vegetables, and diseases.

New Brunswick Department Agriculture and Rural Development
home page www.gov.nb.ca/agricult/index.htm
Weather and climate information, and online factsheets covering diseases, insects, and weeds.

Newfoundland and Labrador Agricultural Services
home page www.gov.nf.ca/agric/
Online lawn and garden factsheets covering topics such as lawn and garden nutrition, insect pests, and pesticide safety.

Nova Scotia Department of Agriculture and Marketing
home page http://agri.gov.ns.ca/pt/hortfact.htm
A variety of factsheets of interest to home gardeners, including information on fruit trees, berries, and organic gardening.

Ontario Ministry of Agriculture and Food
home page www.gov.on.ca/OMAFRA/english/sitemap.html
A good choice of online factsheets, including information on lawns, most vegetables, and fruits and berries.

Prince Edward Island Agriculture and Forestry
home page www.gov.pe.ca/af/agr-info/index.asp
Factsheets include information on soil fertility, growing potatoes, and fertilizing fruit trees.

Saskatchewan Agriculture and Food
home page www.agr.gov.sk.ca/level3.asp?firstPick=Crops&pick=Horticulture
Online fact sheets include information on Dutch elm disease, woolly elm aphids, and browning of evergreens.

Yukon Department of Renewable Resources
home page http://renres.gov.yk.ca/agric
A short description of the Yukon's climate and soil. The following site featuring Yukon government publications was under construction when *Roses For Canadians For Dummies* went to press. Try it, you might like it: http://renres.gov.yk.ca/pubs/

Soil Testing

Here are the addresses for provincial soil-testing services. Prices and tests vary across the country, so check with the relevant laboratory for current pricing.

ALBERTA

Alberta Soils and Animal Nutrition
Laboratory
905 O.S. Longman Building
6909-116 Alberts Street
Edmonton, AB T6H 4P2
403-427-2727

BRITISH COLUMBIA

Griffin Labs Corp.
1875 Spall Rd.
Kelowna, BC V1Y 4R2
604-861-3234

Or try Pacific Soil Analysis
Unit #5, 11720 Voyageur Way
Richmond, BC V6X 3G9
604-273-8226

MANITOBA

Manitoba Provincial Soil Testing Lab
Department of Soil Sciences
Room 262, Ellis Building
University of Manitoba
Winnipeg, MB R3T 2N2
204-474-9257
May give organic results on request.

NEW BRUNSWICK

NB Agricultural Lab
NB Dept. of Agriculture and Rural
Development
Box 6000
Fredericton, NB E3B 5H1
home page www.nbfarm.com/
genfaqs.htm

NEWFOUNDLAND AND LABRADOR

Soil Plant and Feed Laboratory
Department of Forest Resources and
Agrifoods
Provincial Agriculture Building
Box 8700, Brookfield Road
St. John's, NF A1B 4J6
709-729-6638
home page www.gov.nf.ca/agric/
soils.htm

NOVA SCOTIA

Soils and Crops Branch
Nova Scotia Department of
Agriculture and Marketing
Box 550
Truro, NS B2N 5E3
902-895-4469
home page agri.gov.ns.ca/pt/
hort/garden95/gg95-95.htm

ONTARIO

Laboratory Services (a division of
the University of Guelph)
95 Stone Road West
Guelph, ON N1H 8J7
519-767-6242, fax 519-767-6240
home page www.uoguelph.ca/
labserv/

Or try Nutrite
Box 160
Elmira, ON N3B 2Z6
519-669-5401(toll-free in southern
Ontario, 800-265-8865)
Will give organic results.

Or you could also try the
Royal Botanical Gardens
Box 399
Hamilton, ON L8N 3H8
905-527-1158

PRINCE EDWARD ISLAND

P.E.I. Soil and Feed Testing Lab
P.O. Box 1600
Research Station
Charlottetown, PEI C1A 7N3
902-368-5631
home page www.gov.pe.ca/af/
soilfeed/index.asp
Will give organic results, if requested.
Samples may also be left at your
nearest District Agricultural Office.

QUEBEC

Nutrite
Box 1000
Brossard, PQ J4Z 3N2
514-462-2555
Will give organic results.

SASKATCHEWAN

Saskatchewan Soil Testing Lab
Department of Soil Science
General Purpose Building
University of Saskatchewan
Saskatoon, SK S7N 0W0
306-966-6890
home page www.ag.usask.ca/cofa/
departments/hort/hortinfo/
misc/soil2.html
May give organic results on request.

Getting the Bugs Out

These are the provincial bug stations. Well, not exactly, but if you are having serious trouble identifying a pest and your local garden centre can't help, here's where to turn.

ALBERTA

Alberta Environmental Centre, Plant
Services Division
Bag 4000
Vegreville, AB T0B 4L0
403-632-6767
Will also refer to labs in other areas.

BRITISH COLUMBIA

Syd Cannings
Department of Zoology
University of British Columbia
Vancouver, BC V6T 2A9
604-228-3379

MANITOBA

Manitoba Agriculture Entomology
Section 911-401 York Ave.
Winnipeg, MB R3C 0P8
204-945-3857

NEW BRUNSWICK

NB Agricultural Lab, NB Dept. of
Agriculture and Rural Development
P.O. Box 6000
Fredericton, NB E3B 5H1

Plant Industry Branch
Department of Agriculture
Box 6000
Fredericton, NB E3B 5H1
506-453-2108

NEWFOUNDLAND AND LABRADOR

Soil Plant and Feed Laboratory
Department of Forest Resources and
Agrifoods
Provincial Agriculture Building
P.O. Box 8700, Brookfield Road
St. John's, NF A1B 4J6
709-729-6638

Research Station
Agriculture Canada
Box 7098
St. John's, NF A1E 3Y3
709-772-4619

NOVA SCOTIA

Soils and Crops Branch
Nova Scotia Department of
Agriculture and Marketing
Box 550
Truro, NS B2N 5E3
902-895-4469

Horticulture and Biology Branch
Nova Scotia Department of
Agriculture and Marketing
Box 550
Truro, NS B2N 5E3
902-895-1570

ONTARIO

Pest Diagnostic Advisory Clinic
Rm. B14 Graham Hall
University of Guelph
Guelph, ON N1G 2W1
519-824-4120

PRINCE EDWARD ISLAND

P.E.I. Dept. of Agriculture, Master
Gardener Program
Box 1600, Research Station
Charlottetown PEI C1A 7N3
902-368-5619

QUEBEC/NATIONAL

National Identification Service
Room 3119, K.W. Neatby Building
Ottawa, ON K1A 0C6
613-995-5222

SASKATCHEWAN

Meewasin Garden Line
Department of Horticulture
University of Saskatchewan
Saskatoon, SK S7N 0W0
306-966-5855

Online Articles

Sometimes it seems like everybody has written something about roses. Here are a few entry points on the Internet to help you discover more about roses. You'll want to bookmark many of these sites and use them as doorways to the rose world.

- ✔ **Canadian Gardening Online** (www.canadiangardening.com): Quick and easy access to a variety of Web sites selected specifically for Canadian gardeners. They also support the Rosarian pages at www.rosarian.com

- ✔ **Doug Green's Garden Magic** (www.simplegiftsfarm.com): This is the home page of one of the authors: articles and weekly newsletter.

- ✔ **IcanGarden** (www.icangarden.com): Good lists of Canadian links as well as articles about a variety of gardening subjects.

- ✔ **Internet Directory for Botany: Gardening** (www.helsinki.fi/kmus/bothort.html): All gardening Web sites are simply lumped under "Gardening," but this listing is still worth a visit. The collection is searchable.

- ✔ **The Garden Gate** (www.prairienet.org/garden-gate): One of the few remaining noncommercial directories, The Garden Gate offers gardeners and nature lovers a carefully selected and well-organized collection of links to informative and interesting horticulture sites around the world.

Newsgroups

Join an Internet newsgroup to discover another gardening community where you can share and receive information and articles with other rose growers. Try rec.gardens.roses and rec.gardens. Your favourite Internet browser will have newsgroup capacity.

Tools, Books, and Whatnot to Perfect Your Rose Garden

Check any of these sources for all kinds of gardening paraphernalia. Whether it's more books, a better sprinkler system, or stylish planters you need, someone here will be able to help you acquire the right item for your gardening pursuits:

Abbey Garden
Indian Hill Rd.
RR 1
Pakenham, ON K0A 2X0
613-256-3973
Catalogue $1, refundable. Solid bronze, hand-cast sundials designed in Britain.

Amaranth Stoneware Ltd.
Box 266
Kingston, ON K7L 4V8
800-465-5444
Free catalogue with SASE. Natural stoneware garden markers hand-crafted in Kingston; more than 100 herb, perennial, and theme names. Also plaques, pot markers, vinegar labels, herb-drying hangers, garden angels, saints, aromatherapy diffusers, and foot scrubbers.

Arbour Recycled Products
800 Bank St.
Ottawa, ON K1S 3V8
613-567-3168, fax 613-567-3568
home page www.arbour.on.ca
Online catalogue only. Rain barrels, red worms, vermicomposting kits, books, solar lights.

Atlantic Hydroponics & Greenhouses Inc.
Box 807
Moncton, NB E1C 8N6
506-858-0158, fax 506-855-0164;
e-mail ALPHYDRO@nbnet.nb.ca
Catalogue $2. Greenhouse supplies and organic hydroponic products.

Berry Hill Ltd.
75 Burwell Rd.
Box A
St. Thomas, ON N5P 3R5
800-668-3072, fax 519-631-8935
home page www.berryhill.on.ca
Free catalogue. Garden equipment, country-kitchen equipment, decorations, and hobby-farm supplies.

Bowker & Scudds for Gardeners
46 McRae St.
Okotoks, AB T0L 1T0
888-938-1161, fax 403-938-0068
Free catalogue. Garden gifts.

Brite Lite
1991 Francis Hughes
Laval, PQ H7S 2G2
800-489-2215, fax 514-669-9772
home page www.brite-lite-hydroponix.com
Free catalogue. Indoor gardening equipment: lights, hydroponics, nutrients; books.

Cambridge Metalsmiths
347 Lynden Rd.
Lynden, ON L0R 1T0
519-647-3326, fax same
Catalogue $3, refundable. Personalized cast-aluminum signs, brackets, and poles for home, cottage, and business.

Courtyard Creations
7-841 Sydney St., Ste. 167
Cornwall, ON K6H 3J7
888-327-1130, fax 613-933-1987
Catalogue $3, refundable. Garden signs made of handcast stone; decorative garden stones. Products made in Canada.

Ferme et Centre de Preservation
Bruno Messier
15 rue Chenier
Lac aux Oiseau
Gore, PQ J0V 1K0
Free catalogue with SASE. Ducks,
geese, swans shipped for weeding,
pond clean-ups, and slug, snail, and
insect control in the garden.

Frank's Magic Crops Inc.
480 Guelph Line
Burlington, ON L7R 3M1
800-668-0980, fax 905-639-9190
home page www.lara.on.ca/~fmci
Free catalogue. Hydroponic growing
and lighting systems made in Canada
for vegetables and flowers.

Garden Possibilities Bookstore
1065 Davis Dr.
Newmarket, ON L3Y 2R9
905-830-9693, fax 905-830-0996
Free catalogue. Books for amateur to
professional gardeners. Seasonal
catalogue/newsletter.

Garden Room Books
2097 Yonge St.
Toronto, ON M4S 2A4
416-932-8318, fax 416-489-7933
Free list of 150 to 200 books; $3, list
of used and rare books. New, used,
and rare books on horticulture.

Gardenscape Ltd.
2255b Queen St. E.
Box 358
Toronto, ON M4E 1G3
888-472-3266, fax 416-698-9068
home page www.gardenscape.on.ca
Free catalogue. Garden tools and
accessories by Haws, Felcos, Fiskars,
Dramm, and others.

Gardens Past
22 King St. E.
Cobourg, ON K9A 1K7
905-372-5847, fax same
Catalogue with SASE. Gear for
gardeners, includes gloves, tools,
books, and zinc plant markers.

International Irrigation Systems
Box 1133
St. Catharines, ON L2R 7A3
905-688-4090, fax 905-688-4093
home page www.irrigro.com
Free catalogue. Drip irrigation
systems for home gardeners and
commercial growers; growth
accelerator/protector tubes for
saplings and grapevines.

Iron Age Originals
9 Grenville Cres.
Kingston, ON K7M 3A9
613-549-6608, fax same
e-mail ironage@kos.net
Catalogue $2. Designer garden
structures, obelisks, and sculptures.

Jacobs Greenhouse Mfg. Ltd.
371 Talbot Rd.
Delhi, ON N4B 2A1
519-582-2880, fax 519-582-4117
home page www.jacobsgreen
house.com
Free catalogue. Free-standing and
lean-to greenhouses and atriums.

Lee Valley Tools Ltd.
1090 Morrison Dr.
Ottawa, ON K2H 1C2
800-267-8767, fax 800-668-1807
home page www.leevalley.com/
e-mail customerservice@
leevalley.com
Free catalogue. Hundreds of unusual
tools and work-saving products
imported from around the world.

Limestone Trail Company Ltd.
4290 Bartlett Rd.
Beamsville, ON L0R 1B1
905-563-8133, fax 905-563-7526
home page www.limestonetrail.com
Free catalogue. Manufacturer of
gazebos, garden sheds, and cabanas.

Linden House Gardening Books
148 Sylvan Ave.
Scarborough, ON M1M 1K4
416-269-0699, fax 416-269-0615
home page www.icangarden.com/
linden.htm
Free catalogue. Books on gardening,
landscaping, and horticulture.

Martin House Garden Pottery
299 Penetanguishene Rd.
Barrie, ON L4M 4Y8
705-722-6535, fax same
Catalogue $3, refundable. Metal obelisks, topiary forms, sculptural furniture, and terra cotta planters.

Natural Insect Control
RR 2
Stevensville, ON L0S 1S0
905-382-2904, fax 905-382-4418
home page www.natural-insect-control.com
Free catalogue. Non-toxic insect controls, including ladybugs; drinking-water systems.

The Kentish Man
66 Peach Willoway
Willowdale, ON M2J 2B6
416-499-4725, fax 416-502-1265
Free catalogue. Sussex trug baskets made of willow and sweet chestnut.

Randall Prue
Box 545, N.D.G.
Montreal, PQ H4A 3P8
514-984-4385
home page www.jacinet.com/~randall
Catalogue two 46¢ stamps. Mineral products for plants, pets, and people, derived from seaweed, sea plasma, and volcanic rock.

Schindler Crafts
Box 1383
Cardston, AB T0K 0K0
Catalogue $1. Garden ornaments, including bunnies, skunks, frogs, geese, and ducks.

Sitting Pretty
RR 4
Lanark, ON K0G 1K0
613-259-3033, fax 613-259-5568
Free catalogue. Hammocks and stands, rope chairs, garden and porch swings, and portable canvas chairs.

Sundials of Distinction
148 Hillsview Dr.
Richmond Hill, ON L4C 1T2
905-737-4922, fax same
Catalogue $2, refundable. Sundials, weather vanes, and wall fountains.

The St. George Company Ltd.
20 Consolidated Dr.
Paris, ON N3L 3T5
800-461-4299, fax 519-442-7191
e-mail stgeorgeco@sympatico.ca
Free catalogue. Tom Chambers hanging baskets, stainless-steel garden tools, cutting tools, and garden furniture.

Thomas Wildbird Feeders
30 Furbacher Lane, #4
Aurora, ON L4G 6W1
905-727-3110, fax 905-727-3565
Free catalogue. Hand-crafted pine bird feeders, 28 models.

William Wallace Garden Furniture Ltd.
Box 159
Fordwich, ON N0G 1V0
519-335-3759, fax 519-335-3096
e-mail wwallace@wcl.on.ca
Free catalogue. Teak and iroko garden benches, chairs, tables, and planters made in Canada.

West Coast Creations Ltd.
Unit 6C
13136 Thomas Rd.
RR 1
Ladysmith, BC V0R 2E0
800-939-9933, fax 250-245-0530
home page www.island.net/~wstcstcr
Free catalogue. Cedar planters, birdhouses, feeders, birdbaths, pottery, and objects made of ceramic and glass.

Index

• C •

• *N* •

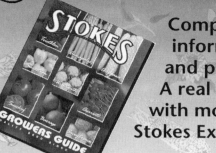